THE ENDS OF GREATNESS

BY THE SAME AUTHOR

THE ENDS OF GREATNESS

HAIG, PÉTAIN, RATHENAU, AND EDEN: VICTIMS OF HISTORY

GENE SMITH

Crown Publishers, Inc.
New York

Published by Crown Publishers, Inc., 201 East 50th Street, New York, New York 10022

CROWN is a trademark of Crown Publishers, Inc.

Design by Lauren Dong

Manufactured in the United States of America

Library of Congress Cataloging-in-Publication Data

Smith, Gene.
   The ends of greatness: Haig, Pétain, Rathenau, and Eden: Victims of history / by Gene Smith.
   p.   cm.
   Includes bibliographical references.
   1. Haig, Douglas, Sir, 1861–1928. 2. Pétain, Philippe, 1856–1951. 3. Rathenau, Walther, 1867–1922. 4. Eden, Anthony, Earl of Avon, 1897–   . 5. Europe—History—1871–1918. 6. Europe—History—1918–1945. 7. Statesmen—Europe—Biography. I. Title.
D412.6.S6   1990
940.2'8—dc20   89-25352
                                                                          CIP

ISBN 0-517-57733-X

10 9 8 7 6 5 4 3 2 1

First Edition

INTRODUCTION

"We met all the tests," the soon-to-die Winston Churchill said of his England of the wars and between the wars.

"It was useless."

That concept is applicable to the four men with whom this book is concerned, all of whom survived the events of 1914–18 and so can be counted among those to whom Erich Maria Remarque dedicated his *All Quiet on the Western Front*. He said his work was for those who lived through the Great War but yet had died, and into this classification fall the four men hereinafter discussed. They saw the ending of what was called the suicide of nations, and the war that cost the world its soul, but during and after the long years of struggle they saw killed all that they had known, and what they were. *C'est la guerre*, the French are often portrayed as saying. That is the somber theme of this book. It is the war.

This book was originally conceived of as a discussion of the observable fact that men put into positions in which they resoundingly fail often do so precisely because of those abilities which brought them their promotions in the first place—the Peter Principle. In the ordinary course of events such individual failures are of trivial importance for all save those directly concerned. The stock shares decline. Enrollment falls. The team falters. It hardly matters. Another factory will take over production, the team will move somewhere. This was not so in the case of the four men with whom I have been concerned. Their failures were for their countries, for their times, for history itself—the Peter Principle brought to grand scale.

Yet why was it so—how was it possible—that they should not succeed? That is the question I asked myself. All ingredients for brilliant and everlasting triumph were present, or so it seemed. Douglas Haig, after all, was Great Britain's most accomplished soldier, compared to Grant for his pertinacity and determination, to Lee for his adherence to duty as he saw it, to Wellington for vast knowledge of war, to the Maid of Orléans for faith. Henri Philippe Pétain was the most noble of France's Marshals of Victory of 1914–18. He made no military mistakes. Beyond that, he cared for his men. Of no other high officer was it said that he could not pass a loaded ambulance without a tightening of the throat. He never kowtowed to Power. He was honor personified.

Of Walther Rathenau it is impossible to say other than that his brilliance was breathtaking, blinding, that he was—to use that overworked term—awesome. It was almost as an incidental addition to his other achievements that he kept First World War Germany on its feet for years. Many who knew him considered him the most gifted Jew of that German-speaking world which produced his contemporaries Freud and Einstein. Robert Anthony Eden, late Captain the King's Royal Rifle Corps, was the symbol of what Churchill called the Mutilated Generation, those who had come home from the Great War. Through the thirties he was the world's model of firmness, intellectual acuity, love of peace backed by knowledge of war. The night Eden resigned from Prime Minister Chamberlain's Cabinet was the sole night of his lifetime, Churchill wrote, that he, Churchill, found himself unable to sleep. So deep was his despair and so heavy his forebodings at Eden's departure from office. It was a high estimate that Churchill offered. No less honors were offered to the other three men mentioned above.

So what happened? Why such sorry fates for each, so tragic for their countries and the world? That is what I asked myself, and for a long time I sought the answers in the men themselves. It was my task, I felt, to define the flaw in each of my subjects that led to the terrible events with which their names are associated: Haig the symbol of the endless catastrophe of the Western Front; Pétain the architect of collaborationist France in 1940; Rathenau the first and most significant victim of what came to be called the Holocaust; and Eden the final suicidal destroyer of what England and the West had been for so long.

But in time it came to me that I was pursuing a false trail. No coincidence could be so all-encompassing as to explain why four men of such diverse types put to high tasks of vastly different nature would all similarly fail with devastating effects and portents. No. The matter was larger than particularized inadequacies or individual poor luck. Yet disaster and sadness hand in hand attend each as they reach high estate. They meet each test, and it is useless. I believe I understand why. *C'est la guerre.*

Many years ago, more than thirty years ago, I attended a series of lectures given by the historian Hans Kohn. It is understandable that I have forgotten almost the entirety of what he said. One memory remains. At that time I was fresh from United States Army occupation duty in Germany. The remains of the Second World War were all about our troops quartered in the caserns built for the military forces of the Third Reich. When you walked through streets of which few were free from smashed buildings and recently cleared lots, deferentially smiling Germans got out of your way, or asked for a cigarette. Other European nations, the victors in the war, were in hardly better case. On leaves in Paris one saw a bitter, nasty people. In London everything was cold, bleak, tired. People's clothing was shabby. As for countries east of Berlin, one could only imagine what it must be like out there. All of Europe was poor, beaten, seemingly down and out for generations to come. The Continent looked to be finished, or near-finished. Then I came home to Hans Kohn's lectures. In one of them he remarked that while the Second War was a frightful tragedy, the First was far more terrible.

I did not understand how Kohn could say what he said. I think I do now. What he meant was that the *meaning* of the First World War, its portent, overrides the physical devastation and human suffering, horrible as they were, of the Second. It is possible today to see the events of 1939–45 as essentially beneficial to mankind. Colonialism came to an end, racial and ethnic discrimination no longer possess credible adherents. Fascism, the concept of dictatorship, Europeans warring endlessly against one another, the rulership of countries and empires by virtue of an inherited class position—all that is gone. Of course there are new problems which do not need enumeration here, but democracy and openness and a fairer distribution of goods and privileges appear enshrined in places where previously they were inconceivable. The millions die, and the cities hit by air attack lose many treasures, but a better world, although purchased at a frightful price, comes into being.

But the First War? Its results? From practically the moment that the guns ceased, a great desire for the vanished past possessed the world along with a conviction that the four years' sacrifice was all for nothing, for less than nothing. A thousand years of tradition, order, religion, the rule of civilization, appeared done in by a crucifixion without redemption or rebirth. The bells were tolling, it was said, for all that was fine in what was now a broken world, unbeautiful and not like an ancient ruin of fallen sculptures and overturned columns, but instead cold and lonely. Through the carnage that shell-shocked even those who never heard a shot fired, one saw walking dead men out of time, ghosts of a lost civilization, attended by the permanently bewildered. Here inflation and racial hatred met spiritual emptiness. Worst of all, it appeared that this was to be normal. It would be like this forever until a final explosion, a second war immediately predicted, would finish the job. The phrase "the good old times" became common to every European language. It denoted disdain and hatred for the then-present, which was low and base, cheap, dispirited, formed of scrabbling, cheating, lying, steady decay.

All this is alluded to in the body of this book, sometimes directly and sometimes by indirection: a hideous fear that the caveman safely sealed in his lair during the long centuries of scientific and intellectual advancement had now by the earthquake's horror emerged from his hiding place to take dominion of humankind's estate so that he might make of it the then and future Kingdom of Death both physical and spiritual. From his fangs dripped the blood of what he had murdered: all that made life worth living. With his Flood he brought eternal war and eternal privation, and hatreds forever aflame. Hitler was, then, a logical development, Mussolini and Stalin something to expect along with brutal Horthy of Hungary, corrupt King Carol of Rumania, Japan's warlords, France's degeneration, and Britain's weakness and new class strife. The Four Horsemen rode. Even the grand and seemingly isolated United States was not immune, for the Great Depression directly stemmed from the war's overexpansion, and even the Dust Bowl storms were traceable to the plowing under of lands better left undisturbed but put into production to feed a Europe starving because those who should have worked her fields were hanging on the wire in no-man's-land. It is worth mentioning that the sole American to emerge from the war with high reputation and universal respect, Herbert Hoover, became in time its victim through its exploding time bomb, the Depression.

It is not contestable, the dismal view held by our grandfathers' generation, or that of our great-grandfathers. It cannot be mistaken. They had gone singing to what proved the slaughterhouse of their youth and of their world—we have seen them in the jerky-moving films of television documentaries, laughing as they piled into the trains taking them to perdition. Then they found out what it was, the Great War. Before, there had been universal expectations that the twentieth century would be prosperous, advanced, progressive. Afterward, those who remained looked back on the brilliantly sunlit summer of 1914 as the twilight of the golden age.

No one can range through the books, the newspapers, the *memories* of the twenties and thirties without knowing the terrible depths of depression and loss which seized the world and the Lost Generation and that generation's elders and its children. It was frightful, this, the dead men walking vampirelike to seek companions in the cemetery of the world-that-had-been. Such was what the war had brought, the universe's long shriek, the Witches' Sabbath, the planet's collective insanity.

Yet the world kept turning. Life went on. Haig's public life was over and he had nothing to do but linger on as a noncomprehending remnant of the Victorian and Edwardian days whose problems he had been trained to meet. He was far from being alone among those to whom it was not given to understand that he and his war had destroyed, shattered, buried, their past. It became the work of the other men discussed in the following pages to go on and to do. The Great War marked their every act when it was over, and I have attempted to make them stand as representatives each in his way of that immeasurable tragedy which overcame the world and whose end is only now coming. Always regretting the past, Rathenau became as a prophet speaking of the future, with his death a final prophecy pointing signpost-like to appalling tomorrows. Caught up in what he had been, the Pétain who had done so much for France became the symbol of much that was taken from her—her honor. It was given to Eden to entomb what England had been. This is not a cheerful book. Hans Kohn was right. *This* was the terrible night of, not our times, but all times. I have attempted with these four men to show why this is so.

But it passes, doesn't it, even the blackest night? Now it is past. Everything, seen from here, might well have occurred in never-never land, those trenches, the poor silly cavalry horses, the pointy-shaft German helmets, the concept, bitterly laughable, that here was the War to End Wars. For it was all so long ago, was it not, the eleventh hour of the eleventh day of the eleventh month, Armistice Day now turned Veterans Day in the United States, the song about Tipperary— where *is* that?—and "Oh Madelon" and "The Rose of No Man's Land," "There's a Long, Long Trail a-Winding" somewhere in France "Over There." Who remembers the Somme, the Trench of Bayonets at Verdun, the Menin Gate at Ypres? Twenty or thirty years ago the obituary pages in the newspaper described leaders of industry or statesmen as former colonels of the Great War; then for a time one read of the deaths of former captains. Today when one reads of the passing of a ninety-year-old one learns he was a long-ago second lieutenant. Soon there will be no more mentions of that time and day. Who lived then and knew the war will be as one with these four who knew it but too well.

. . . On the sand,
Half sunk, a shattered visage lies . . .
. . . . .
And on the pedestal these words appear:
"My name is Ozymandias, King of Kings:
Look upon my works, ye Mighty, and despair!"
Nothing beside remains. Round the decay
Of that colossal wreck, boundless and bare
The lone and level sands stretch far away.

PERCY BYSSHE SHELLEY

THE EDUCATED SOLDIER

As old as history itself is the vision of Glory carried in the train of the conquering warrior, reposing there with the laurels alike his. Yet there was a British soldier who slew the dragon his country opposed, took prisoners, took territory, commanded an army the size of which Marlborough and Wellington before him never dreamed of, nor Montgomery afterward, and found his sword adorned with neither glory nor laurels.

Douglas Haig, his contemporary Winston Churchill wrote, stepped ashore at Dover in early 1919, his war won, and disappeared. "He did not join in the counsels of the nation; he was not invited to reorganize its army; he was not consulted on the Treaties; no sphere of public activity was opened to him. There was nothing for him to do; he was not wanted any more. He became one of the permanently unemployed."

There was more that could have been said. Field Marshal Earl Haig, Viscount Dawick and Baron Haig, 29th Laird of Bemersyde, OM, KT, GCB, GCVO, KCIE, became and remained the eternal symbol of that revulsion with which the world has always looked back upon the horrible wastage of the Western Front of 1914–18. To those who lived through it the mention of his name at once brought to mind endless artillery barrages producing fountains of earth rising in the air to fall back on moonscapelike battered useless fields, hopeless barbedwire entanglements upon which hung dead men shot through a dozen times, wretched trench lines unmoving for years on end, rats, shell shock, machine-gun sweeps, casualties never seen before or since, the Lost Generation: a world gone sick and never to recover, not to the present day. Haig was marked down as unfeeling, the perfect symbol of military stupidity, an ignorant Colonel Blimp of colossal scale who mindlessly sent legions to die in conditions of which he knew nothing. His obstinacy and callous indifference, thought Prime Minister David Lloyd George, his "inexhaustible vanity" and "narrow and stubborn egotism," cost Great Britain her dead of 1914–18, and he would rather the million perish than that he own himself, even to himself, a blunderer.

Termed a heartless butcher during the years of fighting, Lord Haig lived ten years after to read of more denunciations. Those who defended him were at once denounced in turn. He himself had nothing to say, no replies to make, no explanations, and certainly no apologies. It would have been utterly unlike him to rally back at his accusers, beneath the dignity of the gentleman he was born and the gentleman he was. He neither said nor wrote a word about his rôle in the war. To argue the raised points would have been completely out of character— he never argued. He considered it un-British, something foreigners like the French did. And Lord Haig was above all things a Briton. "The distilled essence of Britain," wrote the great military expert B. H. Liddell Hart, "the embodiment of her normal virtues and defects."

He had been raised to high position, reflected Churchill, for good and sufficient reasons. He had been before the war "the head boy and prize pupil of the military school," had done all things "requisite and proper," fought well as a cavalry squadron leader, played polo at international levels, graduated from staff college, held an important post in India, commanded at Aldershot, led a corps and an army. He failed no test. Then came supreme command and the destiny of Great Britain and the Empire in his hands, which physically wrote the orders (for so tongue-tied and inarticulate was he that he could not dictate to an aide) to bring the slaughters of all those mournful places associated today with endless cemeteries, Crosses of Sacrifice, Stones of Remembrance engraved THEIR NAME LIVETH FOREVERMORE, the Ypres Salient, Passchendaele, the Somme. Then the Germans fleeing before him—but how empty a victory!—the coming ashore at Dover, the silence never broken.

He was born in Edinburgh in 1861 to John and Rachel Haig. The father, nineteen years older than the mother, founded the Scotch whisky firm which still bears his name. His wife's social background was such that her family looked down on a husband engaged in "trade." Douglas was the fifth and youngest son of nine children. All his life he was very close to his sister Henrietta, ten years older. He seemed largely indifferent to the others.

As an infant he had no perambulator, but took his airings nestled in a pannier or chair strapped on a pony's back. As a boy he had long blond hair and invariably wore a kilt. Sent away to boarding school, Clifton, as was the custom of the time for persons of his class, he proved an indifferent student. It was notable that he had no close friends and was extremely reserved and self-contained for someone of his age. He spent much time with horses.

His father died in 1878, and he came into part of his inheritance. Outfitted with several polo ponies, he enrolled at Oxford. On the evening of his first day he discussed with another entering student what the longtime head of Brasenose College had said to each when first meeting them. "Drink plenty of port, sir," the other boy was told. "You want port in this damp climate." To Douglas: "Ride, sir, ride. I like to see the gentlemen of Brasenose in top boots." Douglas followed the advice and played for Oxford's polo team. He did little else. His grades were average. There was no drinking or carousing, and he never sat down at a card table. Each night he followed his lifelong practice of writing several pages in his diary—discussions of where he had taken dinner, the times his train had left one place and arrived at another. There was never mention of any romantic attachment.

He was quiet, reserved, controlled, unconcerned with the opinions of others. He did not go about in society and never danced, and struck his fellows as solitary, aloof, alone, a sturdily built dour Scotsman with an unflinching look on a handsome face. Three years into his studies he fell ill and so did not receive a degree along with the others of his class. It did not trouble him. When he recovered he decided not to bother to return to Oxford but instead entered Sandhurst, the Royal Military College, Great Britain's equivalent of America's West Point and France's Saint-Cyr. By then his mother was dead, and he made up his mind entirely on his own. There is no record that he ever indicated to anyone why he wanted to become a soldier. Perhaps because it was a profession much involved with horses.

An astonishing change came over him as soon as he became a cadet. The purposeless young man of means turned into the most determined and focused of students. Haig took careful notes on everything he was taught and sat up nights studying those notes. Older than most of his fellows, for they had gone to Sandhurst direct from their boarding schools, and as ever withdrawn and uncommunicative, he took no part in after-hours frolics. He could never be popular with, and existed apart from, the officer-class sons of privilege who decided to enter the army because it was a gentleman's profession, an amusing existence, a pleasant sporting life with months-long leaves readily available for hunting, hacking, foreign travel, the social round. Sandwiched in were brief adventures with Fuzzy-Wuzzies or Wogs as one did one's bit toward painting the map red so that the atlas would show more and more of the color indicating the Empire—one-third of the world eventually. It was like a point-to-point or fox-hunting, exhilarating and spiced with a touch of danger as a column in sola topees moved out under tropical sun through exotic places to scatter the natives with a volley and *arme blanche* cavalry charge which would add another faraway name to the regimental colors—Tel-el-Kebir, the Hunza-Nagar campaign, the expedition in the Mahsud Waziri country, the Uganda mutiny and Sierra Leone rebellion, the Second Sikh War and the Second Afghan War, Bechuanaland and Zululand, and the crushing of the Dinizula revolt.

Exerting what proved to be unusual powers of concentration and entirely undisturbed by any interest in art, the theater, food, liquor, or reading unconnected with his studies, Haig was the outstanding Sandhurst cadet of his day, the number-one man in his class and Senior Under-Officer, his appointment as such the highest honor the school offered. "A Scottish lad, Douglas Haig, is tops in almost everything," an instructor said, "books, drill, riding and sports; he is to go into the cavalry and before he is finished he will be top of the army."

His regiment of selection was the 7th (Queen's Own) Hussars, one of the most fashionable units of the most elite branch of the British Army, the cavalryman for thousands of years having been regarded as the highest form of the soldier's calling. To serve as a subaltern in the 7th called for expenses of at least four or five times one's annual pay. The purchase of rank, which earlier in Victoria's reign meant the expenditure of fabulous sums to buy commissions—Lord Cardigan of Light Brigade fame paid forty thousand pounds for a colonelcy—had been abolished fifteen years earlier, in 1871. What replaced it was a system in which only the rich could meet an officer's payments for keeping the meals up to accepted high standards, for his chargers of first-class quality, for race meets and balls, for the regimental band, and for what future Chief of the Imperial General Staff Sir William Robertson thought were an "absurd amount of costly uniforms" adorned with gold cord and gold-braided epaulets, feathers on the headgear, choker collars, sashes, buttons, sword with gold braided knot and heavily filigreed guard, elaborately done-up sleeves, shining boots, gleaming spurs, smart gauntlets, brilliantly polished harness and straps and reins and hardware for the horses, scarlet jacket with facings of the regiment's colors for meals at long tables in the officers' mess laden with the unit silver.

The 7th Hussars fielded the crack polo team of the British Army. It had won the Inter-Regimental Cup three years running. With Haig as a new starter it won for the fourth time. He was then offered a place on the British team scheduled to play against an American contingent at Newport, Rhode Island. The matches were a slaughter, the British winning by scores of 10–4 and 14–2. The players returned to England and Lieutenant Haig to his unit preparing to depart Portsmouth for Indian service. They made Bombay and then entrained for Secunder-abad, the largest military cantonment of southern India.

It was 1886. Great Britain was at the height of her power, the Queen-Empress the aunt or grandmother of half the world's monarchs, the British pound the world's standard for currency, the City of London the world's banker and insurer, the iron and coal and railroads and shipyards unchallenged anywhere. The heyday of the British race. At the very tip of the Imperial social structure, above any manufacturer or anyone in "trade," stood the officers of Her Majesty's Forces, which had won and now kept secure the Empire. Each army unit had a defined position. That of the 7th Hussars ranked with, and perhaps above, that held by the Guards. Yet there was really very little that a cavalry officer actually had to do. His day's work was usually concluded by 11:00 in the morning. He had almost no contact with the enlisted personnel—"other ranks," in British parlance; they were seen to by sergeants. In fact, the officer could hardly speak to a private, for they shared not the slightest bond of experience. The other ranks were the sweepings of British life, slum dwellers and the sons of the rural poor, dregs who for taking the Queen's shilling were esteemed by respected citizens to be brutes. As such they were treated. Barracks in the United Kingdom were surrounded by high walls, the tops of which were embedded with broken glass put there not to keep interlopers out but to incarcerate the soldiers.

Seen as machines of an inferior nature, or almost as kin to the horses and mules, although of lesser value, the men were handled in a manner handed down by the Duke of Wellington, who had defined his Waterloo troops as the scum of the earth, enlisted for drink and booty. Ramrod rigidity on parade and blind obedience to orders were the criteria by which they were judged. His Royal Highness the Field Marshal Commanding in Chief, the Duke of Cambridge, was in 1886 in the thirtieth year of his command of the British Army; for all that period plus the nine more years he would serve he held to the view that "change, even for the better, is to be deprecated." So no effort was made to improve on the formations and drill which had served for the Peninsula Campaign in the century's teens and during the Crimean War in the 1850s.

Yet away from England even the lowest private in the rear ranks, one of "the blackguards commanded by gentlemen," according to Kipling, held a high position. He was, after all, British, and a soldier.

(Once an "other rank" was called upon to give testimony in an Indian trial. He mentioned seeing "two coolies" and was called to order by the judge, who pointed out that one of the two individuals referred to was His Exalted Highness the Nizam of Hyderabad, richest of all native princes. The soldier then defined the two men as the "Nizam of Hyderabad and the other coolie.")

Inestimably above the other ranks and in a sense even such as nizam and maharajah, the cavalry officer of the Raj was in but not of the India of heat and dust, the nights filled with the sound of chants, cries, bells, piercing music, gongs clanging, the whistle and crash of railroad couplings, the odor of open sewers, spices, wood smoke. He lived in a bungalow on a luxurious cantonment, with garden and magnificent flowers, and his butler and dressing boy and head groom, and their many underlings, saw to his needs. On field exercises he moved about followed by a dozen to a score of his bearers, grass cutters, khansa-mahs, syces, sweepers, dhobis, and bhistis,* plus two or three genera-tions of their families riding in the officer's bullock-drawn wagons, with strings of elephants to carry gear, including tables and chairs, wines, carpets, and lounge chairs.

Servants pulling ceiling fans, palms in brass urns, silver candelabra, stuffed tigers in the corners, fire-jugglers in the garden, pig-sticking and cricket and race meets—"Princes could live no better than we," remembered Winston Churchill of the 4th Hussars. In the glittering officers' mess with its crystal, fine plate, and shining silver, the band playing softly, it was forbidden to discuss sex, women, religion, and politics. But the supreme prohibition was against talking "shop." There must be no mention of anything relating to work, such as it was. Few felt any incentive to disobey the rule. To do so was to identify oneself as kin to the scrubs, swats, smugs who spent their free time back in boarding school discussing geometry or irregular verbs. What was important was to have what was called the Cavalry Spirit, which had proved decisive on the Indian plains at Gujerat and Chillianwallah and Shabkard. That spirit was expressed by being good at polo and in

---

*Khansamah = cook; syce = stable boy; dhobi = launderer; bhisti = water boy.

horse shows and hunting. One had to be a fellow who would never let down the regiment and was willing to die, if that proved necessary, like a gentleman, with his saber in his hand and his face to the enemy. Cavalry officers spoke in a particular drawling manner and walked in such fashion that their spurs distinctively chimed; they knew about tennis, billiards, gentlemen's steeplechases at the Turf Club, about winning as if they were used to it and losing as if it did not matter. Playing the game.

They lived in their closed order of society, unanxious to know of anything else, apart not only from India but from the industrial England* of mills and factories, High Victorian anachronisms more rooted in the days of feudalism and aristocratic privilege than in the last two decades of the nineteenth century. Regimental customs and rights of dress concerned them; they spent their energies in being good fellows who would play up, would show well at lance and sword contests reminiscent of medieval tourneys, could contribute at evening amusements, music, theatricals, singing, whistling, games. Haughty, rich, snobbish, an officer was to be an unconcerned amateur. The Duke of Wellington himself was known to have been strongly against educating soldiers in military knowledge. The extremely rare senior officer who expected his juniors to know their work and to instruct their men in it was considered, Sir William Robertson remembered, to be more a drill sergeant than a cavalry commander by the juniors, who, Robertson said, knew nothing and could do nothing.

It was not so in the case of Lieutenant Haig of the 7th Hussars. He kept up his brilliant polo and was always immaculately turned out, the smartest of smart cavalry officers, but for the amusements which concerned his fellows he cared not a whit. Such things were in the same category for him as going to an art museum or reading a novel. As he had at Sandhurst, he worked. He subscribed to the cavalry journals of every nation in the world, and cut out articles which particularly interested him for pasting in scrapbooks. On his leaves he

---

*The United Kingdom was often referred to as "England."

went to Europe to observe Continental practices—one autumn to France to see mobilization exercises at Limoges; to Berlin the next year to see German training and meet the Kaiser, who offered a toast to the visitor's health. Afterward he wrote reports on what he had seen and noted, and those reports attracted the attention of the cavalry chiefs in Horse Guards Parade.

By 1892 the 7th Hussars had been transferred from Secunderabad to Indore, three hundred miles northeast of Bombay, and Captain Haig was a squadron commander after having fulfilled staff duties few of his fellow subalterns cared to undertake. He had no close friends, was respected but not popular, and was notable for lack of sentimental attachment to his regiment, an attitude rarely found in the typical British officer, who having once joined a unit usually determined to make it his home for the length of his career. Withdrawn and reserved in the company of his peers although perfectly willing to perform many of their ignored or disregarded duties for them, Haig was un-failingly polite, never too busy to be a gentleman. His batman always found him respectful to the other ranks even as he addressed each of their members as an individual "who was somewhat a stranger to him." He never shouted, swore only very mildly, and detested off-color stories.

Always cool and imperturbable, he was entirely undemonstrative and appeared to seem always in repose, looking out of uniform like a country squire, with a noble forehead, clear blue eyes, and a head always held high. Perhaps beneath the unbending calm there were fires burning, for he suffered agonies from poor digestion, his batman remembered. So he ate the simplest foods. Gourmet eating would never have interested him in any case—he wasn't the type. He lived on a boiled egg and a piece of toast for breakfast, a luncheon of plainly fried sole with no garnishing or sauce, and a dinner of a couple of cutlets perfectly dry and plain and taken with some potatoes and followed by milk pudding. He might take a glass of wine or a whisky-soda with dinner and perhaps a brandy with his coffee, but in summer as often as not he only drank water.

Apart from the stomach problems there was not the slightest indication of any emotional distress, and the only sign that something had disturbed him was a slight broadening of his Scottish accent. He never used gestures of any kind beyond a stiff motion of the forearm as if he were discarding a used match. "Friendship in the ordinarily accepted sense of the term was almost unknown to Haig," said John Charteris, perhaps his closest aide for more than a decade. If anyone showed a disposition to unburden himself to Haig he found his listener turned completely tongue-tied and abrupt. "Aloneness" was a word Charteris repeatedly used to characterize Haig. "Don't be a damned fool; stick to facts," he often said. "Don't ramble, say what you have to say." To anyone showing excitement of any kind: "Don't fuss." To his brothers-in-arms, even those with whom he had soldiered for years, he was inevitably cold and formal, always polite and even kind but always with that pronounced remoteness he had owned even as a child and would display to his last moment on earth.

In 1896 he was accepted for the Staff College at Camberley. In the 7th Hussars he had mastered far beyond the ken of other officers cavalry training, equipment, communications, administration, organization, and transport; now he left without the slightest sentimental qualm and went on to Staff College to study strategy, tactics, artillery, fortifications, topography, and administrative duties. His performance was breathtaking. It was noted by the college's G. F. R. Henderson, the leading military intellectual of the day. "There is a fellow in your batch who one of these days will be Commander in Chief," Henderson told a group of Captain Haig's classmates. It was not a prediction remembered long afterward when it proves right, for one of the classmates recalled it in a letter to Haig years before it came true. (Employing what for him was a light touch, Haig wrote back that "dear old Henderson must have been talking through his hat.")

It cannot have hurt his standing with Henderson, the definitive biographer of the Confederate Gen. Thomas "Stonewall" Jackson, that Haig was a careful student of the American Civil War, entirely unlike the vast majority of British and European soldiers, who, like the German military genius Helmuth von Moltke, dismissed it as a matter of "two armed mobs chasing one another around the countryside." It was in character for Haig, ever the earnest military scholar, to give the records of the North-South conflict his conscientious attention.

With the coveted *psc* for "passed Staff College" now following his name in the Army List, he worked as an aide-de-camp to the Inspector General of Cavalry at home. His much-beloved older sister Henrietta was by then married to William Jameson of the Irish whisky family. Very rich, very social, an international yachtsman whose *Shamrock II* had only just missed winning the America's Cup, Jameson was a close friend of the Prince of Wales, soon to be King of England. Prince Edward found Jameson's brother-in-law appealing, for Haig did not play up to His Royal Highness in courtierlike fashion—that would have been beyond him and utterly out of character—and Edward, shrewd despite his notable self-indulgence, appreciated his firm character and open manner of expressing himself.

In January of 1898 he was gazetted to the Anglo-Egyptian force outfitting for service against the Khalifa's dervishes in Sudan, the River War along the Nile in which Great Britain would paint the area red on the world's maps and avenge the death of Gen. Charles "Chinese" Gordon at the hands of the fanatical Khalifa's predecessor, Allah's Servant the Mahdi, who had hung his vanquished opponent's head above the palace at Khartoum. Directly before shipping out for Cairo, Haig spent two days at the Enfield Small Arms Factory acquainting himself with the Maxim machine gun. Commanded by the Prince and Princess of Wales to Sandringham, he had long talks with Edward about cavalry tactics and departed carrying an invitation by HRH to write from Egypt.

A major temporarily in Egyptian service, Bimbashi Haig Bey, he equipped himself with tarbooshes, several locally purchased horses he drilled on the army's Cairo polo grounds, camels for the field, a cook, a body servant, a groom for each of his horses, a camel boy. He departed Wadi Halfa for Berber and the command of a squadron of conscripted fellahin cavalrymen more used to camels or donkeys than horses. Instructing them as best he could in the Cavalry Spirit, he joined them with the others going up against the Khalifa's vast host of robed warriors, who in tone, weapons, outlook, and hatred for the infidel differed little from the Saracens who had opposed the Crusaders half a millennium and more earlier. Rows of gorgeous white-and-yellow standards danced above the dervishes and the sunlight glinted off their waving swords while their elephant-tusk trumpets sounded and their war drums rolled, but they were facing the weaponry of the Industrial Age. The Battle of Omdurman across the Nile from Khartoum was a slaughter, a thousand of the Khalifa's men falling for each hundred of the invading force. In the cavalry melees Haig was coolness itself, directing not only his own men but those of other units. He found battle not unlike a prolonged chukker, darting horses in swirling dust.

And indeed the polo-like work of the cavalry, and the orderly Napoleonic-style volley firing of the British infantry, convinced the great majority of the victors' leaders that their methods and outlook were alike correct. Sir Herbert H. Kitchener became Viscount and eventually Earl of Khartoum, and the Union Jack floated where once the desert hawks circled the decapitated head of General Gordon; and the maps were painted red.

But Haig's methodical years of study told him there were tremendous deficiencies in the British manner of making war, that Kitchener had been fortunate that his foes were so ill-armed and officered not by logic but by religious faith. Never hesitant to speak frankly when discussing military matters, he analyzed the battle in reports back to England for the higher-ups of the British cavalry and the Prince of Wales. He drew maps and wrote of the force deployments in his ever-attended-to diary.

Back from Egyptian service, "blooded," given his baptism of fire, he went out to South Africa, where what would be called the Boer War was breaking out as the Dutch-background Afrikaners opened fire on the British overlords. He was assigned as chief of staff to Gen. Sir John French, commander of the Cavalry Division, and together they lay flat in a railway compartment of the last train leaving a besieged town. The war was going badly. All the arrogant inadequacies of British military theory and practice bore bitter fruit as Boer farmers ran rings around soldiers who had thought that British pluck and what was good enough for Wellington would serve in the modern world.

It was all very well for the Queen-Empress to declare that in her house the possibility of defeat could not be mentioned because it did not exist, but one British embarrassment after another darkened London until Sir John French with a dashing rush came to the relief of Kimberley in one of the great moments of Victorian England. Haig issued concise outlines for the movement and disposition of the horsemen as he rode alongside Sir John, as quick and accurate with his written orders as he was fumbling and inarticulate when called upon to speak. Sir John French was acclaimed as the greatest British cavalryman since Oliver Cromwell, but even then Haig esteemed him as something other than that, and even then perhaps foresaw that Sir John's star would never again burn so brightly.

There followed a protracted winding-down of the far from glorious war, with Haig overseeing the work of six mounted columns rounding up rebellious Boers in Cape Colony. He was then given the colonelcy of the 17th Lancers, the Death or Glory Boys for their skull-and-bones insignia, among whose battle streamers was one for the doomed charge at Balaklava in the Crimea—into the valley of death rode the brave six hundred. The 17th was stationed in Scotland. He gave its polo team his usual attention, and with himself as forty-year-old playing captain it took the Inter-Regimental Cup, the glory of winning which he had shared in as a youthful subaltern of the 7th Hussars.

After a year his posting to India was requested by the military commander of the subcontinent, Lord Kitchener of Khartoum, with a temporary rank of major general to go with the post of Inspector General of Indian Cavalry. He was the youngest man ever to hold that position. Behind his back he was referred to as "Lucky" Haig, but luck had little to do with it, as all who knew him realized. With active service in two wars added to his store of theoretical knowledge, he began to remodel the mounted units of India. He set his face against all the ingrained panoply of British military method, massed frontal attacks with fifes and pipers and drums and flaunted ensigns, with gleaming steel expected to scatter His Majesty's enemies—for Victoria was gone and Edward King. Haig emphasized musketry, which, Sir William Robertson remembered, had earlier been "a sealed book to most cavalry officers." The effects of his work were seen when cavalry regiments began beating infantry regiments in rifle competitions.

Traveling in a special railroad car attached to regularly scheduled trains, the Inspector General had himself dropped off at cavalry posts which he then toured on one of his several horses, Knight of the Deccan being his favorite. He observed masses of drilling lancers coming to the "engage," listened and looked as trumpets sounded for a right wheel into line, and never voiced an opinion to anyone save the officer just below him in the chain of command. It would never have occurred to him to make his opinion on anything known to a lieutenant or captain, and he was light-years away from that type of fatherly senior officer who pats the youthful private's cheek and inquires the name of his hometown. To the proper ears General Haig offered a searching analysis and recommendations. Solitary, aloof, alone, the hardest of workers possessing the deepest technical knowledge of all points of the soldier's profession, he studied in the most methodical manner the disputed issues of the cavalry of the day, the question of whether horsemen should be swiftly brought to a point of contact with the enemy and then dismounted to fight on foot or if they should stay horsed and deliver a shock-action blow; whether the rifle was superior to the carbine, the lance to the sword, to cut or to thrust. With his officers he was severe, fair, scanty with praise. He made it clear there must not be the slightest familiarity from those who served under him. No one, his batman remembered, was permitted to presume an inch. There was no personal intimacy with any of his subordinates, and his relationship to them was that of an older brother or teacher. To his few superiors he was formal and polite. "But his courtesy," remembered his longtime aide John Charteris, "had in it something of the frigid. There was ever an intangible barrier that effectively prevented any approach to intimacy or even cordiality." At the end of a day, no matter how dusty or tired he might be from the merciless Indian heat, he always saw Knight of the Deccan looked after before he saw to himself.

Immune to charm from others, the Inspector General made no effort to exert anything approaching a quality so entirely foreign to his nature. As inarticulate as ever, he spoke in half-sentences, unfinished, often with verbs omitted. One had to know him well to take his meaning completely. King Edward remained his patron. In June of 1905 when Haig was on leave in England, Edward invited him to Windsor Castle for Ascot Week. On Thursday after the races, General Haig was asked to make up one of a foursome at golf, his partner being Maid of Honor to Queen Alexandra the Hon. Miss Dorothy Maud Vivian, daughter of the third Lord Vivian and sister of the fourth, who had served in the 17th Lancers. Haig's opposite number of the couple opposing them was the Duke of Devonshire, a golfer who continually hit his ball into bunkers and made slow work of getting it out. The general and Miss Vivian had plenty of time to talk as they waited.

The next day, Friday, they went to the races. They golfed together, alone this time, in the late afternoon, and he took her in to dinner in the evening. They parted that night with plans to play a before-breakfast round of golf the next day, Saturday. Haig was forty-four years old and is not known ever to have had a serious, or even trifling, romance. When she appeared for their game he told her he did not wish to play and tipped and dismissed the caddies and then looked about for a place where they could sit down. There was none. So he blurted out, "I must propose to you standing." They had known each other less than two full days.

She accepted. They agreed to tell the King and Queen their secret; it would remain unknown to the rest of the Household. Alexandra appeared delighted, and Edward jokingly upbraided Haig, "What do you mean coming to my house and trying to take away one of the Queen's best maids of honor?"

There remained the question of securing the permission of Miss Vivian's mother. Queen Alexandra wrote a letter of introduction, and Haig took it and went to Lady Vivian in London. Not caring to receive a stranger whose name was entirely unknown to her, she had him informed she was not at home. He simply refused to leave. Eventually she had to see him. The Queen's letter and the daughter's acceptance won the day. They were officially engaged. An acquaintance expressed surprise that this situation had been arrived at with such speed, and Haig replied: "Why not? I have often made up my mind on more important problems than that of my own marriage in much less time." King Edward charged the bride-to-be with ensuring that nothing interfere with the career of his "best and most capable general."

The wedding was on July 11, 1905. Queen Alexandra gave them the use of the Private Chapel at Buckingham Palace for the ceremony. At breakfast the next morning he sat at the left of the Queen and she at the right of the King. They went off for a two-week honeymoon at Radway Grange, Warwickshire, which the villagers decorated with archways of flowers in their honor. Then they departed Marseille for Bombay and the resumption of his work, occupying two adjoining cabins with a third reserved for their luggage. The marriage was a success. In time Dorothy Haig bore three daughters and a son. He entrusted to her the typing of his diary, sending her written notes every two or three days by courier when he was away.

Mornings in India they rode a great deal to exercise his chargers and polo ponies, and played golf and tennis. Lord Kitchener had them to his hot-weather vacation place in the upland country around Simla, and Mrs. Haig became a great favorite of the Viceroy, Lord Curzon, and his wife the Vicereine. As a bachelor Haig had rarely dined out and never gone to balls, as he did not dance, but under his wife's guidance he blossomed to lead a very gay life with her, dinners and gymkhanas and stately affairs at the Curzons', where the level of formality exceeded that of Windsor Castle or Buckingham Palace, natives touching their foreheads to the floor in front of the Viceroy and all guests walking backward in his presence. There were arcs of blooms in rooms decorated with masses of every kind of flowering creeper. Haig wore the red ceremonial uniform no longer used for field service, khaki having replaced it. His wife put her hair up, either backcombed or with horsehair stuffing added, and discovered that Indian maids, ayahs, "have rather cold, clammy hands." To those who saw Curzon and Haig, each so stiff and somberly formal, it would have seemed in order if both wore eighteenth-century costumes with perukes and frills.

The Duke of Cambridge's thirty-nine-year-long command of the army had finally ended, and in the wake of the dismaying South African War revelations, a wave of reform-minded thinking swept in. A new Secretary of State for War was appointed, the distinguished lawyer Richard Haldane. He had no background in military affairs but applied a logical mind and saw the manifest problems. He realized he needed an aide with extensive specialized knowledge, and so General Haig was, as Haldane put it, told to "come over to this country and to think for us." He was, Haldane said, "the most highly equipped thinker in the British Army."

No two men could be less alike, for Haldane liked to sit up late over brandy and cigars and discuss all manner of things, including his student days in Germany when he studied philosophy, a subject upon which he had written much. Haig did not smoke and drank sparingly and as a man hardly able to get a coherent sentence out of his mouth seemed an unlikely companion for his expansive chief. Yet they got on very well together, Haldane understanding what he saw as an underlying shyness in his adviser, and working in adroit and kind fashion to tap the deep military knowledge beneath the frigid exterior. Together they remade the British Army and instituted the greatest reforms in its long history.

Both the Secretary of State for War and his deputy the Director of Military Training and Staff Duties realized that a day might be coming when a British return could be required to the Continent which that country's forces had quitted after Waterloo more than eighty-five years earlier. No one could know whether the opponent would be Germany or France, both Great Powers with enormous conscript armies. Drafting men into uniform was an accepted way of life for most European countries, but impossible for a Britain always expecting to fill its formations with sons of impoverished farm families or the type of boy who hung around taverns hoping to be given a penny for holding someone's horse. The answer was to raise and equip a Territorial Army* of weekend and summer-camp soldiers who could join the reservists, men recently discharged from active duty, in support of any possible British Expeditionary Force across the Channel. Outfitting such a group presented difficulties, for there was a widespread disinclination to allow Territorials even the right to drill on village greens. (Lord Roberts, the Commander in Chief during the Boer War, said that if they were given artillery they would constitute a danger to the country.) It was deadly work to extract money from a Parliament which historically had resented doling out every penny the army said it required.

Haldane and Haig saw it through and worked also on plans for the possible British Expeditionary Force, on the place that Dominions troops could fill, and on the creation of an Imperial General Staff, a centralized military governing body whose invention in Prussia was given much of the credit for that country's several victories in the 1860s and 1870s. As always before, Haig threw himself into his work, which in a sense was not difficult for him because of that complete lack of any other interests which John Charteris said so amazed all who met him. (His sister Henrietta Jameson took up spiritualism, and when she took him with her to visit a medium the only question he could think to ask was whether a future expansion of the Territorial Army should be on a company or battalion basis. The medium said that the spirits with whom she had communication favored a company basis. Pressed for additional questions, Haig inquired after Napoleon and was told, he recorded in his diary, that the Emperor "had become changed for the better in the spirit world.")

He wrote or supervised the writing of new manuals for field service and organization and administration, radical activities for an army quite content with the rituals of one hundred years before. (When it was decreed that lancers would no longer carry their eight-foot spears in the field, reserving them for ceremonial purposes alone, numerous affronted lancer officers resigned their commissions.)

---

*The equivalent of the National Guard in the United States.

He commuted to the War Office from a house he shared with his wife and two young daughters, kept in the closest possible touch with all developments in the Russo-Japanese War, and saw his health decline from the long indoor hours and lack of exercise. At the end of his three-year stint he was named chief of staff to a new Commander in Chief in India. King Edward had seen a good deal of the Haigs during their stay in England, inviting them to shooting parties in Sandringham with luncheons served under a marquee, and just before their departure had them to Balmoral along with the two little girls. The King had knighted him, and so as Gen. Sir Douglas Haig, KCVO, he sailed to India with Lady Haig. The girls were left behind in the care of their mother's twin sister, India with its heat and fevers being considered dangerous for children of gentle birth.

It was 1908. They returned to the life they had known, cavalry displays with masses of horsemen charging the reviewing stand to skid to a halt a few yards away, racing at the Turf Club, dinners at the viceregal Lodge with its furniture of dark curved walnut and yellow muslin curtains to keep out the heat, and, for him, long hours of instruction and study and inspection. King Edward died and his son George succeeded. As Prince of Wales the new King had learned to esteem Haig, and was to be as good a friend as his late father. When the monarch came to India to hold a durbar at Delhi, a great levee, the Haigs delayed a scheduled return to England to be with him. The event was magnificent, King George and Queen Mary in purple state robes wearing crowns, pages carrying their trains as they walked to the Royal Pavilion with its huge golden dome to sit on golden thrones, the assembled maharajahs, princes, and governors salaaming before the King-Emperor in this the great and final display of the supreme majesty of the British Raj in the Jewel of the Crown. An Indian prince sulked in his gorgeous tent; Haig was asked to see him and make clear that his attendance was required. It was done with great courtesy and reserve but with unmistakable firmness; and the prince soon came to be with the others, whose turbans were like masses of flowers, or jewels flashing in the sunshine, with the soldiers in scarlet, silver, brass breastplates. Three days after the ceremony, Sir Douglas and Lady

Haig took ship for England. It had been three years since they had seen their daughters, who had then been two years and nine months respectively.

His new post was one of the plums of the British Army, the command of Aldershot, the chief military post and the center of all army activities in the United Kingdom. He took up his duties in early 1912, bringing with him a nucleus of officers who had served him in India—"The Hindoo invasion." The house assigned the post's ranking officer stood in open surroundings and was grand. A country gentleman in his off hours, on duty he enforced a rigid discipline exerted in his cool and remote manner. Once at an outpost he appeared with his staff and an escort, all mounted. A sentry was standing with a cigarette in his mouth. He flung it down and square-bashed to attention. Haig halted his horse and with the other officers sat in absolute silence watching the column of smoke coming up from the ground. The sentry remained standing at petrified attention. Not until the last ash died out did Haig move his horse. No more smoking on duty at Aldershot was noted afterward.

He was tireless in organizing sports and competitions for the men, agreeing with Wellington that upon playing fields future battles are decided. His ineptitude with the spoken word remained unchanged. "I congratulate you on your running," he told the winners of an inter-regimental cross-country race. "You have run well. I hope you will run as well in the presence of the enemy."

Summer of 1914 came and with it the assassination in Sarajevo of the Archduke Francis Ferdinand, heir to the Austro-Hungarian throne, and the coming into force of those many treaties and engagements which led to what was initially called the European War and then the Great War and then, sadly, the First World War. Great Britain mobilized on August 4. The British Expeditionary Force Haig and Haldane had planned was alerted for immediate shipment to France with at its head Field Marshal Sir John French, Haig's old commander in South Africa, and with Haig as chief of one of the two corps which would compose it. Together the two soldiers went to 10 Downing Street and a conference with Prime Minister H. H. Asquith.

There Sir John French spoke in such fashion that Haig wrote in his diary that he had to "tremble at the reckless way" French saw things. The field marshal wanted to concentrate the British force, tiny in comparison with the French and German armies, so far forward that it would have to take on alone the entire German right wing.

The idea was dangerous beyond words, Haig told the Prime Minister, saying also that this would be a war lasting years and that a large number of officers and noncoms should be left at home to train the levies that would be required. His views were not in accord with most of the world's experts, who believed the troops would be home, as the German Kaiser put it, "before the leaves fall." Haig was overruled. The entire strength of the British Army in the United Kingdom, 100,000 men, was put into motion for France, the operation proceeding with absolute smoothness as Haig and Haldane had long before worked out, eighteen hundred special trains carrying all the Tommy Atkinses to the embarkation points, where their masses made the transports resemble floating anthills. At Rouen people waved the Union Jack and shouted, "*Vive l'Angleterre*," the soldiers with their well-groomed horses and heraldic and painted drums and mascots responding with hip-hip-hurrahs not entirely concealing their Regulars' disdain for foreigners: Wogs begin at Calais. King George came to Aldershot and asked Haig his opinion of Sir John French and was answered with complete frankness. "In my heart I know that French is quite unfit for this great command at a time of crisis in our nation's history," Haig wrote in his diary.

By August 14 he had followed his I Corps and was ashore with a luncheon basket well stocked by Lady Haig and destined to be with him for all the years of the war. His command was some forty thousand men and contained battalions of many storied regiments of the British Army—the Coldstream Guards, the Black Watch, the King's Royal Rifle Corps, the Scots Guards, the Grenadier Guards. Kaiser Wilhelm allegedly termed the BEF England's "contemptible little army," and that is what the men immediately and forever called themselves, those who lived: the Old Contemptibles.

They entrained for the Front and then swung up cobblestoned roads and under tall poplars lining the *chaussée* and came to coal pits, slag heaps, and piles of shale in Mons in Belgium. It was a Sunday, August 23, 1914. Church bells were ringing. Peasants in Sunday clothes went past the troops in their flat caps. In thin mist and light drizzle the officer commanding I Corps of the British Army was up and about, first in an automobile and then on horseback. He heard the rumble of artillery, like distant thunder. The countryside seemed peaceful, but refugees came running, people pushing baby carriages filled with their possessions and pulling carts. German shells began falling half a mile off.

Haig went to one of his divisional commanders lying on his stomach on a hill looking across a valley at a stream where British troops were firing their field guns. Within two or three miles were masses of gray figures coming on in great strength. The entire BEF had only forty machine guns, but the well-drilled Old Contemptibles opened up with rifle fire of such speed and accuracy that the Germans were convinced they had a plentitude of automatic weapons. But the disparity in numbers told. Off to the right the French began to collapse. Liaison between the Field Marshal Commanding His Majesty's Forces and the French general on the right, Charles Lanrezac, was frightful. Earlier Sir John had called to ask where Lanrezac thought the Germans might try to cross the Meuse. The Frenchman spoke no English and was known for disliking the British. He appeared to believe he did them a favor by permitting them to fight alongside the force that was the descendant of La Grande Armée. Sir John's command of Lanrezac's native tongue was such that officers standing outside speculated that in *la plume de ma tante* fashion he was inquiring what had become of the penknife belonging to the gardener's uncle. "*Mon Général,*" asked the British field marshal, "*est-ce que—*"; and broke off and asked a staff officer, "How do you say 'to cross the river'?" Told, he asked if Lanrezac thought the Germans might do this at—and attempting to pronounce the name of Huy, which needed practically to be whistled, he got out "Hoy."

"What does he say? What does he say?" asked General Lanrezac.

Told, he contemptuously said, "Tell the marshal that in my opinion the Germans have merely gone to the river to piss in it."* The conversation did not improve, Lanrezac gaining the completely incorrect impression that the British field marshal declined to use his cavalry as reconnaissance to locate the enemy columns and their line of march. He never bothered to return Sir John's call, and when on the first day of British battle he decided to retreat he did not bother to inform his allies. When they found out, in the evening, they realized they too must fall back or face certain annihilation.

So began what was thereafter called the Great Retreat. To about-face a confident, forward-moving, hardly blooded force and withdraw it from contact with the enemy while avoiding a rout and a slaughter is the most difficult of military endeavors. Perhaps no more delicate assignment exists. The disastrous possibility that the British would be caught "on the hop," divided, and decimated was always present. Fear of such an eventuality unsettled Field Marshal Sir John French, and in quick order he permitted himself momentarily to give up as lost his II Corps, half his force, to think about withdrawing every last man into any convenient city and simply holing up there, and finally to consider rushing off somewhere to the north where, entirely withdrawn from the fighting, he could catch his breath. No such excitement possessed Lt. Gen. Sir Douglas Haig of I Corps. Perfectly turned out, his horse flawlessly groomed, each day of the Great Retreat he rode along his lines wearing the calmest of expressions and giving the impression that all was quite in order. By his orders and example the march discipline of his men was maintained as though all this were no more testing an experience than Aldershot Field Day exercise.

Writing instructions in his own hand as usual from his headquarters at the tail of the march, always in close touch with the rear guards, he gave such complete, detailed, and accurate orders that neither food nor ammunition was ever a problem. When he learned a Moroccan division on his left was suffering from the faulty French supply arrangements he sent over ten thousand rations and received in return a note from the divisional commander saying nothing could touch

*Many earlier versions of the remark have General Lanrezac speaking of a German desire to fish in the river.

him more deeply than Sir Douglas's kindnesses. There followed a case of champagne.

It seemed to his aide John Charteris that the corps commander permitted himself to drop somewhat his customary curtness; Charteris saw him walking a rattled brigade commander up and down in the road, soothing him "just like a nurse with a nervous child," assuring people that the world contained no bogeymen, saying that everything was in order and that the Germans were just as tired as the British. He remained of course for the most part the stiff soldier, entirely true to himself then as ever, and when the strain caused a staff officer's voice to rise to a high pitch he asked, "What's the good of an s.o. who *squeaks*? If he *squeaks* like this now, what'll he do if there is real fighting?"

Fending off the pursuing enemy but adamant about not getting involved in a serious battle which would risk his trained force upon which the Empire depended, he skillfully kept the Germans at arm's length, touching them only with his fingertips so that there would be the fewest possible British casualties. Marching toward the foe just days previously the men had endlessly sung and resung "Tipperary." Now the singing was not as steady, but the units of I Corps stayed correctly formed up and did not intermingle, their demeanor strikingly different from that of their comrades-in-arms of II Corps. There was no singing at all there, but disorder and mixed-together units and men bedraggled and unkempt—"hardly recognizable as soldiers," wrote the liaison officer Edward Spears of the 11th Hussars.

Through the heat and dust the British marched thirteen days with their faces to the setting sun and their backs to the enemy, towers of smoke rising in dense clouds from the shelled villages behind them. The infantry averaged four hours a day rest, the mounted men three. Off to the left the backs of the horses of the French cavalry galled so that the sight was painful and the odor frightful, but the British troopers led their horses except when scouting about for the Germans. The always-shaved I Corps commander only once appeared to lose for an instant his glacial calmness, and indeed it was the only time he did so for the entire period of the war. At Landrecies it seemed that he had been overtaken and must give battle. Field guns, lots of them, were rumbling from nearby, and with them came the sound of infantry fire. The Uhlans were very close at hand. "If we can't get away," he said, "we will fight to the last man. If we are caught, by God, we'll sell our lives dearly." He ordered the town barricaded with anything at hand. The troops rushed into the houses and flung out of windows furniture and chairs and mattresses, one carefully aimed so that it landed on the head of an unpopular officer. But no real fight developed, and Haig moved out over village tracks through a misty night as the Great Retreat went on.

A captured Uhlan officer was brought to the corps commander to say that his own misfortune did not matter because the Kaiser would be in London by Christmas in any event; "I am afraid not," Haig replied coolly, adding that perhaps the Kaiser would be in London upon some Christmas in the future, if the British so desired, but that he would be there as a prisoner. The Great Retreat came to its finish and the French gathered themselves and with the BEF along the Marne drove the Germans back. There followed the digging of hasty entrenchments and the realization that there could not be an immediate breakthrough by either side. So the armies began to stretch themselves out to the north in a race to the sea and a hoped-for flanking of the enemy. The British hurried to Ypres in Belgium. It protected the road to the Channel ports. If the Germans took Ypres the war could find its ending there.

Upon the ancient city was turned the full power of Germany. Shells crashed in the streets to destroy the medieval buildings. In a protecting semicircle before Ypres the BEF prepared to fight, Haig designating a line little more than a mile out from the city and saying that beyond this he could not retreat, that upon this point he must commit himself to fight to the last round and the last man, that he and his command must die together if necessary. His defensive arrangements were masterly usages of barbed wire and reinforced strongpoints. He shifted his troops to thicken here by thinning out there. His cavalry he utilized as mounted infantry, a fast-moving reserve. He was always aware of the need to bring some relief to the most forwardly placed troops, to get them out of the line for a while.

The blows fell. British losses were enormous, terrible. Ypres was to be a monument to the Regular Army, the Old Contemptibles—a monument raised on the death site. There came a moment when all seemed lost, for the line broke. Shells landed near the chateau where Haig made his headquarters. Splinters flew and glass from a shattered window crashed down on the map he was studying. "For heaven's sake come, sir!" cried an aide. Haig replied that he was busy.

"The next shell may be the last—come!"

"I said I was busy."

After a time he went to a safer place, but soon it too came under German fire. The walls vibrated from the shelling. General Haig washed, brushed his hair, did up his tie, stood waiting while his kneeling batman saw to his spurs. A dud hit, and failed to explode. "Mr. Krupp would be very vexed," he said. Another shell, live, struck the house, killing two orderlies. The huge glass candelabra crashed on the table. Along the Menin Road came broken and routed British formations, the men disheartened and exhausted. It was the supreme critical moment of what history would call the First Battle of Ypres. Haig ordered his staff onto their horses and with an orderly riding with a pennon on a lance he slowly moved up the road toward the enemy. His face was entirely immobile and inscrutable as for one of the last times in modern war there was revived the personal element of the leadership of the past.

At the slowest of trots he moved with his group. He did not say a word or make any gesture, but by his presence and calm gave to the fleeing men what could only be called an inspiring example. They formed up. The Germans were held. Ypres was safe.

There followed the commencement of that trench war which almost no one had foreseen and which would last more than three years. In November of 1914, Haig was promoted to full general; on Christmas Day his I Corps was created an army. The French attacked and were bloodily repulsed, and attacked again and were bloodily repulsed. Haig was ordered to attack using the Territorial Army men and Reservists who had replaced the dead Old Contemptibles, and did so and appeared to be about to pierce the German line. But Sir John French greedily held control of the reserves which might have done the job and did not release them until too late. It was a misjudgment too great to be overlooked, and in December of 1915 French was relieved of his command of His Majesty's Forces in France. His replacement by Haig was the obvious and universally approved choice.

By then a terrifying proportion of British officers and men had been "expended." Britain raised to follow them an army of a million volunteers drawn by the everywhere-pasted-up poster of Secretary of State for War Lord Kitchener pointing his finger directly at the viewer and saying Your King and Country Need You. The New Army. Enthusiastic, educated far beyond any previous British force, of social background and standards entirely different from the old sweats of the past, they were drilled in United Kingdom posts and then sent out to France to join Dominions contingents under the command of Sir Douglas Haig. There came a day when with three million shells dumped forward to be fired by fifty thousand gunners the British prepared to attack. (Napoleon had brought twenty thousand shells to Waterloo.) A heavy-caliber piece was in place for every fifty yards of a sixteen-mile front. The shells weighed from thirty-five pounds to fourteen hundred pounds each.

The preliminary bombardment went on for seven days and seven nights without interruption. At a given instant the firing ceased. It was a beautiful summer's day. In the sudden silence the waiting soldiers were astonished to hear the trilling of birds. Whistles blew and 150,000 infantrymen rose and scrambled up ladders to the ground above their trenches and over the top: 7:30 A.M., July 1, 1916, the Battle of the Somme.

THE ETERNAL JEW

The German lines against which Gen. Sir Douglas Haig flung himself on the first day of July 1916 would never have been there had Walther Rathenau never lived. The German soldiers who held those lines would have been dead, or the discharged veterans of a defeated army.

"We must win, *we must!*" Rathenau wrote a friend when August of 1914 came; and, the only person of authority in Germany who saw what the future held, he set into motion three days after the first troops marched undreamed-of processes which would make his country far stronger than she or her enemies could ever have imagined. "*We must*," he wrote, "and yet we have no clear, no absolute right to do so."

He cried when the war came, a weeping prophet amid people delirious with joy gathering in tremendous crowds to cheer and exalt that what they called the Day had come. No one had ever seen him weep before. "Wherever I turn I see shadows before me," Rathenau wrote just before the fighting began. "I see them every evening as I make my way through the shrill noise of the Berlin streets; I see them when I consider the insane way we flaunt our wealth; when I hear the empty, saber-rattling speeches. It is a mistake to think all is well simply because the lieutenant is spick and span and the attaché optimistic." Yet he worshiped, literally worshiped, Germany and Germans—Siegfried, German rectitude, German might, the Nordic gods, this "marvelous blond people of the North whose every migration becomes a conquest." The German Army must advance into that Russia who had "loved all her past conquerors as the Russian peasant woman loves a beating. We must march to St. Petersburg and Moscow and occupy a larger part of Russia for a prolonged time. The discipline and restraint of the German soldier, the justice and incorruptibility of the German administration, will become legendary in a short time." (He also said Germany must take over Latin America. The world could not allow such a rich region to be a "demi-civilization.")

To many in Germany and to many in all the countries of the Continent, the war was of a piece with all those age-old conflicts which marked the course of European history. Rathenau recognized at once with that lightning, that blazing brilliance of his, how seminal a change was occurring, what a sea change the world faced. Time and its hindsight were not required for him to see what was happening. "I am contributing," he wrote before August was past, "to the overthrow of the gods to whom, before August 1914, the world prayed, a world to which I belong." He was, he said, a Saul who wished to recant but hesitated because in seeking salvation he might leave behind a better world. Perhaps, he wrote, Europe might now decline but a better order might replace the old crumbling one. But then, two months later: "We shall live through more difficult times than we have ever seen. A hard race will grow up and perhaps it will trample on our hearts. This war is not a beginning but an end; ruins are what it will leave behind." Even Germany's first brilliant victories, the French and British flying before von Kluck and the Russians shattered by von Hindenburg, did not cheer him. "Can you not detect the false note?" he asked a friend. "We shall be victorious unto death."

Yet he labored on in such fashion that by late 1915 the London *Times* said that Germany's successes were due to three generals and one civilian—Dr. Walther Rathenau, the only man in the German War Ministry who did not wear uniform, and whose offices were closed off by hastily erected wooden partitions put up to protect the soldiers from the civilian and the Jew. "If this man *has* helped us," said one officer, "then it is a scandal and a disgrace." The words were widely reported, and a man who ran an anti-Semitic hate sheet sent them on to the individual they concerned. That perhaps was not so remarkable, but nothing could more precisely define Rathenau than that for some time past he had addressed the hate sheet's proprietor with the familiar *du* and that he wrote thanking him for his "kindly" letter. He was not joking. He did not joke.

It was not the only example of the discordance or dissonance seen in this profoundly uneven man. "The day will never come when the Kaiser will enter through the Brandenburg Gate as a conquering hero astride a white charger," he wrote. "If that event occurs then the history of the world will have lost all its meaning." Yet to oblige the Kaiser, he, Rathenau, bought from him a royal palace for use as a summer retreat, and after receiving Wilhelm there kept a chair cordoned off so that no one could sit in it. "That is where the Kaiser used to sit," he told people.

One of the richest men in the world, he said no family in Germany should have an income of more than three thousand marks a year.* So brilliant as to cause people to say his was the finest mind the Jews of Germany ever produced, he rated intelligence as far less important than soul, blood, spirit. Dark-haired and dark-eyed, he felt only the blond and blue-eyed were destined to be lords of this earth. Passionate about many things, he is not known ever to have undertaken a sexual relationship.

His range was breathtaking. "He knew *everything*," said the woman closest to him. His mind worked so quickly that before you were finished saying a sentence he knew what he would reply and what you would then say. A recognized artist, scientist, musician, architect, designer, one of Germany's two greatest businessmen, at one time its best-selling author, he was found fascinating and repellent in equal measure. The life he lived and the death he died told the story of his Germany and Germany that would be.

His father was Emil Rathenau, the son of a well-off family of pronounced artistic and musical interests. Emil's mother, Walther's grandmother, had little time for her son. (She died in Berlin leaving

---

*Less than one thousand dollars.

Emil little in the way of fond memories, but piles of forgotten and unpaid bills.) Emil married a woman somewhat in his mother's image, the daughter of a Frankfurt banker who loved painting and her piano and came to Berlin with retainers, carriages, *objets d'art*. They had two sons and a daughter. The marriage was not a happy one.

At the time of Walther's birth in 1867 the father was running a rather modest foundry principally engaged in making steam engines for gas and water works. The family lived in a house attached to the little factory. As a child Walther possessed an unshakable equanimity. Ordered to go stand in the corner for some boyish mischief, he did so serenely, seemingly quite content to do it for so long as was required. Other punishments left him calm and smiling. He had a phenomenal memory, describing towns seen when he was two or three years old. School he found unbearable. He never failed a subject, but his grades were mediocre. German was his best subject. He read widely. Once his father awoke to find him going through *Macbeth* by candlelight and was enraged, for he did not hold with wasting one's time on such matters when one's grades were poor. It was difficult for the mother, although she appreciated Shakespeare, for she also wanted to see better marks. Walther smiled his unshakable smile and showed no bad temper, remorse, sulkiness.

In 1881 the father visited Paris and saw there an incandescent lamp exhibited by the American inventor Thomas A. Edison. Emil Rathenau saw the future. He bought the European patents. He then virtually vanished from any aspect of life beyond his work. He worked Sundays, nights, holidays; he hardly permitted himself a free afternoon. He talked business constantly. He seemed like some priest dedicated to a new religion—art did not exist for him, or literature, or the theater. He worked his German General Electric Company up to one of the industrial giants of the burgeoning and dynamic Wilhelminian Germany that followed upon the triumphal wars of the 1860s and 1870s. His undertakings were huge, and he proved a genius at arranging gigantic financial backing. His was the first modern big-scale industry in Germany, with vast undertakings in municipal power stations, electrical distribution to rural areas, exploitation of water power, mass production of electrical implements, the substitution of electrical power for steam. He became an equal of the Krupps, richer than Croesus.

Emil Rathenau was a direct opposite to his son Walther. Extreme highs and lows characterized the father, now daring in his plans and willing to talk to everyone of new projects, now darkly secretive, distrustful, brooding. His attitude toward money was strange. His family said of him that he could understand everything that involved purchases below three marks. Then he became uncomprehending until purchases of three million marks were mentioned. Of sums between he understood nothing.

His son Walther, impenetrably cool as he entered young manhood, was hooded and shrouded even when dealing with his mother, to whom he was far closer than his father. His letters to her were veiled, unrevealing. He had no close friends. Yet there was something about him that commanded respect and even awe. Thomas A. Edison once came to dinner at the Rathenau home and remarked that he believed he could read one's future by one's face. His hostess asked what the inventor predicted for her younger son, Erich. A born technician, Edison replied. And Walther? "He knows things I have no idea of. This chap will one day accomplish more and know more than we all. This is a marvelous person."

The time for Walther's obligatory military service came, one year for those of his education as opposed to three years for those of limited schooling. The regiment of his choice was the Garde Cuirassier. To serve in it required that a man be tall, and he was that, a slim figure over six feet. Also required was a private income, for the unit's uniform with its burnished breastplate was expensive. (His father grumbled at the cost.) To be an officer required something else: one must not be a Jew. It was impossible. A way out was offered: convert. It was not so rare a thing in Germany; it was far more common there than in any other country. Many German nobles had married off their impecunious sons to rich Jewish girls who became Christians before the ceremonies.

It was in that moment when he had to make his decision, Rathenau said later, that he came face to face with a question whose answer he was never to find. A German Jew "entered the world as a citizen of the second class and no amount of ability or merit can rid him of that status." The fact was to bedevil him to the last day, indeed the last moment, of his life. Liking to tell Jewish stories, which he did quite well, he at the same time considered himself first the Prussian and second the Jew. He said a thousand times that the Jews were another branch of the German nation, like the Saxons or Bavarians. Jews in general were more foreign to him, he wrote, than Brandenburgers or Holsteiners although perhaps more akin than Silesians or Lorrainers. Zionism he found incomprehensible: "The vast majority of German Jews, among whom there are many whose ancestors have lived in Germany for countless centuries, have only one national feeling, and that is German. We want to live and die in Germany and for Germany as our fathers did before us. Let others found a state in Palestine. Nothing attracts us to Asia."

He would not convert. An endorsement of an unjust system, his baptism would be a lie and an incorrect method of viewing the world. He served his military year as a private in the Garde Cuirassier. When it was over he went to university. One day he came into his home dressed in a frock coat. His mother inquired what the occasion was and learned that when one was formally awarded one's Ph.D. such attire was required. He had never mentioned he was getting his doctorate.

It was in electrochemistry, the only electrical field not touched by his father's business affairs. With his new degree he obtained a job in Saxony. He stayed there seven years. He was brilliantly successful in his work, securing several patents for new processes and inventing a system for producing chlorine and alkalis by means of electrolysis. Nights he read enormously in half a dozen fields, remembering everything, wrote heroic plays and poems, and painted. In his cool manner he came to realize his written sagas concerned with the Wars of Liberation and love and sacrifice for the Fatherland were unpublishable. His paintings were better, of professional caliber but not works of genius. For years he persisted with them, hoping to raise himself to a higher level. He was never able to do so.

He took up with the lovely blond daughter of an old family. But the girl was entirely unintellectual. He realized they could never be happy and broke off the affair, an act for the coldness of which he was condemned in both their circles. To his sister Edith, nearly fifteen years younger, he appeared to be a hopeless romantic, but not a romantic for women. It was an idyllic Germany that commanded his worship. He sublimated love for individuals to love for an idealized Fatherland. "If you had met Siegfried or Arminium,"* she told him, "you would have run away from them because you would have thought their hands too dirty." It was Germany, not the Germans, he called Beloved. "I hate the smell of little people," he once said.

Toward the end of his stay in Saxony he published his first piece of writing save for a few technical efforts. He was nearly thirty. His subject was the Jews of Germany, and the piece was a magazine article for the renowned editor Maximilian Harden's *Zukunft*. "In the midst of Germany live an alien and isolated race of men. Loud and self-conscious in their dress, hot-blooded and restless in their manner. An Asiatic horde on the sandy plains of Prussia."

The Jews lived, he went on, in a "stifling ghetto, invisible," which they had chosen for themselves in preference to "the pure air of the German woods and hills," they the "dark people" so unlike the "blond and marvelous people." One saw them thronging Berlin streets of a Sunday morning, or in the theater foyer in the evening. They came with industrial civilization and democracy and capitalism, but they were governed by fear while the German was the man of courage. The dissimilarities between the two were a terrible tragedy, the solution to which was that the Jews must consciously assimilate, unloading "racial qualities whether good or bad." It was his first public mention of the abiding concerns of his life: the contrast between fear and courage, Reason and Soul, materialism and idealism, art and business, pleasure-seeking and partaking in purer joys, intellect and visionary intuition, the mechanical age and spiritual values, nobility and baseness, the insider and the outsider. His vast later writings on this series

---

*Arminium = Hermann the Conqueror, annihilator of Roman legions.

of contrasts were turgid, tortured, boundlessly heavy, unreadable to modern eyes but wildly popular among the readers of the day, who were allured by elaborate metaphysical philosophizing. His works were filled with discussions of the "race of the instinctive," which was proud, passionate, principled, imaginative, and of the "race of the intellectuals," which was cold, feeble, clever, slanderous, and unprincipled. Only the mixture of the two, he said, produced genius— adding that he was a German of Jewish stock. ("Nature has so intermingled the two streams of áncient blood in me that they are in foaming opposition.")

A man the writer Emil Ludwig called a "more perfervid German patriot than Nietzsche," Rathenau remained, Ludwig thought, the proud Hebraic aristocrat who carried the shield of his ancestry "showing the dents and fractures that he himself had made in it." Imperial Chancellor Prince von Bülow recalled in his memoirs how Rathenau first introduced himself: he stepped forward, put his right hand on his left breast, and "with a bow as flawless as his dress, in the manner of a *jeune premier* of the Théâtre Français, said, 'Your Highness, let me, before I am honored by the favor of being received by you, make a statement that is at the same time a confession.' He paused briefly and then, winningly: 'Your Highness, I am a Jew.' "

In 1899 the board of directors of his father's German General Electric Company asked him to go abroad to construct power stations. With some misgivings he accepted the offer and was off to Manchester, Buenos Aires, Amsterdam, Baku. Four years later, in 1903, his younger brother, Erich, died—he had always been sickly. Almost overnight the relations between the members of the Rathenau family sustained a change almost indescribable. Never well suited to one another—their battles at the dinner table in the days of his childhood often saw Walther departing for his room—the mother and father appeared almost to exchange their roles relative to the remaining son and daughter. The father, always remote from his older son, became close to him. The mother turned hard, cruel, harsh, suspicious, almost insanely jealous of Walther. When he and his sister Edith wanted to talk together they had to hide from Frau Rathenau.

His personal difficulties with his father ended, Rathenau became his right-hand man at the German General Electric Company and began the great business career that propelled him to the very top ranks of European industrialists, to membership in the group of three hundred men who, he said, controlled the world. (It was a remark open to unfavorable interpretation. Anti-Semites said that the story of the Elders of Zion pulling strings was proved correct; Rathenau had admitted it for all to know.)

In the years before 1914, the last happy years Europe was to know for so very long, Rathenau guided German General Electric ventures into metal production, glass, chemicals, telegraph companies, cotton mills, tramways, motor cars, shipbuilding. He supervised mines in Africa, electrical railroads in South America, undertakings in England, Spain, Russia, Italy, France, Austria. He took up positions of leadership in eighty-six German companies and twenty-one foreign ones. His wealth became unimaginable. Yet he never seemed to enjoy making money particularly, nor spending it. There were no yachts, racehorses, magnificent carriages or limousines, no hordes of servants, never a retinue of hangers-on. His friend Emil Ludwig said he never opened a bottle of rare wine for his personal pleasure. His home in the Grünewald at 65 Königsallee he designed himself down to the colors of the rooms and the carpets; it was luxurious but in a very quiet, cool, restrained late-eighteenth-century Prussian style. The same form was applied to the small Palace of Freienwalde forty miles northeast of Berlin, which he purchased from the Kaiser, and to the pied-à-terre he maintained in his parents' home in the Victoriastrasse a hundred yards from the Roland Fountain. Each piece in each residence was exquisite but understated, and the effect, people felt, was that of a frigid museum, of a way of life gone into history. He was not a philanthropist of great note, restricting his generosity to small grants for promising artists, writers, and musicians. (When the Society for the Improvement of Convicts asked for a contribution he wrote: "I cannot refrain from pointing out that your name offends my sensibilities. It does not correspond to my ideas that one part of mankind should proclaim of itself that it has the intention of improving another part.") His wealth seemed to create one more barrier between himself and the world, and he said carefully that it was difficult to have many friends when so many people desired something from those "whose situation presupposes that they can fulfill certain kinds of wishes."

As a businessman he was a tough and shrewd negotiator with people on or approaching his level. On the level beneath he was painstaking and meticulous, carrying out unannounced and careful inspections of his plants. With workers he was just, remote, somewhat paternal, anti-union. To a great extent he rejected the values of Wilhelminian society, using that society to increase his worldly success while saying that a new set of spiritual values was required, that the Machine Age's materialism was whittling down, reducing, what he called Soul. Modern life's Reason, he said, carried a death germ and longed in its heart for freedom from the "chain of purposefulness." As he rose to be one of the two most important industrialists of Germany, his only rival to be Hugo Stinnes, he moved at the highest levels of the country and in Court society, but always as the outsider. The invisible wall through which one can see but never pass was always there because he was a Jew and because of that unalterable apartness. Perhaps he was lonely, for he was prone to sudden explosions of friendship directed at new acquaintances, either men or women, which would see him writing that never before had he met such a soulmate, that his home was filled with the impression that the prized visitor had left behind. Then suddenly it would be over and the chosen person would be out of Rathenau's life—"the Don Juan of friendship," he was called.

Yet among those friends were the intellectual and artistic elite of his day: André Gide, who wrote that Rathenau spoke French, "it really must be said, with no accent whatever"; Robert Musil, who made him a barely disguised character in his *The Man Without Qualities*; Emil Ludwig, who thought he spoke the most beautiful German Ludwig had ever heard; the writers Hugo von Hofmannsthal, Rainer Maria Rilke, Hermann Hesse, and Stefan Zweig, who found his manner of speaking awe-inspiring, each sentence perfectly rounded and so clearly formed that if it were taken down in shorthand it would have proved a completely finished exposition of whatever he was discussing; the theologian Martin Buber, for the study of whose works on Hasidic mysticism Rathenau learned Hebrew; the dramatists Frank Wedekind, Gerhart Hauptmann, and Hermann Sudermann, who said he was the most brilliant intellect of the age; the theatrical luminary Max Reinhardt; the artists Max Liebermann, his cousin, and Edvard Munch, who did his portrait. "A nasty fellow, isn't he?" Rathenau said, looking at Munch's presentation of himself as masterly, appraising, proud, astute. "That is because when you have your picture painted by a great artist, you become more like yourself than you are." It was the only work of a modern master he ever bought; he preferred the more sedate efforts of the artists of the past. (Van Gogh's productions he termed "an eyesore.")

Moving as he did among mutually suspicious elements of society— for the artists and writers generally found little in common with the tycoons with whom Rathenau spent his days, nor the nobles and state ministers with whom he spent his evenings—he spoke to each in his own language and on his own level. His ability to transcend all barriers, but always with that outsider's view, extended even to his relationship with the All-Highest. Few men could be more opposite in temperament to Rathenau than the hysterical and flamboyant Kaiser, and he found the monarch's flashing eyes and wild statements ridiculous and his garish uniforms and multitudes of rings and bracelets repellent, but somehow the two managed something like a close personal friendship, and spent many hours talking together. Sometimes the heroic look and piercing blue eyes of the leader of the German race captured this most complicated of His Imperial Majesty's subjects and he could term Wilhelm "a true prince" possessed of "dignity, strength, mastery." Then immediately he could write—and there were those who thought the words could apply equally to their author—"There was scarcely an unselfconscious moment; the only unconscious thing, and that was where he began to be a touching human being, was the struggle within himself, a nature set against himself." At the time Rathenau wrote the words Wilhelm was in disgrace, and it took a certain kindness and bravery for Rathenau to speak well of him. But earlier, when Wilhelm was riding high, master of the world in the making, it seemed, Rathenau said of him: "He is an enchanter and a man marked by fate. A nature rent, and yet not feeling the rent. He is on the road to disaster." Again there were those who thought the words could describe all too well the man who said them.

Looked upon by each of the worlds he frequented as a stranger, as something like a nobleman from some distant Oriental land—"an Arabian prince, tall and slim, dark-skinned and dark-haired, gentleman and sahib in appearance and manner," Emil Ludwig said—he tried to suppress all in himself that he disliked. He wanted to overcome, he said, overzealous critical tendencies, enjoyment of the failures of others, the desire to shine and to argue, and above all, fear. Always in English clothes of exquisite cut, taller than almost anyone with whom he spoke, he physically as well as intellectually dominated people, leaning over to take an arm, putting a hand on a shoulder, the glittering intellect joined to an almost menacing physical presence. Perhaps timorous in his soul of souls, he fought timidity by keeping always lowered that impenetrable veil. It would never lift for a woman. The nearest approach to a romance he ever made was with Lily Deutsch, the sister of the immensely rich and prominent German-American financier and patron of the arts Otto H. Kahn and the wife of Felix Deutsch, an important German General Electric Company executive.

Yet even for her the all-pervading ambivalence of his life was always present. He could write in answer to a letter of hers that his only merit was that he loved her, of how his heart "by your dear words has been awakened and set throbbing and your beautiful image hovers before me so that I have been able to feel warmth, light, and peace"; and the next sentence was: "But early tomorrow morning I will tear up your letter and go into the country."

By Lily Deutsch's testimony their relationship was never physically consummated. "He never had any real feelings," she said years later when he was dead. "He just had a longing for feelings. He had a *very* sensuous nature, but to this day I have no idea what vent he gave to his passions. He held them in check." He was a romantic, she said, as his sister had said, for Germany and its idealized blond Teutons. "This romanticism was connected with his Jewishness; sensitive Jews are often romantic. But he struck deep roots in German culture and could not detach himself from Germany.

"That part of him was real."

In August of 1914, Germany went to war. For half a century the campaign had been in the making, and the war was meant to be a lightning war. A very brief fight was planned. All the decades-long perfecting of the dispositions and allotments along the lines of the quick victories of the 1860s and 1870s counted upon triumph before the year was out. Not a person in the government had calculated otherwise. Yet within forty-eight hours after the first troops marched, and tears overcame him as they had never before, not even in childhood days, Rathenau saw and said that all plans were based upon a false assumption and must fail. Four days after the beginning of the fight, he presented himself at the office of War Minister Erich von Falkenhayn to say that the British fleet would blockade Germany and make it impossible for the country to conduct a war lasting more than three months. For one thing, Germany had insufficient nitrates, he pointed out. Nitrates were indispensable for the manufacture of explosives, and the imported supply on hand would be exhausted within a few weeks.

Von Falkenhayn listened and realized Rathenau was right. This war, Rathenau went on, could not be won with the methods of the past. It must be a total, economic, war that required rationing and organization. The incisiveness of his presentation seized the coldly logical War Minister. Rathenau was named chief of a state apparatus of a type that had never before existed in history. In his Raw Materials Section, behind the wooden partitions, Rathenau worked every day until midnight. He forged a great national machine which commandeered nitrates from the farmers of occupied Belgium, who were preparing to spread them on their fields. Then in time he set up factories to manufacture nitrates from the air. He wrote regulations for the use and distribution of all raw materials, entirely rationalized German industry, seized all supplies of metal, cotton, leather, skins, flax, linen, and chemicals or bought them from neutral countries, began to manufacture synthetic substitutes.

He ordered price ceilings for goods, a practice never heard of before. He put into motion a plan forcibly to transport 700,000 Belgians for work in German factories to replace soldiers at the Front. He made German industry cease all nonessential production, completely subordinating private concerns to the needs of the state. His orders affected every segment of German society, agriculture, business, industry. Without his work Germany would have been strangled in months. He saved his country for four years of war.

Even as he did so he wondered at what he was doing. Nothing could have been more in dissonance with his lifelong emphasis on the value of the Soul as opposed to bigness, efficiency, mechanization, impersonality. He turned Germany into a great war machine, but "Do you know what we are fighting for?" he asked a member of the German Parliament. "I do not. And I should be glad if you could tell me." The war he was helping to fight—"It is the funeral pyre of the social structure of Europe, which will never rise again from the flames." He knew as few others did that an era was ending or perhaps had already ended; he was participating in the murder of the past, he wrote. "Who has not asked himself when reading one of the earlier authors of the vanished epoch, say Stendhal or Balzac: how is that possible? Only thirty years ago the Gay Century was at the height of its mother-of-pearl brilliance, and now . . ."

That past his work was slaying was, he wrote, the age of gallantry now quickly become "of a sort of fossil, dead and decayed, an antiquated ghost." Yet he worked on, saying that the Prussian officer class would never forgive him for saving them, and that he could not forgive himself for having done it. What was it all for? Rathenau questioned all of Germany's ideals and values, saying that Jesus Christ had never recognized them as worthy. "Fatherland, nation, wealth, power"—the only absolute value was the Soul, from which he had turned away to ally himself with Junkers and army and guns and high explosives and death. Yet by his doings the Germans roared forward in the east and held in the west. The *Times* of London expressed awe at "this miracle of industry, this inventiveness, this genius of organization. It is a story which explains the fall of Warsaw and the great Eastern offensives and the impregnable Western line."

Rathenau dreaded the future. Richard Wagner, he wrote, composer of heroic music and proponent of German nationalism and anti-Semitism, was perhaps as great a listener as he was a musical interpreter, for he had heard what was meant by "a kind of theatrical, barbaric military pomp, the monuments and buildings of Berlin, the modes of behavior and cults of certain groups. There is always someone, Lohengrin, Siegfried, Wotan, who can do everything and knock everything down, who can release suffering virtue, punish vice, and bring general salvation, striking an exaggerated pose, with the sound of trumpets and lightning and scenic effects. People want the word of salvation to be spoken on every occasion with a great gesture, people want to see historical turning points presented before them, they want to hear the clash of swords and the flapping of banners."

The conflicts within himself were as the conflicts of the glittering Europe of pre-1914, and his impotency to change matters the impotency of Europe to control its long suicide, the war. He came to be unable to stand crowded rooms or houses other than his own. The streets themselves oppressed him. When President Wilson's emissary Edward M. House came to Berlin to seek a negotiated peace, it was Rathenau who impressed him most of all he met; but "It saddened me," House wrote the President, "to hear him say that as far as he knew, he stood alone. He said he had begun to wonder whether all the rest were really mad, or whether the madness lay within himself."

VICTOR OF VERDUN

In early 1914 an aging French infantry officer facing mandatory retirement decided to buy a home, the first he had ever owned. Army regulations were that one must go upward or get out, and in his military dossier there was a binding recommendation that there be no more promotions for him. So he must go.

The home he selected was a modest cottage outside Saint-Omer in the northern part of the country. He had been born nearly sixty years earlier some twenty miles away and had gone to boarding school in Saint-Omer after a not notably happy childhood; his mother died when he was three and his stepmother disliked him. He had as a child seen light infantry lieutenants of the local garrison in the streets and decided then that he would like to be in their position. Or perhaps it was the inspiration of his mother's uncle, his granduncle, who had served under Bonaparte in Italy before becoming a priest, and liked to say he wished the men of his family to bear either the cross or the sword. (It was he who paid for the boarding school.) In any event, having become a soldier, the officer had served thirty-eight years and had ended as Colonel of Infantry Henri Philippe Benoni Omer Pétain, a tall, bald, blue-eyed, silent figure most men—but not all women—considered cold. His career had been far from brilliant. He had been essentially an instructor, moving slowly up the ladder of rank, twelve years a lieutenant, a decade as a captain, a major at forty-four years of age, and finally a colonel when he was fifty-five. "I was old as a lieutenant, as a captain, as a colonel, I have been old in all my ranks," he remarked. He had never served one day outside France, never seen France's Senegal, Indochina, Madagascar, Morocco, never heard a shot fired in anger, never seen a skirmish. The son of a family he knew once asked why there was not a single campaign ribbon on his chest and was told, "Major Pétain is not a fighting officer like our other friends. He is a theoretician, a teacher of the art and science of war, and these do not win medals."

It was the teaching, not the lack of decorations, which placed Colonel Pétain in a position to be bundled off into retirement as a pensioner of no great distinction. Everything he taught was in direct contradiction to the military concepts of the French Army and the French nation, to the spirit of France. He believed what he believed, and no amount of hints, words to the wise, or official pressure could make him change. It was a mixture of temperament and intellectual conviction which made him so. A northerner, calm, dispassionate, businesslike, disciplined, imperturbable, utterly different from the southerner of tradition fiery and excitable, he was completely opposed to the prevailing doctrine that French spirit, French élan, *furia fran-cese*, dash, boldness, were what had brought the French their great victories of the past and that it was the lack of such which brought them their defeat by Prussia in 1870–71. Napoleon, the men of the French Army said, had won by recklessly attacking. To maneuver and hesitate and estimate, to calculate—that was passivity and meant defeat and the enemy marching down the Champs Elysées.

Pétain could not agree. Once after a mock battle he was asked his opinion of the goings-on. There had been a fixed-bayonet assault against a hilltop village. A band played the troops on. The cuiras-siers went forward exactly as had their predecessors under Napoleon, dressed in the same uniform of high crested helmets with horsehair plumes, heavy breastplates, and tall boots. There had been no real artillery preparation. The charge was magnificent. Everyone was de-lighted. The proud officer commanding stood by. "I am sure," Pétain said in his deep and hollow voice, "that General LeGallet, so as to make a greater impact on your minds, must have set out to present a synthesis of all the mistakes which a modern army must no longer make."

As a teacher in the advanced schools of the army he harped for years on his favorite theory, which was that heavy artillery fire, powerful and destructive, must precede any forward movement by troops. Shells conquer a position, he said. Troops occupy it. Nothing could be more opposite to the views of the chieftains of the French Army, led by their mystical high priest, the fiery theorist Loiseau de Grandmaison, who said and said again that infantry, not artillery, was the queen of the battlefield, that the bayonet was the most useful of all weapons, that an attack *à l'outrance*, the only kind of attack which wins, must be made with drums and bands and with no attempt to utilize the cover of hills or valleys, for that might dilute a formation's shock effect. Maneuver and flanking movements, it was agreed, weaken the offensive spirit. The thing to do was seize the enemy by the neck and throttle him, never mind your own defense and what he might do before you got to him. Combat was a matter of will, élan, morale.

Pétain might argue that dense formations attacking in the open against rapid-fire weapons would lead to catastrophe, that opposing such weapons called for supple and flexible shifting, use of the terrain, and sharpshooting. The prevailing doctrine was that marksmanship in an attack was unnecessary in an age of modern magazine rifles and that what was required was a cone of undirected fire followed by a roaring charge, boldness, dash, a hurling of oneself upon the enemy. One prevailed if the soldier in the ranks had the right attitude and his officer the right fortitude. That the traditional red trousers and kepi, the blue jacket, white gloves, and dancing plume of the officers made a perfect target was beside the point. "Rashness is the safest policy," de Grandmaison said. Imprudence was the best of safeguards. The French Army could know no other law.

Always, then, a discredited rebel, Pétain put in his time. He was popular with the officers serving under him for his attention to their welfare, but there were few willing to ally their destinies to his. An exception was an almost freakishly brilliant young man who, admiring

Colonel Pétain's lucidity, requested service under him in the 133rd Infantry after graduation from Saint-Cyr; but then, Charles de Gaulle was always an exception to every rule.

Dour and unyielding where professional matters were concerned, Pétain in his private life was more relaxed. He liked dirty jokes, puns, funny stories, mild practical jokes. As a junior officer serving in Marseille it amused him to walk the Canebière, the city's main street—which was believed by the Marseillais to be the subject of awed conversation by all the world; they were certain the President of the Republic asked his Premier each morning, "What do you believe they are saying on the Canebière today?"—and ask a citizen kindly to tell him the name of the street upon which they stood. Invariably the response, Pétain said, was that the infuriated citizen would pound the pavement with his cane and shout, "What do you take this for, a pile of *merde?*"

In the more intimate aspects of his private life he, the confirmed bachelor, was known as a master of the boudoir. He was never without a mistress or two, or more, and nothing was more typical in his life than that when the moment for his rendezvous with destiny came he was found in bed with a woman by a messenger come to tell him the news. A splendid rider and crack shot, fond of children, he ate well, maintained a great handlebar mustache, kept so youthful an appearance that he furnished formidable opposition for young Lieutenant de Gaulle in pursuit of a garrison beauty, and showed no bitterness over the entire disavowal of his views by the ruling military hierarchy. His cold impersonality in many situations he never lost. Once he met with an officer with whom he had had some differences in the past, discussed cooperation between their two units, and ended by saying, "It was Colonel Pétain who received you. Pétain himself wants to have as little as possible to do with you." He turned and saw an embarrassed lieutenant who had overheard. "You. Get the hell out of here."

He was fifty-eight when the war came in 1914. They gave him a brigade in the northern army of that Gen. Charles Lanrezac whose view of Field Marshal Sir John French's command of foreign languages set so unhappy a tone to initial cooperation between France and Great Britain. The mission of the Allied forces in the north was to attempt to hold the onrushing Germans. In the south the French poured forth into Lorraine and flung themselves at sight upon the Germans with all the fiery determination desired by Loiseau de Grand-maison and none of the artillery support and coordination of all arms taught by Henri Philippe Pétain. The results were horrible for the Republic. Germans firing from concealment and with machine guns sent to heroes' graves in a matter of days some 10 percent of the French officer corps. (The cadets from Saint-Cyr rushed to the attack in their white gloves and shakos with tossing tricolored ostrich plumes, waving their swords. Not a single man of the graduating class of 1914 survived the war.)

In the hot August days of the Great Retreat from Belgium the men under Colonel Pétain made the Germans pay for every inch they gained. There were no death-or-glory heroics, and the brigade losses were far less than those of adjacent units. On night marches he walked with the men, the only concession to age and rank being that he hooked his arm through a stirrup strap to let a horse help him along. All around him officers were being relieved of their commands, but on the 29th of the month he was given command of a division. "Are they already reduced to revolutionary procedures?" he asked in his ironic manner. He joined his new unit to participate in the Miracle of the Marne, where the Allies turned and flung the Germans back. A woman in whose house he stayed learned the guest was now a general and cut from a deceased relative's old uniform the symbols of the rank and sewed them on Pétain's jacket. A general's cap would have to be found later.

Crossing the Marne, the 6th Division, disorderly and demoralized by the long retreat, learned something of the new commander. The men broke ranks and went running into an orchard to shake the plum trees for their fruit. General Pétain drove his horse through them, firing his pistol in the air as he ordered them back into formation. They scurried to comply. On September 6 he was ordered to attack. He, personally, saw to each gun of the division, ordering each in turn to fire a registering round so that he could correct the range and telling his brigade, regimental, and battalion commanders that not one soldier could be sent forward until the general commanding judged the right moment had arrived for it to be done. The last thing from a staff officer pushing pins on maps despite his wholly academic career, he sought information from all levels down to sergeants and corporals. There resulted a near-perfect attack, with low losses. The Germans lunged back at him and he coolly held them off with barbed wire and trenches, innovations at a time when creation of entrenchments was held by many French officers to make troops unlikely ever to leave them and go forward—to make them "sticky."

Tall, bald, cold, imperturbable, free from all illusions, the Pétain who for years had been out of step with his nation's military thinking was suddenly looked upon as a coming man. They gave him a corps and made him a lieutenant general. Eleven weeks earlier he had been a colonel on the verge of forced retirement; but much had occurred since then, including the death General de Grandmaison might have chosen for himself: he fell at the head of his troops.

In the spring of 1915 the French attacked. Pétain's XXXIII Corps, meticulously trained under his exacting direction, its morale high because of the frequent leaves he allowed and the behind-the-lines theatrical performances and workshops he sponsored—something no one had ever thought to do before—broke through the enemy lines, captured artillery pieces, machine guns, three thousand German soldiers. He decisively outperformed the units on his flanks. They gave him the Second Army in Champagne—thirteen divisions and a full generalcy. He had achieved what headquarters ordered in every instance, but he remained a skeptic, believing headquarters staff did not yet understand the war. For he was the first man and for a time the only man to know that no amount of gallantry and dash would prevail, that what existed on the Western Front was a siege war, that what must be harnessed was not French élan but the stolid holding qualities of the French peasantry. To serve that concept he was efficiency personified. When he sent soldiers to an attack they found no unexpected obstacles in front of them, and the artillery barrage arrived on time. He assumed nothing, and did not permit blind bombardments "lifting" at predetermined moments and then automatically moving on to the next targets: his advancing infantry carried with them colored boards so that artillery observers could tell precisely where they were and control the guns accordingly. "You went into the assault singing 'La Marseillaise'; it was magnificent," he told a group of his men. "But next time you will not need to sing. There will be a sufficient number of guns to ensure your attack is a success. Let us first crush the enemy by artillery fire and afterward we shall win our victory."

No officer on either side was so niggardly in the expenditure of lives. At a meeting of corps commanders the question of hand grenades was raised. The other generals felt five thousand per corps would be sufficient for a coming push. "I want fifty thousand," Pétain said. He wished, he said, to spend metal, not blood; he did not believe in victory at any price, but victory at the smallest price. He made no secret of his cool disregard for what others had said in the past and might say and think now. Many officers eagerly wined and feted ministers, deputies, and senators when they came to view the war, but General Pétain treated them with notable reserve: no one could browbeat him from on high. His staff officers he forbade to gild the lily when issuing communiqués; he would not lie or come close to it.

He inspired faith in all who knew him or served under him, and it seemed that daily he grew stronger, more imposing and majestic. "A soldier before all," said the chief military correspondent for the *Times* of London. He gave himself time for reflection and regularly took walks alone, his head down, thinking. It came to be said of him that during the Great Retreat and on the offensive in the spring he had surpassed all competitors. "He was always successful," said the British liaison officer Edward Spears, "for at every stage of the war he was just a little ahead of the practice, theory, and thought of the moment." He did not order pointless minor attacks and petty trench raid patrols to keep the men in fighting spirit, as other perhaps too ardent or too ambitious generals did, but if he felt it necessary he could mercilessly enforce discipline. When an epidemic of self-inflicted wounds broke out, with men shooting themselves in the arm or leg to get out of the lines, General Pétain had offenders tied up and flung over the trench parapets to spend a night in no-man's-land, their fortunes there to be determined by a stray shot or shell or the lack thereof. The self-mutilations ceased. In the winter of 1915–16 he was made chief of training for the entire French Army.

Underneath the glacial exterior so different with its masklike appearance from that of the blood-and-thunder fire-eaters—Foch, Mangin, d'Urbal, Franchet d'Esperey, Fayolle—emotions no less strong than theirs possessed him. "They are madmen," he said when they still called for attack regardless of preparation or equipment. They thought of Eternal France and cried that they could not endure it that the enemy owned even a square foot of French soil. He thought of the ruined places where people had lived—"The whole city, with decapitated belfry, was no longer anything but a heap of ruins," he said sadly of Arras—and of his soldiers. He thought of God—"It's curious how in getting older I am moved by religious ceremony"—and again of his soldiers. "I played the part of a butcher," he said when his men suffered losses. When to the French it seemed all was in danger of being lost, when the battle of battles came, when there impended the turn of the card which would decide the country's fate, when there hung in the balance faith, the soldiers, France itself, they knew for whom to send. He went to Verdun.

Erich von Falkenhayn, his forceful analytic powers allied to his ruthlessness, the image of the popular idea of a Prussian general, had before 1914 was over moved up from his post as War Minister to replace Helmuth von Moltke, who had always doubted, correctly, his own abilities, as the leader of the German Army. Behind him he left a profound, complex, contradictory, and tortured Jew, Walther Rathenau, who used the Raw Materials Section to mobilize Germany into a gigantic machine for the purpose of making war. For a time the new Chief of the German General Staff sat on the defensive. But when eighteen months had passed since the commencement of hostilities, von Falkenhayn decided that Germany must make a move in the west. For the east he had no concern; the Russians seemed to be on their way out of the war. But the stalemate in Belgium and France was

damaging Germany's position with her allies and with wavering neu-
trals. Time was not on her side. The British were training a gigantic
force. Despite Rathenau's work the Allied blockade was having its
effect.

A breakout through the Allied lines with large territorial conquests
would be a task of the utmost difficulty to perform. What was instead
required, Falkenhayn decided, was to strike the chief sword from the
enemy's hand. He would destroy the French Army and in so doing
bleed France herself white. In his cold fashion he planned a battle
which would do that. His battle was not designed to take a point or a
line. It was designed to provide a killing ground upon which Germany
would execute the French Army.

Falkenhayn studied his maps. One of many German officers brilliant in his understanding of the French—that had been their profession for centuries—he knew that for his Operation Gericht—tribunal,
judgment, place of execution—he needed a site which the French
could not, would not, give up. The city of Verdun met that test. It had
been a fortified strongpoint since Roman days. In more modern times
it had been so studded with dozens of outlying forts and emplacements
in a great semicircle facing Germany that it was known as the strongest
land position in the world. Verdun had heroically held in the Franco-
Prussian War before surrendering, and it had held in 1914, a bastion
sticking out into a large area of German penetration. The French high
command could not think of abandoning it. If they did that, if troops
once fled Verdun, they might very well keep going and never form up
again. France had lost her rich northern provinces during the Great
Retreat. To give up Verdun in the south was impossible. Yet surrounded as it was by German troops above it, in front of it, and below
it, it was open to German artillery from three-quarters of the compass.
The Germans held fifteen roads and railways heading toward the city
and its environs, while the French communications consisted of one
narrow-gauge railroad and one two-lane country road only seven yards
wide.

In addition, although the French public did not know it, the
outlying forts had been largely stripped of their big guns. They had

been taken away to support the failed French attacks of 1915 in Artois and Champagne. It was possible, Falkenhayn knew, that a German rush might successfully capture all the forts and the city itself, and the troops under his command joined battle thinking that was their task. But that was not their commander's intention. If he took the city he was still 140 miles from Paris. He would menace Verdun, certainly. Then the French would come to it and to him. There he would destroy them. In late 1915 and early 1916, as the British built up their New Army for Sir Douglas Haig in the north, the thickly wooded hills surrounding Verdun in the south on three sides sprouted battery emplacements. Tunnels to protect German soldiers from French guns were dug. Railroad lines and roads were strengthened for heavy use. Orders to marshal a vast army were dispatched.

The French were not unaware of the German preparations, although enemy agents seeded neutral capitals with rumors that the whole operation was a feint aimed at sending French reinforcements into a cul-de-sac to be held there as a real attack came in another sector. The officer commanding at Verdun, an elderly engineer, asked General Headquarters for the return of the departed guns. They were not forthcoming.

On February 21, 1916, at 7:00 in the morning, a gigantic German shell aimed at one of the bridges of the Meuse River, which ran through Verdun, crashed in the Bishop's Palace there. It was the signal for hundreds of thousands more to come down on an area hardly larger than New York City's Central Park, a monstrous bombardment sounding like gods beating on drums the size of lakes, like express trains roaring through the sky. Some of the shells came slowly weaving through the air, turning end over end as they came. From Big Bertha, a weapon so huge that when dismantled it was carried in no less than 172 wagons, shells came weighing a thousand pounds and taller than a man. In a matter of moments the forts were all cut off from one another with their communications trenches entirely destroyed. The Germans came on, but by Falkenhayn's design only in probing strength, not in numbers enough to overrun the defenses.

French General Headquarters realized the attack was no feint. As

Falkenhayn had predicted, they instantly determined to hold Verdun at whatever cost. The elderly commanding officer would not do. Word was sent to Pétain that he report to General Headquarters at Chantilly. Then he would go to Verdun.

The summons arrived at Noailles, Pétain's headquarters, late in the evening. He was ordered to Chantilly at 8:00 the next morning. But Pétain was not to be found. Staff Capt. Bernard Serrigny ordered up a car and had himself driven at top speed to Paris. There, at 3:00 A.M., he presented himself at the Hotel Terminus at the Gare du Nord. The proprietress said no General Pétain was registered at her establishment. Captain Serrigny told her that finding his chief was a matter of life or death for their country. She led him upstairs to a room before the door of which stood a pair of Pétain's yellowish boots waiting to be shined by the night porter. They were, Serrigny remembered, "agreeably accompanied by some charming little *molière* slippers, utterly feminine." ("I have two passions, sex and the infantry," Pétain often said.)

It was not a situation in which an aide ordinarily wishes to find himself. But as Serrigny had said, the life or death of France was involved. He knocked on the door. Wearing "the scantiest of costumes," Pétain opened it. Serrigny gave him the summons to Chantilly. Pétain told him to find a room in the hotel. They would depart when it was light. He closed the door and returned to his companion, who, he told Serrigny later, first wept when he told her the news and then displayed such passion as would make the night memorable in the recollection of one who had known many passionate nights. In the morning he and Serrigny drove to Chantilly. Pétain spoke with Commander in Chief Joseph Jacques Joffre and then they made for Verdun, stopping for lunch at Châlons-sur-Marne with an old friend now a general. In the course of the conversation the old friend spoke of Nini, the garrison belle of the Amiens of twenty years before, and of his love for her then. Nothing could have been more delightful than for Pétain to reveal that he had enjoyed Nini's favors. He departed Châlons "in complete serenity."

But as he and Serrigny went through snow and ice toward Verdun they saw disorganized men running from what so soon would be called

the furnace, the mincing machine, Moloch, Minotaur, the devourer
of men. Down the slippery road came broken formations, civilian
refugees, ambulances jammed with wounded. Pétain looked at mud-
stained men of the shattered 2nd Zouaves; and their lieutenant saw
that he was crying.

He met at Dugny with the officer he was replacing, and found him
and his staff to resemble the inmates of a lunatic asylum, talking,
gesticulating, in a panic and out of control, able only to offer the
horrifying news that due to calamitous French oversight the Germans
had without casualties just taken Fort Donaumont, the most powerful
of all the outlying posts in front of Verdun. "We shall install ourselves
at Souilly, where I hope we may find a little more calm," Pétain said in
his cold fashion, and went toward the little village eleven miles down
the single road from Verdun that France owned. He arrived after a
slow trip over icy footing and walked into the reception chamber of the
town hall. The room was empty, echoing. Its only adornment was a
bust of Marianne, symbol of the Republic. Pétain was wearing neither
boots nor puttees, but long wool stockings of the type used by cyclists.
Officers arrived. Expressionless, he shook hands with them. Orderlies
pinned on a wall a large-scale map. He took up a stick of charcoal and
with his chill light-blue eyes silently looked at his positions.

He drew lines on the map. From the inferno to the north came the
sound of German 210s, 150s, 105s seeking to grind to bits everything
in range. Von Falkenhayn's field commander was the heir to the
throne, Crown Prince Friedrich Wilhelm, a strangely dissonant personality part playboy and no less the satyr than Pétain himself, part
insensitive fool, part sharp observer and talented soldier. He was
innocent of Falkenhayn's plan not to take Verdun but to use its
magnetic pull as a means to lure and decimate the French Army; and
so he sought the city Pétain defended. Together they went down into
history, Gaul opposing Teuton, and into correct legend and true
myth, paintings depicting Death, the soldier's last sweetheart, implor-
ing the Crown Prince, "I am weary of work, don't send me any more
victims," and with Pétain remembered always as standing between the

carved balustrades on the steps of Souilly's town hall staring at his men, and they at him, as they went up the road ever after called the Sacred Way.

He talked on the telephone to officers and then went to the house Serrigny selected for his occupancy, a little place with defective heating which belonged to a local lawyer. He ate some beans left over from the orderlies' meal, went to bed, and awoke with a high fever brought by double pneumonia. He did not care. His men were suffering worse as the ring of woods around Verdun belched a long continuous sheet of flame from the German guns—in less than one day a particular rectangle five hundred by a thousand yards was estimated to have taken no less than eighty thousand shells, each splitting upon impact into jagged pieces of metal weighing up to a hundred pounds each. From his sickbed the new commander began conferences with staff officers from each corps by inevitably asking, "What have your batteries been doing? We will discuss other points later."

After five days he arose and mobilized sixteen work battalions of middle-aged reservists in old uniforms, eight thousand men to stand along the forty-five-mile route up from Bar-le-Duc and throw crushed rock fragments on the road so that it would stand up to the pounding of trucks that would carry for ten months an average of ninety thousand men and fifty thousand tons of material a week. When rocks gave out he opened a quarry. Trucks vanished from Paris streets to be used as transport along the Sacred Way. Passing was not allowed as the vehicles went by at intervals of no more than fifteen seconds, often less, day and night, the mileage accrued each week amounting to five times the earth's circumference. No stopping was permitted. If a truck broke down the reservists instantly pushed it off to the side, where eventually it would be taken in hand by one of the thirty tow trucks kept ready. Midwinter thaw put the road awash in six inches of mud and slime, but the line kept going.

Pétain's work began to tell. His artillery barrages began to match those of the Crown Prince. "The poor horses!" wrote home the German artist Franz Marc. He had made his career painting them: the

Blue Rider school. Within a week of writing his letter he himself fell victim to the French guns. In one day seven thousand horses of the German Army perished, ninety-seven killed by a single shell.

Airplanes used as spotters for the artillery soared over the tiny battlefield soon denuded of vegetation and reduced to a dull brown mass of smoking and corrupted earth hit and hit again and so ground down that never again would it grow trees. Flamethrowers made their appearance in war. No shell hole lacked a smashed dead body or bodies, or fragments splattered or chopped to pieces, and the dead were punished beyond death, now picked up by new shells and flung up into the fetid air, then buried in a shower of dirt, now dug up again. It was reckoned that a week in the inferno meant a division's loss of half its effectives to death, wounds, disease, madness. Sometimes forty-eight hours was sufficient time to reach the figure.

It was said that no man who survived Verdun could have stayed still, for each square inch of the battlefield was hit not once but a dozen times. "Humanity is mad!" wrote a French lieutenant. "It must be mad to do what it is doing. What a massacre! What scenes of horror and carnage! I cannot find words. Hell cannot be so terrible. Men are mad!" He died under a German shell.

The German divisions stayed in the line for what seemed brutally endless periods of time, their losses made good by a flow of reinforcements. That was not a policy Pétain would permit for the French. More than any other commander of either side in this war, he felt for his soldiers, for what they were undergoing. They knew that he would order no made-for-show attacks, would keep them in places of danger for as brief a time as possible and then rotate them to safe havens in the rear. It was said of Falkenhayn with his bleed-white concept that he regarded soldiers as corpuscles. General Joffre appeared to see them as sacks of grain which must be consumed. Pétain wrote: "My heart failed, I must admit, when I saw twenty-year-old boys going into the firing line at Verdun. I thought to myself how, at their age, they must suffer. I looked at them as they passed by, either jolting along in a truck or, if they happened to be on foot, loaded with combat equipment.

They sang and joked in an effort to appear nonchalant, and I appreciated the trusting way in which they looked at me.

"But what a change in them when they came back, either maimed or wounded or marching in decimated ranks! Their expressions, indescribable, seemed frozen by a vision of terror, their stance and gait indicated complete exhaustion; they were stooped under the weight of horrifying memories. They no more than mumbled an answer to my questions, and the comments of their older companions did not even seem to reach their ears."

It was said of Napoleon that he once remarked, viewing a field strewn with the bodies of his soldiers, "One night in Paris will make up for all of this." Nothing could be more opposite to Henri Philippe Pétain. Hospital visits to broken men found him seemingly imperturbable, withdrawn, as remote as a surgeon at work; "Luckily, I have a mask of ice," he said. Day after day he stood watching from his Souilly town hall as three-quarters of the French Army rotated up into Verdun along the Sacred Way. The Crown Prince came on and came on again, but the French under Pétain held them. *"They shall not pass."*

Spring came. Joffre implored Gen. Sir Douglas Haig to launch a British offensive in the north that would relieve the horrible pressure on Verdun. Haig spoke of attacking by August 15, perhaps August 1, and Joffre blazed out that if the British waited that long no French Army would be left to save. Haig said he would attack along the Somme on July 1. In Verdun they came to believe that the fire would burn on until the last few survivors on each side would hobble out of their holes to destroy one another with fingernails and penknives. Only then would the nightmare without a morning find its terrible ending. Pétain's old 133rd Regiment of Infantry of the Line suffered in three days the almost complete slaughter of one of its battalions; a company lost 90 percent of its men. Among the officers was one for whom Pétain himself wrote what was believed to be a posthumous citation. It was Captain de Gaulle.

Hill 304, Fort Vaux, Le Mort Homme, the Trench of Bayonets, the Ravine of Death—Verdun—there was the death site of that Unknown

Soldier who would lie beneath the Arc de Triomphe, there on the battlefield the tourist of the future would read: *This ground has been the Calvary of soldiers. Every square foot bears the mark of its bloody progress. Complete silence is requested out of respect for the thousands buried here.* The villages would never be rebuilt, and the scrub undergrowth which would in time grow up would remain forever dangerous because of the unexploded shells and grenades which could blow up at any moment and so kill, as they did, new victims of a war finished decades before. There would be an Ossuary containing the bones of 150,000 unidentified men of both sides: neat piles of legbones, armbones, skulls. "Courage!" Pétain told his soldiers in an order of the day. "We shall have them yet!" *On les aura!*

In the end he was right. The Crown Prince never took Verdun. They did not pass. Pétain had saved his country—not for the last time.

CAPTAIN EDEN, M.C.

Sir William Eden of County Durham in the North lived the kind of life which one day would become familiar to those who watch movies and television programs dealing with the rich and wellborn of an England gone into history, and those who tour the castles and palaces left behind and opened to the public. Twice over a hereditary baronet, with one of his titles, of which he was the seventh holder, dating from 1672, Sir William came from a family which had been large landowners since the fifteenth century. One ancestor was a colonel under Charles I, another commanded a regiment of foot, and another was a captain of horse for the monarch. Edens were in high favor at Court.

The family counted in its number members of Parliament, a colonial governor of what would eventually be the state of Maryland, ambassadors to Berlin and Vienna, governors-general of India, a mistress to Charles II. William Pitt had loved an ancestor, Eleanor Eden. Edens had lived on the same plot of land for four hundred years, their main residence by 1800 being Windlestone Hall, a vast pile of yellow stone built by the fifth baronet to replace an earlier structure at a cost of 100,000 pounds.* It had magnificent gardens and vistas, a park, great trees. Sir William and Lady Eden and their four sons and one daughter lived surrounded by gardeners and blacksmiths, greenhouse workers and footmen, woodsmen and carpenters, tenants of the villages of the estate whose families had lived there as long as that of the landlord.

---

*Some half a million dollars then, the equivalent of several million today.

In the tradition of the landed aristocrat who has many splendid hobbies, Sir William was an excellent rider and a huntsman who was referred to in print as the best shot in the North of England. He was a watercolorist who exhibited and was a serious collector of art, specializing in works of the modern period. There were Old Masters in Windlestone Hall, and portraits of ancestors, and a John Singer Sargent of Lady Eden, but Sir William's truest interests centered on the Impressionists. Above his desk hung works by Degas and Corot. ("You know," said the Marquess of Londonderry, a near neighbor, "something ought to be done about it. Willie actually gave good money for these things.")

Sir William liked to box, and had in leading prizefighters for sparring. (When the Duke of Leeds, a neighbor also interested in the sport, visited Sir William's gymnasium, he made the mistake of landing too forceful a blow on his host. The Duke of Leeds remembered nothing of what then ensued when he awakened on the floor.)

When the Edens went for trips on the Continent they moved with maids, nannies, governesses, and a courier to a rented villa overlooking the Mediterranean at Nice or a house with a garden in Dresden. The children spoke the languages of France and Germany perfectly—they were trilingual from childhood. The family maintained a little flat in London with a housekeeper, cook, and parlor maid always there, but on occasion they rented larger accommodations. When H. H. Asquith departed his home to take up residence at 10 Downing Street, the Edens let it from him.

Lady Eden, the former Sybil Grey, was born in India, where her father was Governor of Bengal. He was a nephew of the later Foreign Secretary Sir Edward Grey. No less typical a figure of what later ages took to be the British aristocracy of the Victorian and Edwardian eras than her husband, Sybil Eden might well have posed as the model of Lady Bountiful. "Lady Eden has, this Christmas, with her usual generosity," reported the society editor of *Woman* in 1893, "distributed a large amount of beef and plum puddings amongst the poor in Shildon, Coundon, and Merrington, as well as sending tea, tobacco, and toys to the Bishop Auckland Workhouse. There has also been a bullock killed and distributed among the workmen on the Windlestone estate. Lady Eden is always busier than usual about this time distributing meats and warm clothing to all who need them."

She was accounted as very beautiful, the fashion of describing her retaining today something of the tone of the times in which she commanded admiration: "Lady Eden is but little seen in London, but when in town is greatly admired. It is left to her to be the almost sole remaining example of the pure Madonna type of loveliness, now so rarely seen," said *Woman*. The artist Henry Bacon: "There is no more beautiful woman in all England."

Yet for all the interest in plants and flowers which saw him create some of the most magnificent gardens in the country, and the concentration upon beauty which found him supervising every two or three years the painting of Windlestone's doors and window trim a dark blue, and the intense interest in modern art which found him discussing it for hours on end, Sir William Eden was impatient, excitable, explosive, an eccentric. He could not stand noise, and so when his children came home for Christmas from their schools, he was nowhere to be found. He ate in a dining room whose chairs were Hepplewhite, and read in a library lined from floor to ceiling with books and with a gallery three-quarters of the way up with brass balustrading, the shelves divided by delicate mahogany pilasters, but among such finery he surrendered himself to almost half-crazed rages. A barometer indicating fair weather could be flung through a window to see for itself that it was actually raining outside, and in fact he appeared to have a fixed idea that when his house was filled with guests, and keepers and beaters of pheasants ready for a shoot, the Almighty deliberately sent rain to thwart the outing. "Oh, God!" he shouted. "How like You!" He terrified his children, using them as butts for cruel jokes and harsh assessments. His volcanic letters to editors and battles with presumed enemies, opponents of his concepts of truth and beauty, were quite legendary.

Lady Eden also had layers unseen upon first inspection. She drove each Sunday after church in a pony cart to distant parts of the estate to succor pensioned-off servants, the needy, sick, aged, infirm, and had in former Prime Minister Lord Rosebery to open the Lady Eden Cottage Hospital for incapacitated miners, but she did so by selling family heirlooms which were not hers to dispose of, and by taking out loans of which she never bothered to note terms which in some cases surpassed 60 percent interest per annum. She was, her children felt, far better a philanthropist than a mother.

In June of 1897, Great Britain and the Empire celebrated Victoria's accession to the throne sixty years before. Troops marched to the beat of thundering brass bands through a London awash with Union Jacks, soldiers of the Queen brought from Canada and Natal, camel men from Bikaner, headhunters from North Borneo, Indian lancers, British Guianans and Jamaicans. Rome and its Caesars had not ruled 372 million subjects and a quarter of the earth's surface as did Victoria at her Diamond Jubilee. It was the highest moment England was ever to know, for just over the horizon lay the dismaying and distressing Boer War, and just beyond that, many terrible things. Ten days before the great day of celebration, Lady Eden gave birth to her fourth child.

Hundreds came to the lavish christening of the infant, who one day in the future would see in the window of a London pawnbroker his christening bowl, put there so that his madly spendthrift mother might have new funds to give away.

Robert Anthony Eden grew up at Windlestone, with its stables for ponies and hunters and carriage horses, its grounds with fountains, statues, and pots of flowers, its carpentry shop and paint shop. The house's billiard room was reached by going up a flight of stone stairs, and there was said to be an ancestral ghost found upon occasion reading in the library. He never saw the haunt, but knew which dummy books hid a staircase giving access to the gallery. A reader no less than an athlete, he wore glasses and was slim, graceful, extremely good-looking, resembling, it was said, his parents' friend the romantic author George Wyndham. In later years he was not sure that the rumors about his mother and the author were incorrect.

The Eden children put on amateur theatricals. Express trains were halted in the village for them when they traveled. Anthony—he was not called Robert—went at the appropriate age to Eton, where Edens had gone for two hundred years. Photographs of him in his collar and topper show the same handsome face almost unchanged decades later. He did not much enjoy school, but still less did he enjoy being with his presumed father, Sir William, at vacation time. Jack, the heir to the titles, was cheerful and openhearted, an outdoor man who learned to take the father in stride; Tim, the next in line, grew able to understand and deal with Sir William; Nicholas, the youngest, was another Jack, cheery and fun-loving and involved with the outdoors and his menagerie of animals; Marjorie, the only girl, was in a different category from her brothers—but Anthony was high-strong, nervous, and a brooder. He did not sustain well Sir William's constant terrifying tempers, which could erupt at any moment, nor his steady jeering. Sixty years on, the son remembered his agnostic father's sardonic reaction to the winning of a divinity prize at Eton which was really for mastery of the Greek Testament and had nothing to do with religion as such: "My son who is going into the Church, my son who is going to be a bishop."

In June of 1914, Anthony turned seventeen. Two weeks later the shots sounded at Sarajevo. Diplomatic notes began passing back and forth among the Great Powers of Europe. School vacation commenced. His brother Jack, nine years older, an officer of the 12th Lancers back from service in India and South Africa and sporting a mustache and monocle, invited him to luncheon at the Cavalry Club. Friends came to the table to talk about the next day's polo match, in which Jack would play for the regiment. Afterward they drove in Jack's Austro-Daimler to watch the cricket at Lord's, and Jack introduced him to a fellow officer of the 12th who had been a great player at Harrow and Cambridge. The next day Anthony sat by his mother and heard her gasp once when Jack fell from his horse. He remounted, and the regiment won on this sunny afternoon of the summer of 1914. Looking at the large hats laden like trays and worn by gaily dressed women, Anthony thought the scene was worthy of Renoir. He had Sir William's interest in art, and would in time be a discerning collector himself.

In late July he went to camp with the Eton Officers' Training Corps. The boys talked over the possibility of a war and agreed that if it came it would be over in six weeks. Their military knowledge belonged to the turn of the century and the later days of the Boer War, which at their age they only dimly remembered. Yet when Anthony read of the Russian mobilization a curious sense of foreboding came upon him. A fight was approaching, he thought. One of the Eton masters serving with the Officers' Training Corps told the boys there would not be a war. British financial interests would not allow it. But if it came it would last only a few days, for the money to fight it would run out after that.

By August 4 the notes and ultimatums came to their ending. Lt. Gen. Sir Douglas Haig crossed the Channel to France, Walther Rathenau went to the German War Ministry to set up his Raw Materials Section, and Col. Henri Philippe Pétain put aside his retirement plans. Anthony Eden and his fellow students from Eton drilled, singing "Tipperary" as they went, as all the British did. Within three months Jack Eden was dead, killed on a cavalry patrol near Ypres as Haig held the Germans off and the Old Contemptibles perished. Within three more months the cricket player met at Lord's was dead. Anthony's uncle, Robin Grey of the Royal Flying Corps, had been shot down and taken prisoner. Timothy Eden, who had been spending the summer studying in Germany, had been interned.

Anthony finished at Eton in 1915. It would have been unthinkable for someone of his type, of his class, to do other than immediately join the British Army a-building by voluntary enlistment to drive the Huns across the Rhine. (In no other case is the concept of a rich man's war and a poor man's fight less applicable than to the Britain of War Minister Lord Kitchener's New Army—"Your King and Country Need You.") The unit he chose was the King's Royal Rifle Corps, one of the most exclusive regiments* in existence in any army. "No one could hope to become an officer without close family connections, and

---

*Despite the word "corps" in its name, the KRRC was a regiment.

even then only after the most searching inquiries had been made
by the Colonel Commanding," remembered Gen. Sir Brian Horrocks.
The new subaltern's contacts included the KRRC Lieutenant
Colonel the Earl of Faversham, who had married the sister of Marjorie
Eden Brooke's husband, and whose aunt was the wife of that Lord
Londonderry who had expressed concern over Sir William Eden's
purchases of modern art.

The King's Royal Rifle Corps dressed in green and wore black
buttons, and officers by long regimental tradition called one another,
all save the Colonel Commanding, by first name or nickname. Lieutenant Eden was so slim and youthful-looking that his address became,
and remained for a long time, Boy. Lord Faversham, "Charlie,"
gazetted him off for recruiting duty among the men of his County
Durham, and he went about to do so in his father's Benz, yellow as
had been the Eden carriages in horse days. He was eighteen. Many of
the men he signed on for his Yeoman Rifles were younger, with only a
few over twenty-one and none more than a year or two older than that.

The unit up to strength, he went with the boys he had recruited to
that Aldershot which Douglas Haig had quitted for the Front. They
lived in long Victorian barracks named for Wellington's victories and
practiced with hand grenades made out of jam tins. They concentrated
on open warfare despite the talk among the returned wounded of
trenches in France and Belgium. With his men of Platoon No. 9 he
developed a comradeship he had never known before and which would
never end—"It links the survivors to this day," he wrote, sixty years
later. He enjoyed training the boys. "After all these years one wonders
why."

Nicholas, his younger brother, was a midshipman in the Royal
Navy at sixteen, serving on HMS *Indefatigable*. They were together at
home in March of 1916 for two days. They rode Jack's horses, which
were still in Windlestone's stables. The following month the KRRC
sailed for France and then made for Belgium and a trench position in
the now much-quieted but still dangerous countryside outside Ypres,
there to await the coming great push Britain had been working toward

during the year and a half the war had lasted. There in the trenches the first of his comrades fell victim to German steel. "The passage of the years has never blunted it," he said of that loss, the first of the many which in quick time would leave only a memory of almost all of the men, and of the officers who called him Boy.

His platoon went out on night patrols and carried poison-gas cylinders through communication trenches to the lines facing the enemy. Sometimes in the dark he talked with his soldiers, and those talks gave him ideas which he held to, he said, even when in the last year of his life, seventy-nine years old then, he came to write of those days. *Another World,* he named his book, published just after he died and filled with memories of his childhood and the war which had been his real education. He rescued a sergeant wounded in the no-man's-land a hundred yards across and took him to safety, and the man gave him a pretty gold penknife from his native Sheffield. He kept the knife on his desk all through the years that were to come. "It is always there."

Toward the end of June 1916, when the big push was days away, General Haig planning to end the war with it, Second Lieutenant Eden was told he was wanted at once at company headquarters, a dugout in the support line. Colonel the Earl of Faversham was there, looking grim. "I want a word with you, Anthony." They found a place where they could talk privately. "A quiet lull in the wood," Eden remembered, "a brilliant summer's day, and Charlie standing there disturbed and unhappy." Sailing with the Grand Fleet to meet Germany's High Seas Fleet at the Battle of Jutland, Nicholas's HMS *Indefatigable* had been hit and blown up. There were no survivors. They had shared everything, nannies, governesses, tutors, and preferred one another's company to any other in the world. Years later he hesitated before naming one of his sons for Nicholas, fearful that regularly to hear and say the name would hurt too much.

He returned to his duties outside Ypres and then with his men entrained for the south. It was just before the light of dawn. He remembered how they sang "There's a Long, Long Trail a-Winding." They went through shattered Albert, from whose church there hung a golden Virgin holding her Child, knocked forward by a German shell but secured in place with thick steel wire by a French engineer because a legend had grown up that if the statue fell England would lose the war. In front of the Yeomen of the King's Royal Rifle Corps the flashes of guns lit up the sky in a great stretching arc from north to south. It was the Somme.

The Educated Soldier

Surgical instruments tinkled as they lay waiting for use on steel trays in hospitals behind the lines, and on still nights in London across the Channel the drumming of the guns rumbled dully. The British pounded the German lines. On Sunday, Sir Douglas Haig rode from Château Beaurepaire two and a half miles out of town into Montreuil for church services. The town before the war had three thousand inhabitants. Now some five thousand British officers and men jammed General Headquarters for His Majesty's Forces in France, preparing to fight the Battle of the Somme.

Montreuil, a few miles inland from the seaside resort of Le Touquet and near the main road to Amiens and Paris, was encircled by massive stone ramparts put up hundreds of years earlier. Upon one of them was a little wooden hut above which flew a flag of the blue-and-white St. Andrew's Cross, the sign of the Church of Scotland. General Haig was bound there, for with the approach of the day of battle he had become pronouncedly religious. As he rode to listen to the Rev. George Duncan's Sunday sermon, the high points of which each week he entered in his diary, two French boys kicking a ball around stopped their play to stare.

To one of the boys, destined in time to be mayor of Montreuil, and to see Nazi German occupiers destroy the statue of Douglas Haig that one day would stand in the town, then to see a new one erected, then to see it threatened with a new destruction by Frenchmen who resented what Haig had to say when long after his death his diary was published, it seemed that the general and his staff riding to church on Sunday, June 25, 1916, positively glittered. Shining in the sunlight were their polished belts, boots, harness, and spurs. All seemed in readiness for the British push that would end the war. Until this moment the fighting in the west had essentially been a French-German struggle. Now Britain would speak. Really she had no choice. The heart of France was beating in Verdun, and French Commander in Chief Joffre had shouted at Haig that unless Britain moved that heart could stop, that soon there would be no French Army to whose aid he might come. In Russia the sagging Czarist government had gathered itself for one last offensive. Brusilov's Galician drive was magnificent. Never again would the Imperial Russian forces show to such advantage. Along the Trentino River, Italy's troops moved against the Austrians. Could Britain stand idly by?

In his hands Haig held all the reins of his great force, personally looking to issues of supply, training, equipment, munitions, development of the air arm, transport, tanks. Across the British zone, a rectangle fifty by sixty miles, so tiny in size, so momentous in meaning, he had drilled and prepared the best-equipped army that ever the British race gave a soldier. In his zone, victorious English yeomen from Crécy had marched—indeed, they had gone past Montreuil's ramparts—and later the town had been Marshal Ney's headquarters as he planned for Napoleon's projected invasion of the British Isles. Here Marlborough and Wellington had maneuvered, and Henry V. Agincourt was near. None of the great captains could have dreamed of what Haig possessed, and the sites of none of the great battles had seen anything like what he planned. All the way back to the coast the British had covered the land with supplies, hiding some of them under camouflage canvas so that the German planes could not see. Vast artillery parks, hospitals, workshops, depots, bakeries, training camps—all the enormous resources of a mighty world empire stood behind the thin cutting edge prepared to slice into the Germans. The guns thundered day after day. Their mission was to destroy the barbed wire that guarded the enemy's lines and eliminate his one thousand machine-gun nests along the eighteen-mile front. Then the British troops would rise up and go across no-man's-land and kill or capture whoever lived in the crushed German trenches. Through the split and shattered line would then pour five cavalry divisions. They would spread out and ravage whatever they found, and behind them would come one million infantrymen to mop up and keep going.

No attacking army ever had higher morale. Secretary of State for War Lord Kitchener's volunteers had enlisted into informally named units of their own choosing, where they could serve with friends from their home localities—the Barnsley Pals, the Grimsby Chums. Or they went with men of like interests—the United Arts Volunteers—or similar employment—the City of Glasgow Tramways Battalion. There were Bantam Battalions composed of men five feet tall or less. Never was an army more free of military crime. They had flocked to the recruiting stations because Britain's old Regular Army was gone, and the Territorials and Reservists too—and their country needed them.

Their commander sat in his office, one wall of which was covered with a great map of his zone, at a desk upon which there was rarely an unattended-to paper. He almost never spoke on a telephone, preferring staff officers to do it for him. A career cavalryman, he seemed to those who studied him to have more the mind of an engineer. Opinions meant nothing to him. He sought facts and reasoning. Instinct, intuition, genius, unconscious mental processes were entirely foreign to his soul. To the great task before him he brought cold logic only, like a doctor, his associates thought, attacking a disease. Among themselves they referred to him as the Chief.

General Haig knew his volunteers were half trained when compared to the Regulars of the past, who had years of soldiering behind them. He believed certain maneuvers would be dangerous for them. To advance in short, darting rushes supported by small-arms fire would be beyond their abilities, he decided. They could not probe, for that required quick individual decisions on the part of subalterns and sergeants, and the real subalterns and sergeants were dead, perished Old Contemptibles. So his men must go forward in rigid lines, dense masses, at a measured beat, as if on parade. So the barbed wire and machine guns must be eliminated. So the guns pounded, day after day.

To keep up his health, General Haig rode as often as possible, always with an escort of the 17th Lancers, his old regiment. Back from an inspection trip conducted by automobile, he had his horse wait for him some distance away from Château Beaurepaire. After a trot he would dismount and walk the final three miles. He arose each morning at exactly 8:25 to do exercises prescribed by his doctor. He stopped work each night at 10:45. This routine was rarely broken, his aide John Charteris remembered, "even by a minute." He conscientiously studied the French language in daily lessons and, astonishingly, ended up speaking it far more fluidly than English.

He was always in correct and immaculate uniform, with gloves and a cane when on foot. (His officers of the assault would also carry canes when they went over the top.) Absolutely confident, both of himself and of his destiny, certain that he was God's tool to lead the British Army to victory and so end the war, a "knightly figure," Churchill said, majestic, calm, of striking presence, he kept as always his rigid control of all emotion and all excitement, and remained the stiff soldier he had always been. Once when he was conferring indoors in a village where a senior ordnance officer had his headquarters, a battalion came marching by. They were singing. Their words came through the window to Haig. "Fetch my horse," he said. He went chasing up the column, heading for the colonel in the lead, who was bawling out the song with his head thrown back. It was a vulgarization of a childhood ditty, with mention of male parts substituted for the juvenile version's "ears." As the unmistakably upright figure of the Commander in Chief cantered up the column the soldiers ceased to sing, leaving the colonel almost solo to roar out, "Can you sling them on your shoulder, like a fucking soldier?" Haig pulled up his horse.

"I must congratulate you on your voice, Colonel," he said.

The singer looked over. "I like the tune," Haig said, "but you must know that in any circumstances these words are inexcusable." He rode away. The column marched in silence until an irrepressible rearranker began "After the Ball Was Over."

The incident was typical both of Haig and of the men he commanded, who were confident, clever, willing, complete opposites to the layabouts and workhouse boys Haig had always known for other ranks. They recognized, as high summer on the Somme approached, that their leader was a perfected soldier-student of great background, hardworking, a master of detail, a master of the field. Something of his earnest single-mindedness came down to them in the mystical manner in which captains and kings reach followers. They believed in Douglas Haig and would continue to do so through all that was coming. For the generals under him, soon enough, they would feel what approached and perhaps surpassed hatred, certainly contempt. But not for him, not then. Perhaps later. During the war the men in the ranks always esteemed their commander—esteemed, not loved. In time the Russian and French and German armies would crack—never the British.

As the day of battle and moment of decision neared, he left Château Beaurepaire and moved to a requisitioned house close behind the jumping-off point of his fourteen divisions along the Somme.* It was in Beauquesne, near Albert with its leaning Virgin. He was there on June 29 to make all last-minute preparations as the sound of a little girl playing exercises on her piano was heard, for he had left free a few rooms of the house so that the owners need not leave. In front of him the Germans waited. In their great drive of the first days of the war they had taken almost all of Belgium and much of northern France, and then to consolidate their positions had drawn back here and there to fortify the best defensive sites, the rises and hills. It was different for the French and British. The former could not draw back even a kilometer to gain a tactical advantage, for they had already given up so much of their country. The latter knew that every step backward meant they were closer to the waters of the Channel and Northern Sea, upon whose shores they could be slaughtered if the Germans pushed them there. Kaiser Wilhelm and Falkenhayn and the Prussians and Ba-

---

*Each division had sixteen battalions; the number of men equaled twenty-six divisions of the Second World War.

varians and Saxons held the high ground, and in the chalky hills had gone down forty and fifty feet to build electrically serviced galleries complete with timbered walls and running water. In their underground sanctuaries they felt the earth rocking as the British artillery thundered on.

To mystify, to deceive, to feint, to mislead and surprise, that was difficult to do on a front devoid of either a northern or southern end—for the lines ran unbroken from Switzerland's unpassable mountains to the equally unpassable seas. To make the enemy have a rear, the first objective of warfare, was impossible. So Haig must make a frontal assault, the most difficult and demanding of attacks. It went against all his cavalryman's instincts to fight a medieval siege battle, but there was no choice. He performed in other sections of the British zone, throwing up barrages and ostentatiously building communication trenches, but that he would fight along the Somme was clear to the enemy. Behind their first lines of defense with their deep dugouts and their ridges with good fields of fire the Germans had two and three more lines, each positioned so that the British must attack uphill. Their soldiers were no recent vibrant volunteers, but veterans with years of prewar conscripts' experience. Their machine gunners, picked men, represented the embodiment of mechanized, of industrial, slaughter, able with the press of a finger to throw forward a curtain of bullets.

Light drizzle fell in the early morning hours of July 1, 1916, along the Somme, to give way to a brilliant sun. Zero hour of 7:30 approached. (Haig had considered attacking at dawn, but was afraid to let his inexperienced men work in semidarkness.) Ten minutes before the signal whistles blew, British sappers detonated a series of underground mines, enormous charges of explosives stacked in tunnels dug under no-man's-land and the German positions. Eighteen tons was under what the British called the Hawthorne Redoubt. The mines and the million and a half shells fired by the guns whose number was such that there was one for each seventeen yards of the enemy's front line, the British troops were told, would completely destroy the Germans. "You will be able to go over the top with a walking stick; you will not need rifles," the Newcastle Commercials were told. "You will find the Germans all dead; not even a rat will have survived." The 11th Sherwood Foresters heard, "You will meet nothing but dead and wounded Germans. The field kitchens will follow you and give you a good meal." A general said to the King's Own Yorkshire Light Infantry, "When you go over the top, you can slope arms, light up your pipes and cigarettes, and march."

Officers looked at their watches. It was very quiet after the noise of the week-long bombardment, the startling birdsong the only sound. Zero hour came.

Whistles blew. It was the 132nd day of France's Battle of Verdun. The British came out of their trenches along the Somme. Each man carried two hundred rounds of rifle ammunition and two days' rations in a haversack, gas mask, water bottle, grenades, entrenching tools, pickax, shovel, bayonet, wirecutters, flares. Some had carrier pigeons or poles with pennants attached to use as markers, some had duckboards to be used for bridges over captured trenches, some stakes for barbed wire. No man carried less than seventy pounds.

The British formed up in a miles-long straight line with each man no farther than two or three yards from his neighbor to right and left. They moved at a steady slow pace of no more than fifty yards a minute. Behind the first wave the following ones prepared to follow at one-minute intervals. The Battle of the Somme was to be a rigid and methodical slow advance, like a vast parade-ground movement eighteen miles long, a set-piece performance which would send forth a successive wave of line after line in a continuous forward flow. Haig had thought of having lightly burdened assault troops, skirmishers, rush out to pounce on the Germans, but had decided it was not necessary. For, he felt, the German front line would be found completely battered in with its defenders entombed. So no local initiative, no breaking of ranks, short dashes, rushes from shell hole to shell hole to lie down and fire from cover, could be permitted. Unnecessary in any event, he reasoned, such moves would in addition be impractical to attempt with such half-trained men as formed the New Army. They could not be allowed to maneuver on their own, but must go forward behind a curtain of shells now by finely delineated orders beginning to fall on the second German line, where the British planned to arrive in a few minutes.

In their deep dugouts were those Germans who had survived the bombardment and the mines which at times had shaken the earth as if, they felt, the Day of Judgment had arrived. In the sudden silence they shoveled through the debris of the least damaged entrances to their caverns—some dugouts had as many as half a dozen entries—and cautiously stuck up periscopes to behold the British. "They're coming! They're coming!"

The German machine gunners got above ground with their weapons and set them up. "The English came walking, as though they were going to the theater or were on a parade ground. We felt they were mad," remembered an *Unteroffizier* of the 109th Reserve Regiment. "These came forward very slowly, either because of their heavy loads, or was it madness, without taking the least cover," remembered a man of the 170th. There followed one of the great horrors of military history. "My God! My boys! My boys!" the colonel of the Newcastle Commercials screamed over and over, tears streaming down his face. For the boys were falling like tenpins, like dominoes, like hay cut by a swathe, to lie in near-perfect rows over which stepped the next wave to meet the same fate. The next wave followed.

Such an effort as seen in that first hour had no precedent and could never be duplicated. It could only happen once. The British artillery elevated barrels and fired on according to the carefully prepared program aimed at continuing the expected walkover, but the British infantrymen lay dying only yards from their own trenches. The sound of the shells falling uselessly, farther and farther off, became dim background music to the sound of the slaughter. Back at headquarters five miles west, General Haig knew nothing of what was happening. It was for officers to send messages, and in many units there was not a single officer left to write one.

Within a couple of hours the fighting was effectively over, and the battlefield fell silent. The midmorning July sun shone on what looked like a pasture empty of all life save for the wounded man here and there who tried to drag himself back to safety. Sometimes the Germans picked him off, sometimes not. For long periods of time there was hardly any firing. Of the 150,000 who had gone over the top, 60,000 were casualties.* The others were crouching in holes or in the few portions of the German front line which they had managed to wrest away from the enemy. The Accrington Pals lost 585 of the 700 who had gone into action. There was a British casualty for every foot and a half of the eighteen-mile front. "We were two years in the making and ten minutes in the destroying," said a survivor of the Leeds Pals. When the roll was called for Platoon No. 14 of the 1st Rifle Brigade, there was one man to answer to his name. There had been forty before the battle.

Back from the casualty clearing stations and the field hospitals came the wounded to be loaded into ambulance trains. Forty thousand men were taken off to hospital ships to clog Britain's hospitals and, in time, the school halls and churches where beds were set up. On July 14, Haig attacked again. Sustaining tremendous losses, he fought his men up to the high ground and took the German trenches of the first line. On the day previous, Erich von Falkenhayn called upon the Crown Prince in his headquarters before Verdun and told him all German operations there must cease. Men and supplies were required along the Somme.

So the British had relieved their ally of the weight of enemy pressure. Some said the General Officer Commanding in Chief of His Majesty's Forces in France had thus decided the war, that he had shown immense moral courage and spiritual stamina. That he had shown the world England's strength and determination, and the fighting power of the British race.

All through the summer and into the fall he flung his men against the Germans. He fought them down from the highlands and to the valley beneath, beyond which were more highlands and more defenders. He perfected the open-ended box barrage which by its expenditure of shells almost bankrupted the Bank of England but prevented the

---

*France's losses during Verdun's worst month, June, barely exceeded what Britain lost on this one day.

enemy from bringing up men and ammunition to reinforce an assaulted point. He fought his battle. He did not mention his losses in his daily diary, nor in his letters to Lady Haig, and no sentiment was expressed regarding those losses save for a reference here and there to the "plucky fellows," the "brave fellows" whose command it was his destiny to possess. He threw in a handful of tanks, the great secret weapon of the war, pawning them prematurely, it was said, for a song. There were those who said it was criminal to reveal their existence to gain a pottage of a little, purely local, success. Others felt it was essential to test the new invention under battle conditions. Haig was, some said, determination itself, the essence of British bulldoggedness, tenacious and brave, a finely trained and experienced and thinking soldier dealing with a situation for which there were only hard answers. Others used different terms to describe him.

The men themselves never faltered and never cursed him. That might have been saved for later, might have appeared in plenty later on, but such reactions were no part of the then present reality.

At home the members of the government quailed at the terrible butcher's bill. Minister of Munitions and soon-to-be Prime Minister Lloyd George said privately that rather than sustain another Somme the government should resign in a body; Lord Lansdowne circulated a written question among the members of the Cabinet: "Are we to continue until we have killed *all* our young men?"

On November 18, after 141 days, with winter coming on, General Haig called off the Battle of the Somme, closed it down. Britain's casualties were in the vicinity of half a million men—no two authorities agree on the exact figure. For that cost the troops had gone forward six miles. They were still four miles from the key town of Bapaume, which the cavalry had been marked to take on the first day of battle. Cold weather came with its rain and ice and trenchfoot and frozen bodies hanging on the wire in no-man's-land, and the soldiers remained in their trenches. The King appointed his commander a field marshal—"a New Year's present from myself and the Country." Haig planned new battles.

6

THE ETERNAL JEW

The Teutonic race, the sons of Wotan and daughters of Brünhilde, had placed its soldiers turned machine-tenders along the River Somme to feed unending belts of bullets into rapid-fire automatic weapons. That this was so constituted the most exquisite of tortures for the man whose efforts in his Raw Materials Section kept those men there.

All his life Walther Rathenau had preached the opposition of the Soul to the devil-god Mechanization. The only use to which industrialization should be put, he said, was to remove economic hardship so that life might move to a higher spiritual level and to the evolution of the Soul. Now by cruelest circumstance Mechanization, served so well by his work, was killing bodies, and minds and spirits as well. Modern technical developments and organization were ruthlessly diminishing the Soul. The battle between practicality and something higher was being resolved, not least by his doing, in favor of the base and ignoble over the pure and noble. The sickness of the age, he felt, was due to materialism and Reason as opposed to Soul, and in Germany and the rest of the world the Soul was dying along with the men of Verdun and the Somme. Soullessness, bigness, efficiency, impersonality, all that he had always opposed and all that now he fostered, were in the ascent. As much as he hated the war from its earliest moments, he hated it more as each day passed.

His reaction was to pour out a flood of writings aimed at rescuing or at least giving voice to his values. He wrote a series of books which became immensely popular. It was quite amazing, for when he had first tried book-writing, in 1908, his effort had been a thundering failure. At his own expense he had brought out a huge biblelike quarto printed in two colors on the most expensive paper. The work consisted of his philosophical observations and aphorisms. Its readers, who were few, and those who heard about it, who were many, agreed that something comic attached to a director of companies who labored on about the Soul, that a rich man who attacked luxury was grotesque, that it was pathological for Rathenau to advocate nationalization of business monopolies, the abolition of inheritance, ruthlessly high taxes for the wealthy, the liberation of the proletariat, and a classless society. The great industrialist, people said, put to shame the radical tendencies of the wildest agitator in any of his numerous factories. And he did so in a book so physically elaborate and *luxe* as positively to shout its author's wealth. Having pulled down the ever-present veil to reveal his deepest thoughts, remarked Rathenau's friend Count Harry Kessler, he found himself greeted with indulgent smiles. Rathenau himself said that what he had done made him seen as "a dilettante in sixteen subjects."

It was different as the years of the war dragged on. Rathenau's mystical and elaborate style—"A mysterious Cosmos, the whispers of the Unspoken and Unspeakable, a second Nature, lies veiled behind the visible"—spoke then to those who had once believed there was little to learn beyond Nietzsche's order to live dangerously. Yet not only Germans read his books. They were eventually to be translated into no fewer than twenty languages.

A philosopher and prophet whose only superior as a social educator, Emil Ludwig believed, was George Bernard Shaw, Rathenau in his books reached beyond his familiar themes that idealism must be substituted for dirty materialism, that the "urge to reality" was overcoming the "link with the spiritual," that intellect must be secondary to vision, spirit, imagination, and intuition. He offered concrete proposals. Long before it came to Woodrow Wilson's lips Rathenau spoke of a League of Nations. Before Lenin Rathenau advanced the idea of the Soviet, a local county or provincial council. He wrote of control of armaments by means of a universally enforced limitation of expenditures on weapons calculated for each nation by its other national expenditures, with the proportion of men in each country's army to be guided by the proportion of men in other fields of endeavor. He spoke of a "People's State" in which merit alone would determine an aristocracy. The war, Rathenau said, would one day end, but unless certain procedures followed there would only be an armistice before another war came. To prevent that future disaster there must be a league of industry, with common distribution and administration of raw materials, products, and finances. He spoke of a United States of Europe, holding that London was already merely an outpost of New York. Backward and primitive regions must be aided. Countries must be forbidden to export if they forbade imports.

Rathenau spoke of the food chain, and gave healthful recipes. He was, Emil Ludwig thought, like a lighthouse flashing in the distance. Rathenau's *In Days to Come* said that future generations would not understand how the will of a dead person could bind the living, or how it was possible that a man could fence off miles of land for his personal gratification and allow fertile ground to stand untilled, or erect or demolish buildings as he pleased and ruin a beautiful landscape. The future, he said, would look with amazement at a time when the public called for state intervention if a cab horse was mistreated, but thought it entirely natural for one class to enslave another for its aggrandizement.

It was absurd, he taught, that women's styles should constantly change at ridiculous cost and useless waste. The effort expended in mowing lawns around great houses should be invested in growing corn; the existence of a private yacht was a loss to world transport. The labor which produced delicate needlework or woven tapestries should be used to clothe the poor. If the production and distribution of coal were rationally organized, Germany's consumption of that substance could be cut in half.

There must be equality of education as there must be equality of material holdings. The keys to a closed society, knowledge and property, must be offered to all. There would be no castes in days to come. If things did not change, "one single hour will witness the downfall of what was believed capable of enduring for centuries."

Yet Rathenau knew the resentment his economic and moral vision of the future aroused in multitudes of his readers for the menace he presented to their privileges and because it was perhaps inherent in human beings to resist change. He knew the figure he cut in people's eyes. In the most blatant way, he knew, he seemed to be saying that he must be judged by words, not deeds. He knew, he said, what people said: "We are to become humble Christians again; he remains, needless to say, the cunning Jew!"

His work with the Raw Materials Section came to an end in 1915, for its organization was complete and others could run it. He returned to the leadership of the German General Electric Company. It was his entirely to control when Emil Rathenau died later in the year. The funeral shocked the Jews of Germany. There was no rabbi. Instead the dead man's son presided, and invoked the name and concepts of Jesus as much as those of Moses. His father gone, Rathenau became as close to his mother as in childhood. No matter how demanding his engagements, he lunched with her each day at her home. They played piano duets together, Bach often.

In August 1916, von Falkenhayn was removed as leader of the country's army, to spend the rest of his life finding it difficult to sleep for thinking of Verdun. His replacement was Field Marshal Paul von Hindenburg, whose alter ego was Gen. Erich Ludendorff. Rathenau had visited them often as they performed miracles on the Eastern Front. He was with them often when they came to the Western Front, and got along particularly well with Ludendorff, who was the brains of the combination, Hindenburg filling the role of an upright and commanding figure around whom the army and country could rally. Yet there was never a man with less of what Rathenau called Soul, for Ludendorff was a harsh technocrat interested only in efficiency. It was another sign of Rathenau's profoundly dislocated personality that he could see eye-to-eye with this military robot, an avowed anti-Semite with obsessions about Jews which in future years would make people think him half mad.

As the war went on and on, the Germans turned toward the idea of an unrestricted submarine campaign which would cut Britain off from the world. Rathenau opposed it, saying such warfare would not work and would in addition bring America into the field. He had it out with Ludendorff, who in the end admitted Rathenau was right but said it was against his feelings not to use submarines. Germany unleashed its underwater fleets. Rathenau ended his relationship with Ludendorff as he had ended close relationships with so many others.

He retired within himself, feeling the war was going to be lost and much of what was worthwhile in life along with it. In his hothouse at his country home he grew things. He got a magazine to run a contest with a prize for anyone who could discover one single new idea in any of the writings of Walther Rathenau. He put up the prize money himself. An enormous gloom overcame him. The war, he wrote, was "the funeral pyre of the social structure of Europe, which will never rise again from the flames."

When he thought of the future he could see no light save in the hope that the younger generation, they who had seen "the end of a dying, the beginning of a new epoch," would be ready for a great spiritual transformation. Perhaps they could make a new Germany, idealistic and pure. Perhaps when they came to take the leadership of the country in their hands, they would redeem the mistakes of the Wilhelminian Era, and by their Germanic purity, and spirit, and blood, in which he still believed wholeheartedly, make whole the Germany at whose shrine he yet worshiped, the Germany he had always called Beloved. He wrote them a book, *To the German Youth*. He could of course not then know of what they would do to him, the German youth.

7

There was an officer who had served with distinction under Pétain, Gen. Robert Nivelle. As the Germans ended their pressure on Verdun to hold the British on the Somme, Nivelle mounted a series of meticulously prepared attacks upon them. The attacks were uniformly successful.

Nivelle began to think in larger terms. He became the successor of the dead high priest of the School of Attack, Louiseau de Grand-maison. He dreamed of a Napoleonic assault upon the German lines, one tremendous blow that would end the war. Nivelle was handsome, dynamic, verbal, the son of a French father and British mother who spoke his mother's language perfectly. He hypnotized the British statesmen, who had watched in horror as their own generals squandered British lives and treasure along the muddy Somme, and he infused the French statesmen with his enthusiasm. He would have no Somme, he promised. If in forty-eight hours he could not rupture the German line he would call off his battle. In the sector between Rheims and Soissons he would break the enemy, and he would do it economically. He would not advance across a miles-long front, but as with a thrusting spear that would pierce the heart of the enemy and stop its breathing. "I can assure you that victory is certain."

Nivelle gathered 1,250,000 French soldiers, 5,000 guns, 500,000 horses. There was never any attempt to disguise his aims and objectives. German headquarters knew everything. They contracted their lines, withdrawing a few miles from the point of the projected attack to a crest in front of Soissons called the Chemin des Dames, "Ladies'

8 3

Way," either because it had been constructed for the riding pleasures of the daughters of a king of France or because the women of nearby towns made it a favorite place for a Sunday promenade. The Germans put concrete machine-gun nests there to face down the steep slopes up which the French must come, if they came. The leaders of the French government had in their generals to ask what they thought. Some indicated skepticism in the light of these new developments. Not Pétain. "It is impossible," he said in the blunt and cold manner that he always used when addressing politicians.

But the attack went on as planned, on April 16, 1917. One month earlier the Russian Czar had abdicated. Days earlier the United States, driven to do so by the German submarine campaign, had declared war. Rain mixing with late-spring sleet poured down on the troops as they gathered around their company commanders to hear Nivelle's order of the day. "The hour has come! Long live France!" At 6:00 A.M. the whistles blew and the French went over the top. A portion of their sledgehammer slammed down upon nothingness, a vacuum from which the Germans had withdrawn. The remainder found waiting machine guns, barbed wire, bursting shrapnel.

Nivelle had estimated he would take ten thousand casualties on the first day. The French medical service figured five thousand more for safety. But there were ninety thousand. Nivelle had said he would cut off the battle in forty-eight hours if he had to. But he could not do that, for to do so would mark it as a calamitous failure. So for days he shifted men through the frozen mud as he sought a way through. There was none. He had promised no Somme. One was in the making.

But Nivelle would know no Somme, nor any other battle. For his army was broken, destroyed, finished. Near a bend in the River Aisne, in the cabbage fields between Soissons and the Chemin des Dames, France's soldiers found the end of their endurance in this war. "It's over," the letters passing through the censorship said. "We did not get the Boche this time. We'll never get them." "They are giving us citations and medals, but we feel like telling them, 'Keep the medals, but have done with this stupidity.' "

Soon the men went from writing to direct action. It was all very swift. A unit would be ordered up to the trenches. The men would resist, shouts of "Long live peace!" and "We're through!" coming from the ranks. "Down with the war!" They refused to form up, to get on the trucks.

Officers would order, then entreat. Military police would be brought up. Arrests of supposed ringleaders would take place. But the same thing was happening in a dozen, a hundred, other units. Men in a rest camp, ordered forward, smashed up the quarters of the camp commander. Others refused to pick up their rifles or shoulder their packs. Masses deserted, went off into the woods. One heard "The Internationale," the song of the Russian Revolution. The British liaison officer Edward Spears was told over and over the same thing: "What's the good? We are fed up. We can't beat the Boche, so why get killed uselessly? What's the good? What's the use?"

Soon there were other things to hear. "Death to those responsible! To Paris!" Men no longer companies of soldiers but rampaging mobs marched upon railroad stations, commandeered trains, headed for the capital. Officers telegraphed ahead to cut them off with military police and cavalry, but soon other trains were seized. Back in the lines along the Chemin des Dames men told their officers they would defend themselves if the Germans came, but under no conditions would they attack. There were drunken and half-drunken soldiers everywhere, slovenly and with unbuttoned uniforms. "Enough have died! Peace!" A brigade commander had his cuff stars and epaulets ripped off. Wire cutters were used to free the prisoners in a stockade. Met by military police manning machine guns at the railroad station, a group shouted, "We'll be back—with grenades!"

When, by threats or pleas or by mustering of sufficient police, units could somehow be gotten to go forward to relieve those in the front line, it was to an appalling sound: a terrible baaing which imitated lambs being led to the slaughter. The phrase "collective undiscipline" was carefully used by the generals, but they knew what they faced was something far more frightening. It was mutiny. "Unless it is stopped

we will have no army and the Germans can be in Paris in five days,"
Gen. Franchet d'Esperey, Charles Lanrezac's replacement back in
1914, told a deputy who had seen a night of rioting in Soissons. The
Minister of War was informed that at least half the divisions of
the army had shown evidence of rebellion, and that between Paris
and the Front there were but two divisions that could be absolutely
relied upon. Rocks thrown at railway workers, Red flags flying—"We
won't march!"—drunken uniformed gangs pillaging—"Enough of
dying!"—a Paris incident where Indochinese troops fired on women
demonstrators—"They are murdering our wives! To Paris!"—
frightened officers hiding from their men: "On a day when a choice
had to be made between ruin and reason," Charles de Gaulle later
wrote, "Pétain was promoted."

Commander in Chief of his country's army, 109 divisions on the
Western Front, he held in his hand a broken sword. He must repair it
or the war was lost. Majestic now at sixty-one, tall, frosty, lucid,
forceful, unemotional as always, he established his headquarters at the
Palace of Compiègne in what had been the salon of Marie Antoinette.
Tapestries hung in the high-windowed neoclassical chamber and a
monumental clock on the fireplace mantel stood reflected in a great
looking glass. But he was no château general. Each day he drove out in
a requisitioned Rolls-Royce to visit his men, the winged woman on the
hood which they identified with the *Winged Victory* tactfully removed
when the news was bad.

The disorderly soldiers found themselves listening to a general
known for never breaking his word and for a profound understanding
of what it was they had undergone. Standing on a tree stump or the
hood of the car he did not talk to them of "punch" or the offensive
spirit, still less of glory. Let them for a few minutes forget his rank, he
asked, and speak as man to man of what was on their minds. They
responded with a rush. The war was hopeless. To attack against uncut
wire and into machine-gun fire! "We are not such fools." Behind the
lines the staff officers, drinkers of blood, lived in safety and luxury
while the men who did the fighting ate swill. On their brief rests from

the fighting they were billeted in squalid villages where there were no beds, no showers, no provisions or facilities to cook a decent meal. When upon infrequent and unpredictable occasions they were granted leave, there were no buses to take them to the railroad station, and often no trains for them when they walked there.

The slackers were getting rich in plush factory jobs and stealing the soldiers' women. There was no rhyme or reason to which units saw service at unmenaced sectors and which, decimated from battle, were sent again and again to the most dangerous points. What did the General Commanding think of the army's Medical Service? It was appalling; the doctors were cynical butchers. (A 3,500-bed hospital awaiting casualties from Nivelle's Chemin des Dames catastrophe had four thermometers.) The entire atmosphere of the army, the loathsome living conditions, the indifference in high places, made one feel like a convict. It was too much, too stupid.

Pétain listened. By his orders staff officers, wearing their identifying brassards, were sent to show themselves at the Front. He demanded that the government furnish him with 400,000 cots for rest areas behind the lines and beyond the sound of the guns. There must be sports equipment at these places, prizes for competition in games, either cash or goods; every effort must be made "to blot out the painful vision of the terrible drama." He said he must be allowed to guarantee each soldier seven days' leave every four months, that there must be transport furnished to the railroad station, and exact timetables displayed there, and letterboxes and a canteen with food and wine counters, tobacco and newspaper stands, washbasins and showers. When men returned from leave they must find cheerfully painted buildings at the station so they would not be so shatteringly plunged back into the war—let there be a "humane cushioning process."

He demanded green vegetables of the Ministry of Food, and an end to the red tape that delayed shipments. He ordered army cooks sent to intensified training courses, which junior officers must also attend so that they could supervise. He outlined his desires as to what menus should be like. For breakfast he wanted the men to have coffee, soup, cold meat, pâté, sausage, sardines, and cheese according to availability. Junior officers must see that a meal was cooked as near to the lines as possible, "so that the men should be able to eat it hot, or at the worst still warm." (His own meals at Compiègne he kept rigorously sparse and simple, finishing up with a single slice of cheese and a single glass of wine.) The staff officers of General Headquarters found him the most commanding personality of all the men who had come their way, his face always impassive, his demeanor reserved and masterful. The ex-journalist who had edited the daily official communiqué since early in the war said of Pétain that he gave the impression of a statue come to life, a statue of a Roman senator taken from a museum. "No one evokes better than he what the Romans called 'great men.' Incomparable majesty." Meals were eaten in almost total silence. Hardly anyone spoke save for the Commander in Chief.

Pétain barely slept but continued that activity which characterized him all his life—"I have two passions, sex and the infantry." When his car halted so that he might have some lunch he enjoyed inviting army nurses to join him by the road or in a ruined town. Wearing an ordinary military greatcoat without orders or stars he handed out bread and tins of food and only when the cheese was served said, "Please excuse me, I haven't introduced myself. I am General Pétain." His faithful aide Bernard Serrigny, who had interrupted the general's hotel tryst to tell him of the appointment to command at Verdun, wrote: "A number of these women, I fear, received unequivocal tokens of the admiration of the Chief." (When at Compiègne Pétain admired a bust of the Empress Eugénie in Serrigny's bedroom and asked if he might have it for his own, the aide refused, and referring to the fact that French intelligence had learned that one of the mistresses of the General Commanding was on the payroll of the German ambassador to Spain, said that he had too much to do with women anyway and would have to get along without this one.)

Pétain worked on his army. Weakness would bring complete dissolution of the force, and brutality complete revolt. So in the most delicate manner he kept to a middle course. Yes, he told the soldiers, they had reason to complain. The war was too long and too hard. But it had been imposed upon France and so must be seen through. They must be patient. He would look after them, they would have better food and wine, more leave time. He would guarantee that he would never send them forward unless gigantic artillery barrages preceded them. There would be no more assaults upon undamaged defensive positions; he would never push into a salient within reach of enemy reserves or flanking fire, there would be no blind obstinate battering, but only coordinated probes. Let the soldiers think, then, of their wives, their children, the old people, their region, their land. Let them believe in France.

He employed neither familiarity nor wheedling. Sometimes a tone not harsh but forceful came into his voice. He would promise them no sunny hours, he said, but he must have victory from them. He permitted them to believe that many mutineers had been shot (the actual number was less than fifty men), and he showed them that he could speak strongly to their officers: "Look at these men; there is nothing the matter with them. All they require is leading, all they need is an example."

He was, Edward Spears reflected, like a surgeon operating on his army, his tools human understanding displayed with masterly psychology. To a *poilu* receiving the latest of several medals he said, "Five decorations all by yourself! What have you done?" The stumbling answer was, "My general, I have . . . I have done what everyone else does." "What everyone else does? That's all there is to it, eh?" A band played. He visited between eighty and ninety divisions. In each company there was at least one private who got to speak with him. One of them said he had gotten no leave for eighteen months, and his wife was ill. Pétain ordered immediate leave. Months later private and general met again. Pétain remembered and asked how Madame was. "My going did her good," said the soldier. "But she told me to do something about you, my general, that I dare not tell you."

"Why shouldn't you tell me? Out with it."

"She told me to embrace you, my general."

"And what is stopping you?" They kissed.

The army, his patient, began to get well. Pétain went to cookhouses to taste the food, handed out medals, tobacco, and pipes inscribed with the facsimile of his signature. He looked at the leave rosters. The regal presence never relaxed but the humane understanding shone through. With his word given that miserlike he would husband his men's lives he conducted meticulously prepared minor attacks. They were invariably successful. He told the men in the frankest manner that he would attempt no grand breakout and would press the enemy just sufficiently to keep him off-balance. Let his soldiers hold out, just a little longer. "I am waiting for the Americans and the tanks."

Pétain was enshrined, Spears said, "as a deity." As un-Napoleonic a French soldier who ever lived—"I found him businesslike, knowledgeable, and brief of speech," Field Marshal Sir Douglas Haig told his diary, and continued, "The latter is, I find, a rare quality in a Frenchman!"—Pétain was compared to the Great Emperor for the occasion upon which Napoleon found a sentry asleep, picked up his rifle, and walked his post for him. The Miracle of the Marne in which the French turned on the Germans after the Great Retreat in 1914 had seen beaten and weary masses turned into aggressive armies; but Pétain's was a greater miracle, for in mid-1917 he converted mutineers to soldiers, drunken bands into steady battalions, and strikers into disciplined troops. At home, through his doing, units which had received honors had their names announced publicly by local authorities in the centers of the places of their origin, the county and town councils. The soldiers knew that those at home knew of their deeds, and that there were men in their number who had received certificates signed by the Commander in Chief.

Here was a leader, the soldiers said, who understood what a Frenchman's life was worth, and what he was. No one ever forgot what Pétain had been in those days. He was the commander lavish with steel, stingy with blood. Doctor of an army threatened with death, he gave it resurrection. War, Premier Georges Clemenceau once said, is too serious a matter to be left to soldiers. It was not so in the case of Pétain. "In saving the armies of France," Spears wrote, "he saved the Allied cause. Great as were his achievements as a commander in the field, they pale before this."

In later years, loved and honored and revered, "the noblest of our soldiers," said the leftist intellectual and Premier Léon Blum, named by the United States Commander in Chief John J. Pershing as the finest soldier of the war, Pétain spoke only fleetingly of what he had done. If he deserved to be remembered for his activities in 1914–18, he told people, it was for his helping the *poilus* find themselves again when, for a time, they had been lost. "When his car drove away from a unit, Pétain left behind a memory of integrity and humanity—above all of trust," Spears said. They would one day come for him again, the French.

8

CAPTAIN EDEN, M.C.

All of his life Anthony Eden remembered the days of the war. He remembered the fifteenth of September of 1916 along the Somme for the four officers and fifty-four other ranks of his battalion who died that day. He remembered the days between October 2 and October 8 when twelve officers and 350 other ranks went into the line and six officers and 170 other ranks came out.

He remembered Lord Faversham, who had taken him into the battalion and who had told him of the death of his sixteen-year-old brother Nicholas when the *Indefatigable* went down at Jutland. One day Faversham went into no-man's-land and never came back. He had sought to take an almost completely undamaged German position. A month later his body was found. The German position was still intact. In the night Eden took out a patrol hurriedly and noiselessly to give the dead man a shallow grave. They put up a cross, and Eden whispered lines from the burial service. Soon dawn would be coming to the Western Front and the Germans would see them going back to their trench. Eden and his patrol for the last time saluted their colonel and went away, "leaving him to Picardy and the shells." Sgt. Reg Park was killed. They had talked through many long nights. "I lost a friend I have never forgotten."

He remembered the desolation, the stench, the corpses, the torn and twisted guns and limbers, the mutilated horses and mules, how the Germans had the British range to a yard, to a T. He saw a wounded friend being carried away and asked where he had been hit. The man smiled and, "a little ruefully," he remembered, said, "In the stomach." They had talked with others a few nights earlier about where the worst place was to be hit, and all had agreed it was the stomach. His friend died before reaching a casualty clearing station.

Eden became battalion adjutant, the youngest in the British Army. Like all the others, despite his captaincy and the Military Cross given him for rescuing under fire the sergeant who gave him a gold knife from his native Sheffield, he prayed for a "blighty wound," an injury that would not kill or cripple him, but would get him back to England. It never came. He survived innumerable near-misses, became the only frontline officer of the battalion to go through the war without a scratch, and then and for the sixty years of life remaining pondered the ways of a fate that gave each man his individual result in so haphazard a fashion. The enormous trench rats, as large as cats, unsatisfied with their limitless diet of human flesh, ate the chocolate peppermint creams his mother had sent. Winter came and the campaign along the Somme was closed down.

The King's Royal Rifle Corps went north whence they had come and were there when in July of 1917, one year after the beginning of the Somme, Field Marshal Sir Douglas Haig struck again at the Germans. In the frankest possible manner, Gen. Henri Philippe Pétain had told his British opposite number the mutinous state of the French Army. The news transfixed Haig. If the French caved in, his own force would find itself cut off and pinned up against the beaches with water at its back. The Russians were collapsing and the Americans would never arrive in time. The British, therefore, Haig reasoned, must attack to relieve all pressure on the French. And if they broke through the enemy lines, the Belgian ports harboring German U-boats would be theirs.

He lunged forward as he had done along the Somme, but with far better tactics, with even more artillery. By then Haig had come to an almost Socratic method of asking questions of his subordinates. Were the enemy batteries accurately mapped, what were the changes in German positions, were they reoccupying them after time lapses, were there new camouflaged positions, were the machine-gun sites known,

when were the most recent air photos made of canals and rivers, what
was the bridge situation over those waterways, were the barrages in
depth arranged, were the smoke- and gas-shell determinations made,
were there counterbatteries to protect forward guns as well as infantry,
were there sufficient guns forward to support foot soldiers taking advanced objectives? He asked all questions, the educated soldier, tireless, at the peak of his form. In his diary he drew pictures and gave
specifications of new weapons and analyzed those captured from the
enemy.

Preparing to attack, he permitted himself to dwell on the possibility
that he would effect a complete rupture of the enemy lines, his
horseman's hands sweeping over the map and his blunt fingernails
coming to rest on the German border. Prime Minister Lloyd George
looked on now that Asquith was gone, his son Raymond lost along the
Somme along with his tenure at 10 Downing Street. Lloyd George
never forgot those fingernails resting on the Rhine.

But what it came down to for Captain Eden was: mud. Western
Flanders is one of the flattest sections of the earth's surface, flatter than
the Hungarian plains, flatter than Kansas, a place where rivers mean-
der in curves and never run straight because of the lack of any gradient.
The ground is clay, impervious, so that any flooding or heavy rainfall
produces puddles, swamps, ponds. One cannot dig down more than a
foot and a half on the average without striking water.

Rain falls in western Flanders on the average of every other day
during the year. When the British attacked it came down in torrents for
three straight days. The artillery had destroyed the intricate drainage
system. Thereby mud was created in such quantity that mules and
horses who fell off the duckboards drowned in it, that men sinking in it
could not get out unless someone lent them a hand. The earth turned
almost to liquid eternally sucking at one's legs. Mud-covered bodies
lay everywhere in the polluted stagnant water, for it was almost impossible to carry them away or to bury them. Haig's chief of staff, Gen. Sir
Lancelot Kiggell, went up to the front line, undertaking a trip which
could see hours pass before one got forward even a mile. Kiggell was
one of the very, very few high officers who ever saw the battlefield up

close—a fact, Eden noted, that did not escape the riflemen who had to do the dying. Kiggell saw what the Battle of Passchendaele was, its name coming from the utterly insignificant town which crowned the low ridge the British now sought, their hopes of a breakthrough vanished. He became more and more agitated. When at last he was where the sway of the Allies ended and that of King Death, ruler of no-man's-land, began, he burst into tears. "Good God!" he cried. "Did we really ask our men to fight in that?" He went away, his nerves gone. Field Marshal Haig sent him home.

The British fought on, Eden with the others never losing faith—that would come later—and raving at government leaders in his letters home. "My God! It does make my blood boil. Have we not one single politician who is really out to do his best or are they all an unscrupulous set of narrow-minded, self-satisfied crassly ignorant notaries! My God! It does make me see red. I wish they would muzzle or drown all these infernal politicians until after the war. My God, they are brutes and murderers, they make me see red."

The low clouds and mists and heavy rains of Flanders autumn came, and to carry a wounded man though the depthless bogs back to a medical clearing station required sixteen stretcher-bearers working in relays. Passchendaele went on for 105 days, the casualties more than a quarter of a million, the ground gained no more than four miles at the farthest point. The British never got all of the ridge. The Yeoman Rifles of the 21st Battalion of the KRRC, shattered along the Somme and then replenished, were again shattered at Passchendaele. Captain Eden went off to be a staff officer brigade major, the youngest in the British Army.

Eden was to know high office and great honors. He would live to advanced old age. But his forming, his education, took place in those days along the Somme and in front of Passchendaele's ridge. In later years people knew what it meant to him when the band played the song of the King's Royal Rifle Corps when he came into a room. He had gone to war childish in nature, he said of himself. When he came from it he was mature in his thoughts. They were never to change, he wrote. Anthony Eden was the symbol of England in the Great War,

Winston Churchill felt, the representative of those who had given and lost so much, the group which had come of age in time to spend its youth serving under Douglas Haig. Many of them, a million, were never to come home, but would lie in their endless cemeteries where their relatives and later their descendants might come to write in visitors' books that where the dead men lay was a little corner of a foreign field that was forever England.

Many years after it all was done, become one of those politicians against whom he had railed when he was a soldier, it fell to Eden to complete a chapter in England's life whose beginning came when the Old Contemptibles marched from Aldershot to board the ships that led to the trains and then the roads that ended in the cemeteries. England had been great on the day that trip began, the first power in the world. When one day long in the future ex-Captain Eden of the KRRC sat with ex-Captain Harold Macmillan of the Grenadier Guards for a few sad moments, the one Prime Minister leaving in disgrace, the other in hours to be his successor, it was quite different. England then had become, not least of all through Eden's doings, a small island off the European mainland. They did not talk about the events of the day, but of another time. "We talked for a few minutes about the First World War," Macmillan wrote.

Eventually the war was won, but the world he knew, Eden wrote, was gone. He left the army on the day before his twenty-second birthday.

THE EDUCATED SOLDIER

David Lloyd George, British Minister of Munitions during the Battle of the Somme, Prime Minister during Passchendaele, was accounted by most people who knew him to be the most fascinating human being they had ever met. Lloyd George was a dazzling figure, funny, irritating, filled with song and jest not always suited for the prudish. He was the Wizard to some for his oratory and brilliant insights, the Goat to others for his womanizing. He was buoyancy itself, a whirlwind who liked to dance people about, sing, imitate accents, tell stories, laugh. A village boy from Wales, he held hereditary aristocrats in contempt and did not go about in society, scorning Mayfair hostesses and avoiding Court functions and affairs. Alert and quick-witted, he disliked rules, regulations, barriers. "I hate fences," he said.

No more absolute contrast to Field Marshal Sir Douglas Haig could possibly be imagined, and these opposites did not attract. The Prime Minister, with his long flowing hair, shapeless overcoat, and unorthodox trilby hat, was a fatiguing companion on an automobile trip, Haig wrote. "He talks and argues so! He seems to be so flighty, makes plans and is always changing them and his mind." Lloyd George to Haig was unpunctual, sloppy, a politician whose trips to France were joyrides. "Breakfast with newspapermen and posing for the cinema shows pleased him more than anything else. No doubt with the ulterior motive of catching votes!"

To Lloyd George, Haig was the most unimaginative person in high position he had ever met. The man's tongue-tied speech was infuriating and frustrating. His mind seemed sluggish. In his presence one could not simply remark that four times three made twelve, one had to add that three times four also made twelve. "Haig's part in the conversation consisted of a series of grunts, monosyllables, raised eyebrows and scowls." Haig, Lloyd George said, showed by his confused talk that he was anything but a clear thinker. "Brilliant to the tops of his army boots."

Yet in the hands of this stolid figure rested the fate of the young manhood of the Empire. And in what Lloyd George felt was the most gross and brutal manner imaginable he was in nightmare fashion systematically martyring them. The Somme had been ghastly. When it was over the Prime Minister was terrified at permitting Haig to try again at Passchendaele. Those fingernails on the Rhine had persuaded Lloyd George to go ahead over his better instincts. Then his worst fears had been confirmed as Haig slogged through the hideous arena of depthless Flanders mud, killing men by the tens of thousands to capture some all but nameless country village reduced to a mass of shattered stones. Then he pushed on to seek its duplicate, at equal expense, a quarter of a mile away.

The war was horrible beyond conception, the Prime Minister told his intimates. And he himself was being put in the position of a butcher's boy who drives cattle to the slaughter. There was a savage look on his face when he spoke of Douglas Haig. When France's General Nivelle, who was graceful, who was fluid in his thinking, who could *talk*, was appointed to the French command, Lloyd George tried to put him also in charge of Britain's army, and so save that force from its Commander in Chief. Haig would be reduced to a glorified adjutant who carried out the Frenchman's orders. Britain's forces would be another French Foreign Legion. This plan failed. Haig and Chief of the Imperial General Staff Sir William Robertson said they would rather face court-martial than submit. The King was on the side of the generals, and many in the Cabinet also. Lloyd George commanded no Parliamentary majority. He could not pick up the gage of open battle Haig and Robertson offered. He decided to ease them out.

The Prime Minister went about asking the Allied commanders what they thought. Arriving almost two hours late for lunch with Gen. Ferdinand Foch, bringing eight people after saying there would be two or three, Lloyd George asked the Frenchman why British generals lost so many men for so little ground. He had given Haig, he said, all the guns and men and ammunition he could use—and nothing had happened. What was Foch's opinion of such generalship? Foch said he had no means of forming an opinion. Lloyd George turned to Pétain, who felt the questioning was ridiculous and out of place, and evaded an answer by saying he was wholly engaged in retraining his own men and so could not offer a judgment on the British efforts. When word of the Prime Minister's inquiries reached Haig, he wrote he could not believe Lloyd George "could have been so ungentlemanly as to go to a foreigner and put such questions." But that was Lloyd George, a sneak, so "un-English." It was impossible, he wrote Robertson, "that a man such as he can remain for long head of any government. Surely *some* honesty and truth are required."

All would be easy, he sighed, "if only I had to deal with Germans." But that was precisely what Lloyd George did not wish the British to do. Lloyd George was what came to be called an Easterner. The Western Front, those of that persuasion reasoned, was permanently stalemated. Certainly there must be other places where the war could be won. The forcing of the Dardanelles in Turkey had failed, but there remained locations where the German props could be knocked away— the Italian front, Salonika, Mesopotamia, Egypt, Syria, Palestine, East Africa; anywhere there were no German entrenchments years in the building and where Douglas Haig was not in command.

To Haig and Sir William Robertson, the leaders of the Westerners, Lloyd George's ideas were a completely incorrect departure from first principles. The war would be won by killing Germans, not Turks or Bulgarians or Austrians. To offer battle to such was "like a prizefighter leaving the ring to trounce his opponent's seconds," said Haig's aide John Charteris. Lloyd George, Haig felt, was a man who wanted to go wandering about seeking laurels and political advantage somewhere, anywhere, rather than seeing the war through on the Western Front. "Victory while you wait," said Robertson contemptuously. In Lloyd

George's mind, Haig said, looking good politically was the important thing. "There is only *one sound* plan to follow, viz., *without delay* to

"1. Send to France every possible man.
"2.   "   "   "   "   " aero-plane.
"3.   "   "   "   "   " gun."

It was maddening for the Prime Minister. He asked for details or concrete predictions and received only the deadly information that a drawn-out wearing-down battle was the only way the war would be won. He went out to France and Charteris arranged a tour of German prisoner-of-war camps. The captives were uniformly old and tired or almost childishly young. This was what the Germans were down to, Lloyd George was told. Years later he learned that by Charteris's orders all able-bodied and impressive German prisoners had been weeded out and hidden from his sight. "Those fellows absolutely lied to me," he said. Politicians, he said, did not lie, not like that. Soldiers were another matter. "It is a fatal thing to give in to generals. History shows every time they are wrong."

He did not give in to the generals. This mutual grinding, this endless reciprocal massacre, this pigheaded bulling ahead, it was murder, butchery, it was mad; if people really knew what was happening the war would stop tomorrow! Lloyd George saw war as chess: you checkmate the enemy although many pieces yet stand upright. Did Haig, he cagily asked the man who for years had said the enemy was on his last legs, believe that the Germans were capable of launching an all-out offensive in 1918? Hamstrung by his own statements that Hindenburg and Ludendorff were at the end of their tether, and the memory of his fingernails upon the Rhine, Haig could not now announce that he was going to be attacked. Lloyd George had him. From that moment on the Prime Minister refused all requests for additional men. The British Isles were filled with uniformed soldiers while the lines in France thinned. At least those at home were safe from the madly senseless killing fields where men were shot like animals or squashed like insects, Lloyd George reasoned.

The Prime Minister pressed his advantage. In February of 1918 it was announced that Sir William Robertson, Haig's "echo" in the Prime Minister's eyes, "that one-eyed fellow in blinkers," was resigning his position as Chief of the Imperial General Staff. He had not resigned. He had been told he was leaving. He wrote to Haig, addressing him for the first and only time by his first name: "My dear Douglas." Perhaps he thought Haig would save him. Haig could not. Nor could he give up his own post, for he saw himself as all that stood between Britain's politicians and Britain's Prime Minister—"A cur. What a wretched lot!"—and defeat, perdition, the end of England, the end of the Empire.

In March of 1918, for the first time since 1914, the German Army moved forward in the west. Russia was finished, Italy comatose. Ludendorff had division after division shipped in. He struck with picked storm troops probing forward into the Allied defenses, a series of little rivulets, not a flood, jets and not waves. The rivulets sapped at the dam. Ludendorff pushed his artillery through on portable ramps and heavy duckboards so that the guns would not sink in the mud fought over for going on four years. The French and the British broke. Ludendorff roared forward, forty miles. No such gains had been seen before. Of a sudden the war seemed lost for the Allies. When on a Sunday Haig went to church as usual, Chaplain George Duncan ventured to say that he hoped things were not as bad as they seemed. Haig replied that things would never be too bad. The chaplain said that perhaps after Passchendaele the commander would never think anything was too bad.

" 'Be not afraid,' " Haig replied, quoting Second Chronicles 20:15, " 'nor dismayed by reason of this great multitude; for the battle is not yours, but God's.' " To Duncan he seemed akin to Moses or Joshua or Cromwell or Lincoln, a man who saw a need and in obedience to God set himself to meet that need. That night Haig met with the French Commander in Chief, Henri Philippe Pétain, and found to his horror that something seemed to have broken there. Pétain seemed to have shot his bolt, seemed ready to concede the war to Germany. He was, Haig wrote, "very much upset, almost unbalanced. Pétain had a

terrible look. He had the look of a commander who has lost his nerve."
Pétain told Haig he was going to separate his force from that of Britain
and fall back to cover the approaches to Paris. That meant the British
would be cut off. Perhaps Pétain had come to the end of what it was in
him to do for his army, had reached the end of the miracle he had
performed, was out of fuel, of spirit, had done enough, was empty. But
for Britain his plan meant the end of everything. Haig wired to London
saying that a supreme commander must immediately be appointed
with authority over all Allied forces, and that he must be a Frenchman, and a Frenchman who would fight. There was no question of
rank, nor a Nivelle-like situation such as Lloyd George had tried to
force upon him. It was that their cause was in danger. This was the
only way out.

The next day, retreating troops and vehicles pouring through the
streets, the military and political leaders of France and Great Britain
met in the little Hôtel de Ville of Doullens. Shells were falling outside.
Lloyd George had never liked shells. Premier Clemenceau was taken
aside by Pétain to hear a horrific prediction. "The Germans will defeat
the British in the open country," Pétain said. "After which they will
defeat us too."

Clemenceau had thought of designating Pétain as Supreme Allied
Commander. The expressed sentiments made him instantly change
his mind. "Ought a general to talk or even think like that?" he asked
President Raymond Poincaré. They appointed the fiery and ardent
Ferdinand Foch, whose method of expressing himself made many
people believe him at least half mad. (Others reflected that sometimes
a winning general needs something of the demonic or the deranged in
his nature.) "I suppose you think I can't fight," Pétain said nastily to
Lloyd George. Like many Frenchman, he did not much care for the
British. "No, General," Lloyd George replied. "With your record I
could not make that mistake. But I am certain that you won't fight."
He had done enough, Pétain.

Foch took up the reins, saying he would fight and then fight some
more. But within a short time the Germans struck in enormous force
against the British. The thinned lines broke. The British fled. Field

Marshal Sir Douglas Haig went out to see for himself, traveling by automobile. Upon his return he was as usual met some distance from his headquarters by an orderly holding his horse and an escort of the 17th Lancers. He rode to his residence, dismounted, and went straight to his room to write an order of the day which made Winston Churchill revise the opinion he had held that Haig was entirely insensitive and "indurated" to the torment and drama which was the war. He had thought Haig "inflexible, rigorously pedantic," Churchill wrote, a commander ready to send men home at an hour's notice for refusing to order their troops to certain destruction. "Fight and kill or be killed" had seemed his only thought, Churchill wrote, "obey orders even when it was clear that the Higher Command had not foreseen the conditions, or go at once to the rear, to England, or to the devil." The order of the day which Haig wrote, as usual in his own hand, made Churchill feel he had misjudged his man. There was that in it which made him view a shy and inarticulate and formal soldier who served on while the government searched "high and low for someone to replace him" as something more: a figure "majestic," a "knightly figure."

> Many amongst us now are tired. To those I would say that Victory will belong to the side which holds out the longest. There must be no retirement. With our backs to the wall and believing in the justice of our cause each one must fight on to the end. The safety of our homes and the freedom of mankind alike depend upon the conduct of each one of us at this critical moment.

He did not speak in terms of officers and other ranks, nor call upon the Divinity, nor even offer hope. He simply said, Churchill wrote, what the war had become: "It all worked down to blunt, grim and simple duty." The soldiers knew what he meant, heard his voice through the guns. Nurse Vera Brittain, her husband-to-be dead, her only brother about to die, read what the Commander in Chief had written, "and after I had read it I knew that I should go on, whether I could or not." In later years she was never able, she wrote, to view the author of those words as simply "the colossal blunderer, the self-deceived optimist." All of her fellow nurses took heart. "Though enemy airmen blew up our huts, so long as wounded men remained, there would be 'no retirement.' " Douglas Haig, said the military intellectual Sir B. H. Liddell Hart, "in his qualities and defects was the very embodiment of the national character." The national character of his day and time held it unthinkable that Britain would fail to see it through. So the British held. And as the German drive stalled, Haig saw that the end of the war was at hand.

For nearly four years he had waited to put together those combinations of space and time which, dazzling the enemy, are the soul of military art. He had never had the chance. Now with the Germans extended and out of their fortresslike positions of the trenches in depth of the Somme, the mud of Passchendaele, he attacked, then cleverly shifted his attack to another point and then another. For four months he came on, his forces by far the most important of the Allied mixture that now included Americans. On August 8, less than four months after writing what became known as the Backs to the Wall Order, Haig threw 450 tanks against Ludendorff. The German commander broke. This was the black day of his army in this war, he told the Kaiser that night. Germany must have peace.

The War Cabinet in London could not know what Ludendorff had told his master, and they listened to what Haig had to say with a cynicism and bitterness born of four years of the war. Haig was "ridiculously optimistic," said Secretary of State for War Lord Milner, and the new Chief of the Imperial General Staff, Sir Henry Wilson, wrote out a projected plan for the summer campaign of 1919, with an Easterner's view of attacks launched as far and remote from the Western Front as Albania. ("Words! Words! Words!" Haig wrote on the copy sent him. "Theoretical rubbish!") He pressed on. The Germans fled. King George sent him a telegram of congratulations for his brilliant advance; so did Queen Mary, and even Sir John French. Nothing was received from the British government as such until October 9, when the Prime Minister telegraphed that he had "just heard from Marshal Foch" of the victorious movements of the day previous. Why he had never noted earlier ones he did not say. The implication that he relied only upon Foch for information presaged the decades-long assault David Lloyd George would mount upon Douglas Haig, his works, attitudes, what he represented.

In the last three months of the war the British Army took 188,700 prisoners and 2,840 guns. The other Allies in the west, the French, Americans, Belgians, and Portuguese, between them took 196,700 prisoners and 3,775 guns. Britain's performance was amazing. Only months before, her army had seemed broken. What her soldiers had done, Foch said, was "thanks above all to the unselfishness, to the wise, loyal and energetic power of their Commander in Chief."

The Germans asked for peace. They were beaten. Their people were starving. The war was about to end, and anyone with eyes to see and ears to hear knew it, save for one man who suddenly stepped forward saying it must go on: Walther Rathenau.

10

THE ETERNAL JEW

He had wept while others rejoiced on the day the Germans went to war, and said that although it was summer he felt winter coming on. Now winter was coming, the winter of 1918, Turnip Winter for Germany, when that was what the coffee was made of, and a million old people and children died of starvation. Walther Rathenau plunged forward to publish an appeal that the whole population spring to arms.

"The people must be ready to rise in defense of their nation," said his call for a levee en masse. "There is not a day to lose. There will be enough found who are yet sound, full of patriotic fervor. All men capable of bearing arms must be combed out of the offices, the guard rooms and depots." The wounded must rise from their hospital beds. The women must join them. Guerrilla war against the Allies must follow, if necessary, the war of the trenches. In battling on, Germany would secure just conditions for peace. She must thus offer terms to her creditors, not simply declare bankruptcy.

But what Rathenau called for was impossible, Imperial Chancellor Prince Max of Baden found when he asked the high command its opinion of the proposal. Rathenau did not accept that judgment. He went to the War Ministry to lobby for *Götterdämmerung*, his Wagnerian Twilight of the Gods. Nobody would listen to him. An auto flying white flags with a trumpeter on the running board sounding his instrument drove through the lines to a clearing in the woods at Compiègne where Generalissimo Foch waited. His fiery nature smoldering through in the brutal manner in which he posed the question, Foch asked the German visitors what it was they desired.

They told him: an end to the fighting. He granted them their wish. So it was over, the Great War. As he had on the day it began, Rathenau burst into tears. He cried, Prince Max remembered, "like a child."

Few joined in his sobbing, for the vast majority of Germans were beyond emotion. One other, a lance corporal* lying wounded in a hospital, did cry. An Austrian waif and vagrant who had found a home in the German Army, and a sense of destiny previously unknown along the Somme and at Passchendaele, where he directly opposed the King's Royal Rifle Corps and Capt. Anthony Eden a few hundred yards away, he buried his face in his hospital pillow. He of course knew of Walther Rathenau, but Rathenau of course would not have known of *Obergefreiter* Adolf Hitler.

The war was over. The German troops came home. There were those among them who spiritually were as walking dead men returning to a collapsed society. Germany's lodestars had gone, Kaiser Wilhelm to Holland, Ludendorff to Sweden, and there was nothing to replace them. The kings and captains had taken leave, and those they left behind flailed aimlessly about asking themselves how this could have come to be when they, Germany's sometime heroes, had so steadfastly held the lines for so long, never giving up one square inch of the Fatherland's soil. A kind of mad frenzy seized the nation which had produced the Army of a Thousand Victories and where in the past the law had been seen as a force comparable to thunder or the frost, unable to be disregarded or argued with. Now there was no law, nor code, nor values. Above the shops were empty spaces where once hung Purveyor to the Royal Family signs, and there was soot on the statuary in the park, and the stucco was peeling from the buildings at the bases of which sat legless veterans begging alms of the pale and emaciated people passing by in threadbare clothes.

In the streets one heard bursts of machine-gun fire and the rattle of armored cars going past. Coup followed political murder, to be followed by anarchy. In seventy days Bavaria had five different governments. Children's arms and legs were pitifully thin, their eyes dull. There was no food, for the British blockade stayed in place as the

---

*Equivalent to a private first class in the U.S. Army.

victors met to determine the peace terms they would offer the vanquished.

Coup d'état, general strike, revolution and counterrevolution, hunger, cold, shots in the night, gun runners, continuous elections,
political murder gangs, anemic women, men without work, a broken
society and an entire nation's people wan, haggard, abject, rendered
déclassé and disinherited by the war—and the Allies at Versailles
presented their demands. The government that received them had
found its formation at Weimar, chosen for its association with Goethe,
who had always stood against what the world called Prussianism, and
for the fact that while Berlin was intensely dangerous with its pointless
mad chaos in the streets, Weimar could be more easily patrolled and
defended by what troops could be mustered up by the new republic
replacing the Kaiser. But those troops were very few. So the government came to rely upon armed piratical gangs who bound themselves
to some freebooter leader because they found their lives purposeless
without something or someone to whom they could pledge allegiance.
It was very risky to trust them. Such as they cared nothing for the fine
ideals of the Weimar Republic whose constitution was the most liberal
in the history of any country, nor for the president, the ex-saddlemaker
Friedrich Ebert. Rathenau's name had been proposed for the post, to
be greeted by many of the assembled delegates with roars of derisive
hilarity.

It hurt him deeply that they laughed. One had achieved some
intellectual standing, some business success, one had done one's best
for Germany, he said, and one might have hoped for a little respect.
He did not perhaps understand that all standards were gone, that
nobody was able to believe in anything anymore, that from the Rhine
east to Moscow and beyond not a stone remained in place of the
structure that had been. Inflation, famine, pestilence, lice, looting,
the old tribal hatreds of the new countries formed from the wreckage of
the shattered empires, the little pocket wars, the empty harbors and
silent factories, the broken markets, the fear of Bolshevism, slaughter,
barbarism, a new Dark Ages—all this had ended the nineteenth century and the early years of the twentieth in which Rathenau had found

his being. He had predicted that it would happen, that the war would leave ruins and the funeral pyre of many things; yet some of the madness seized him also, and when the terms of the Versailles Treaty were made known he said they were impossible and could not be accepted. The Allies called for massive reparations, the loss of Germany's colonies, the ceding of large amounts of her territory, the perpetual disarming of her military forces, and the admission by the beaten nation that it and it alone had been responsible for the war. Rathenau declared that what Germany should do was abdicate all responsibility and all government. Let Ebert and his Cabinet resign, let the Allies take on their shoulders sixty million Germans. Thus the world would be shown what Germany thought of the treaty. "For myself I have nothing more to hope or fear. My country has no further need for me and I do not believe that I shall long outlive its downfall. My father and brother are waiting for me in that neutral country to which no railroad leads. They cannot understand why I am delaying."

It was so unlike him, this unrestraint so different from his usual controlled manner reflected in the tempo of his speech, his measured walk, his careful fashion of eating, his extraordinarily clear handwriting. But few were they who kept their heads completely in the Germany of 1919, a place and time uprooted in the earthquake and collapsed in the ruins. Nothing was the same as it had been. A German officer in the past had been the member of society most revered, an almost godlike figure. Now when the too-young-for-the-war Ernst von Salomon wore his Royal Prussian Cadet School uniform in the street people called him a jackanapes, fancy-boy, ninny. In his hometown in western Germany he saw French occupation troops come in at the quick march with fixed bayonets, bugles sounding above their short crisp steps. To von Salomon the "Sambre et Meuse" of their bands was wild music, fierce music against the backdrop of his house with its paintings of the Franco-Prussian War, old epaulets with tarnished tassels, swords. People placed trays on a sidewalk and sold from them what they could to foreigners. For a song the foreigners bought the family silver. Von Salomon heard that Free Corps detachments tacitly encouraged by the government were fighting with Poles along the eastern frontiers and as mercenaries in the once-Russian Baltic republics Lenin sought to reclaim for Bolshevism.

He went out there, out east, to get away from the all-pervading melancholy of a country which in twenty years, Rathenau wrote, might well turn into "a Balkan race among Balkan races," with cities become half-dead blocks of stone, forests down, fields yielding miserable crops, the harbors, railroads, and canals in ruin and decay, crumbling great buildings the only reminder of the ages of grandeur. "The German spirit which has sung and thought for the world will be a thing of the past." In the east von Salomon joined a multitude of other purposeless souls in tattered uniforms to whom the war or at least the thought of war had given meaning and direction, and with them and against them fought the nastiest kind of unpleasant and unplanned fights, which saw prisoners shot and flung into bonfires, beheaded, castrated, dropped into wells with a grenade following so that the blasted-open body would contaminate the water. Soon enough he would have much to do with Walther Rathenau. For the moment he burned and pillaged, living and fighting, it seemed to him, in an absentminded way, not belonging anywhere, he and his fellow strangers from a Germany turned strange to them. Neither he nor his Free Corps comrades ever asked what it was all for, the shooting of corpses, the senseless destruction: "The search for reasons why was lost in the tumult." Madly they ravaged on, completely nihilistic. "What we wanted we did not know, what we knew we did not want. There were many who thought that some message must come; but what this message was no one knew, though all awaited the summons."

In Germany itself a ghastly luxury came into being for those who knew how to scrabble, cheat, buy devalued currency, sell alleged influence, operate through illicit commissions or bribery in a situation where all businesses and business values and institutions had come undone and everything was corrupted. The buttoned-up Germany of before the war was no more. Thirty sailors were massacred in broad daylight on a street, noted the diarist Count Harry Kessler, and at the same time advertising placards for a certain cabaret went up: "Who has the prettiest legs in Berlin? Visit the Caviare-flapper dance." Jazz bands competed with the rattling machine guns, Kessler wrote, in nightmare Berlin. The limousines of the "newly enriched" passed empty bakers' and butchers' shops on their way to frenzied revelry, and hurried by shivering women in rags selling themselves for a quarter loaf of bread. The foundations of civilized life were fading, Kessler wrote; and Rathenau reversed himself and said that the Versailles Treaty must be accepted so that Germany could begin to find its way back to the world. The ground-down and dispirited country must make a start somewhere. Acceptance would mean compliance with the Allied demand that seven hundred Germans be turned over for trial as war criminals, and Rathenau's name was on the list for having conspired with General Ludendorff forcibly to deport hundreds of thousands of Belgians to work in German war plants. It was entirely unfair that such a demand should be made, Rathenau said, and if others on the list attempted to evade punishment he would not blame them in the least. He himself would neither flee nor hide and would stand trial if the Allies so wished. His fate would be as nothing when compared to a nation suffering what Count Kessler described as a continuous St. Bartholomew's Massacre night after night in the streets, the fighting, bomb-throwing, arson, all mad, all senseless.

Rathenau was opposed in his new willingness to implement what came to be known as the Policy of Fulfillment by his only rival for the position of Germany's greatest industrialist, Hugo Stinnes. Colossally rich, with interests in steel, shipping, communications, a hundred other things, Stinnes was an utter opposite to the Rathenau of complicated speech and ornamental style. Dressed in peasant boots and clothing which to Count Kessler's eyes appeared just to have been reclaimed from a pawnbroker, Stinnes held to the opinion Rathenau had but latterly abandoned: defy the Allies, let Germany be occupied, let it be Bolshevized. Then the Allies would see the light. Blackmail the blackmailers. Looking and acting like an untidy terrier just out of a scrap and looking for another—so he appeared in the eyes of Great Britain's first postwar ambassador, Viscount d'Abernon—Stinnes said Rathenau's opposition to his views came from his ownership of the

"soul of an alien race." They had it out before the leaders of the
government and the army, Rathenau carrying the day with a great
speech in which he said of the Policy of Fulfillment that it was similar
to Beethoven's last string quartet: "It begins slowly, 'Must it be?' and
ends with a decisive and powerful 'It must be!' " He had returned to
himself, the man who in d'Abernon's eyes was profoundly mistaken
when he declared that while he was of Jewish stock he was a thorough
German, mistaken because he was far more than either, a fun-
damentally cosmopolitan European who knew the languages, litera-
tures, and philosophies of other lands, knew capitalism, socialism,
Bolshevism, "and every other ism" and was a bold inquirer into new
theories. "Such a man was not limited to or confined by any arbitrary
geographical frontier. He belonged to the universe."

In preference to paying cash reparations it was Rathenau's idea that
Germany offer to repair and refit the devastated areas of Belgium and
France where the war had been largely fought. If she did the work she
would gain moral position and jobs, and in time an atmosphere in
which trade could get under way. Rathenau became Minister for
Reconstruction, met with Allied leaders, worked at eroding the harsher
clauses of the Versailles Treaty. Talleyrand was his model for what he
had done to the Congress of Vienna when the representative of a
power defeated, helpless and occupied. He would express Germany's
desires and hopes not by the use of military power but by cooperation
and understanding, and so help return his country to a place correspondent to her moral, intellectual, and economic resources and
position. He became very close to Finance Minister Josef Wirth, a
mathematician who felt most of his colleagues simply chatted away
and had no grasp of affairs. It was quite different in Rathenau's case,
and so Wirth consulted with him on all things and sent him to talk
with Lloyd George about lowering reparations and to point out that it
was Germany who stood between Europe and Bolshevism. The British
blockade was lifted and diplomatic relations resumed with the dispatch
of Lord d'Abernon to Berlin as ambassador.

The first steps were thus taken toward German resumption of her
role as a Great Power of Europe. The Weimar Republic, so different

from Imperial Germany, became known as the freest country in the world. The private armies of the Free Corps faded away as the foreign loans came in, and there was food and even prosperity and an explosion of new creative energy sweeping away accepted forms in music, architecture, and art, and films were produced of a type never seen before. Yet there was always something disjointed about Weimar Germany. One did not feel entirely comfortable there. There was something strange about the people, the average everyday woman wearing too much makeup, those leather-booted prostitutes carrying whips and soliciting men in monocles and dress-for-dinner batwing collars. One saw people bowing from the waist and heard heels respectfully clicking, but there was that which was sinister about Germany's new music, that ticky-tacky beat for a doomed and corrupted masquerade ball.

In a country where it had been said there could never be a revolutionary storming of the palace because there were Do Not Walk on the Grass signs before the gates, vice, gambling, and exhibitionism reached a peak never before seen in Europe. There were armies of procurers, transvestites, fetishists, boy prostitutes; "Berlin was transformed into the Babylon of the world," Stefan Zweig wrote. "Along the entire Kurfürstendamm powdered and rouged young men sauntered. Even the Rome of Suetonius had never known such orgies as the balls of Berlin, where hundreds of man costumed as women and hundreds of women costumed as men danced. In the collapse of all values a kind of madness gained hold."

Decadent, tragic, sinister, dangerous, the laughter of the damned sounding just below the surface, the ghosts of the dead warriors of the Front hovering everywhere with the memories of that which the war had killed: it seemed to Lady d'Abernon, wife of the ambassador and aunt of that Colonel Lord Faversham who had recruited the young Anthony Eden into the King's Royal Rifle Corps and told him of the death of his brother Nicholas, that the Berliners were down and out mentally and morally. She looked out the window of the embassy and saw a skeleton of a boy passing by, dragging a cart full of some miserable merchandise, and male streetwalkers, one of whom was in woman's clothing with a large hat and floating veil but wearing a cavalry belt to which was attached a saber, and the wives of the vile profiteers with pearls and other jewels on top of their fur coats, and high yellow boots. Back from the east and his Free Corps of nihilistic sallies against he knew not what with other young fighters seeing themselves as the descendants of the colonizing and crusading medieval Knights of the Teutonic Order, Ernst von Salomon entered a world of wild forays against what he and his called the Traitor Republic of Weimar. They held that it had stabbed in the back the soldiers of the Western Front who for long had held the lines before November of 1918. Von Salomon's intellectual qualities and moral form were married, he said, to those who shot to death Mattias Erzberger, who had gone to see Generalissimo Foch to ask for peace. Philip Scheidemann, who had proclaimed the end of Imperial Germany from a balcony of the Kaiser's palace, had prussic acid flung into his face.

All along the border with France the von Salomons threw bombs, roughed up German girls who consorted with the occupiers, ran arms to resistance groups. As in their Free Corps doings in the east, when tearing prisoners' arms from their sockets they wondered why they were doing it, they fought in half-mad ecstasy. "The curious medley of the fumes of beer, sun-god myths, and military music was an expression of the confusion of the times," Salomon remembered. Patriotic clubs— according to certain lights—sprouted up, joining the scraps of old beliefs, German spirit, genius, honor, to the latest catchwords and half-truths. "Quotations from Schiller and patriotic songs were mingled with the muttering of spells."

They saw, the von Salomons, a supine government, ignoble, base, un-Wagnerian—the Weimar Republic—offering to Germany's oppressors paper formulae, notes, protests, appeals. Their murder gangs passed sentence and executed the traitors. There was no reasoning to it—they raved against Germany's humiliations but never suggested any alternative. They simply struck out at everything about them. "We understand logic of this sort," the Minister for Reconstruction said. "It's the fault of the police, the rationing system, the Prussians, the

Jews, the English, the priests, the capitalists." The von Salomons read what he had said and made up a song set to a marching beat:

Shoot down Walther Rathenau,
The goddam dirty Jew.

He smiled when he heard of what they sang. There existed people who had to have someone or something to hate, he said. He went ahead with his efforts to get and keep Germany's feet under her. His mother, terribly worried, was against his becoming so much a public figure, but he said that in life one had to employ one's abilities and fulfill one's responsibilities. Simply to accept gifts from Nature was not right.

Having reached out to the former enemies France and England, he reached out to the former enemy Russia, opening informal discussions about future trade. The setting for the discussions was unusual. Taking with him Felix Deutsch, director general of the German General Electric Company and his lady friend Lili's husband, Rathenau went to a Berlin jail to see Karl Radek, Lenin's close collaborator, whom the German government had imprisoned for too clearly and loudly calling for Bolshevik uprisings. Radek was part political theorist, part blood-thirsty rebel, part street urchin who appeared to be hugely enjoying some colossal prank. He found Rathenau "a very complicated man, a great abstract intellect" who "listened attentively to the sound of his own voice."

A new aristocracy of intellect was going to run the world, Rathenau told Radek. There would not be a society of equality, for that was impossible, but this new order which destroyed inherited power would see the most intelligent and the strongest rule. In a few years, he predicted, he would visit Russia as a technician, and the Soviet notables would receive him wearing silk.

"Why silk?" asked Radek. Because, Rathenau explained, after all the years of ascetic revolutionarism, they would wish to enjoy life. Radek felt Rathenau acted like a one-man control commission, gracious and indulgent. When Felix Deutsch asked if the Bolsheviks would restore to the German General Electric Company their con-fiscated factories, Radek laughed. "He is, of course, clever and witty," Rathenau told Lord d'Abernon, "but very dirty, the real type of low Jew-boy."

That he had gone to see Bolshevism's representative infuriated those who could neither accept Germany's defeat in the war nor bring themselves to go on afterward. The barricades and barbed wire were gone from the cities and there was no more street fighting, and Germany was on the way toward gaining the world's moral acceptance; and there were those who grew to hate him more each day, the fabulously rich Jew who spoke of sacrifice, the brilliantly successful industrialist now on his way to becoming the world statesman of a country still profoundly and nervously ill, the intellectual responding to ancient calls of blood and soil and mystical destiny. They detested him for all they were not and their country was not.

Finance Minister Joseph Wirth became Chancellor. He asked Rathenau to be his Foreign Minister, to hold the highest official position any Jew had ever held in Germany.* Rathenau hesitated. He knew that for the most part the men of the Republic's government were faceless, unglamorous, and uninspiring when compared to the Im-perial government's princes and barons besworded and bespurred, the "vons" of the pre-1914 world. He knew that he was of a different type from the new government's men, and known to be, and seen to be. If he accepted he became the symbol of the new Germany, the Weimar Republic incarnated.

There came a day when Ambassador d'Abernon called upon Chan-cellor Wirth and was met with an enthusiasm he was never to forget. "Do not let us discuss current affairs today!" Wirth exclaimed. He was "boyish" in his excitement, d'Abernon remembered. "There is a great, a most important event: Rathenau has joined!"

He did not dare to tell his mother. She had to find it out from a newspaper. At lunch she said, "Walther, why did you do that to me?"

"Mama, I had to do it."

---

*Or has ever held since.

11

VICTOR OF VERDUN

In the Place d'Armes at Metz one month after the Armistice the commanding general of the French Army was made a Marshal of France. All the great captains of the Allies were there. Haig stood next to Pershing.

Pétain was the least typical of the six Marshals of Victory that the Republic created, and even less typical of the ones of the past, for he stood for caution and restraint while other great French soldiers were filled with dash, inspired imagination, passion, romanticism, *furia francese*. (As the President of the Republic handed over the baton, the fire-eater Foche's aide Maxime Weygand whispered, "We have shocked him to such an eminence by untiringly kicking his buttocks!") For eight centuries a Marshal of France had represented military virtue in a nation of very old fighting tradition which had seen victory seldom desert its banners. A halo surrounded a Marshal. Under the early kings it was his duty to interpret the code of chivalry. To receive the baton was like being ordained a noble.

In his kepi of red and gold and with seven stars on his sleeves, tall, erect, calm, of never-absent regal presence, no man looked more the part. France had needed Joffre's phlegm in 1914 and Foch's fire in 1918, but no less had it needed Pétain's good sense and freedom from illusions in 1917. More than they ever were, he was loved. The French knew what they owed him. He took up the duties of peacetime service to cries of "Long live the Marshal!" when he conducted tours of inspection or escorted foreign royals on visits to the former battlefields now grown quiet. He led the Bastille Day parade of 1919 past eight million viewers, flowers pouring down as he rode a white horse. He was named as automatic Commander in Chief for any future war.

Another war was of course the last thing France desired. Yet it might come. So as early as January of 1920 the Commander in Chief began to plan what might have been called the Pétain Line but what was in fact called the Maginot Line for War Minister André Maginot. It was a series of fortifications facing Germany like an endless fleet of battleships sunk six stories deep into the earth with revolving turrets of from thirty to three hundred tons that rose up at the touch of a button ready to throw a salvo before sinking down for reloading. Below were staircases, galleries, tunnels, barracks, hospitals, diesel engines for electricity and ventilation, airtight doors that would keep out poison gas, stores of food, water, ammunition.

Telephone wires buried under fifteen feet of concrete connected the fortresses. Every foot of ground for hundreds of kilometers was open to bullets from emplaced double machine guns; the land was kept clear of any trees or even a bush that might offer the slightest protection to the Germans if they came. France had nearly a million and a half dead from the war, a third of her population of men aged between eighteen and twenty-eight. Five million soldiers had been wounded. France was finished with anything that smacked of *à l'outrance* or even glory. The Maginot Line was to be a gigantic extended Verdun which would hold Germany at bay forever. It was a monument to the lifetime theory of Marshal Henri Philippe Pétain, who had always stood for the use of material rather than men, the power of defense, the use of artillery. Planning it, he said, would be his last contribution to his country, for he was sixty-four, the owner of a charming house on the Riviera between Cagnes and Antibes bought with the aid of admirers. The Ermitage had ten acres of lovely grounds, vineyards, outbuildings in which he could raise animals, a view of the Mediterranean—and soon a mistress. In a quiet ceremony he married Eugénie Hardon, a lady twenty-one years his junior with whom for years he had had an off-and-on physical relationship. A friend who did not care for the new Mme. la Maréchale wrote sadly that the marriage proved that those who said Pétain was too much the slave of flesh were proved correct.

The thought was both right and wrong. He was too set in his ways to remain faithful to one woman, and married or not there would be many others in his life. He had a trunk filled with perfumed love letters.

Possessed of great energy, he rode each morning and enjoyed the best of health. (When he came down with a heavy cold and accompanying laryngitis and consulted a country doctor who did not know him or recognize him from his pictures, the man remarked that it was obvious that the well-preserved individual in tweeds could not have served in the war. Pétain loved to tell the story.)* He planted vegetables on his estate, new grape cuttings and olive trees, and planned for two cows and a flock of chickens. He represented the Republic at the funerals of distinguished foreigners, inaugurated war memorials, was guest of honor at dinners, sat for portraits and statues, was invited to castles by counts and dukes, met women through King Alphonse XIII of Spain and flirted with Queen Elizabeth of the Belgians, went to soirées where he mixed with statesmen, artists, scholars, journalists. He was always expected to talk about the Battle of Verdun. It was never far from his thoughts, the boys passing as he stood on the steps of his headquarters at Souilly and watched them go up the Sacred Way, the survivors returning and the dead staying forever where one day, he said, he also wished to lie, to be for eternity still at the head of his soldiers. Other generals wrote their memoirs, and it was notable how they never mentioned the suffering of those who served under them. They spoke of casualties sustained as mathematical calculations. Alone of the Great War's high commanders, Pétain was concerned with the human cost. He spoke of it emotionally. It was otherwise when he wrote of the mutinies of 1917. His monograph on the subject took the tone of a college professor discussing a problem whose solution might be applied to similar difficulties.

---

*A companion story was his rendition of a meeting with a woman who ran a restaurant at which he had often dined when a junior officer serving with the mountain troops along the Riviera. It was only with difficulty that she remembered his face. "But tell me," she finally said, "in all this time, and with the war, you must have gotten promoted. You're perhaps a colonel now?"

He hardly mentioned his own role, and when he did so the references were in the third person. Pétain did not care for glory. Even more pronounced was his distaste for attempts to write of him as a public figure who had saved his country. He did not care for personal questions, avoided reporters who asked them, and did not wish details of his life and doings to be given publicity. He was elected to the French Academy, the "assembly of immortals," Paul Valéry welcoming him as the man who during the fighting embodied the spirit of Resistance.

Always at his side in those years was the officer whose supposed death he had regretfully noted during Verdun days. Escaped from German captivity and recovered from wounds, Captain de Gaulle became a speech and ghost writer for the Marshal, whom he addressed as "Boss." In the eyes of others de Gaulle remained what he had been at Saint-Cyr when a cadet, the Tall Asparagus whose outstanding traits were coldness, ruthlessness, an inhumanly Olympian intellectual arrogance—someone entirely unlovable. Pétain esteemed him differently. "What a style, what magnificent language," he said of his aide as they worked together for a book on the French soldier through history. "He is brilliant." When the Marshal learned de Gaulle was to be given a low grade in a Staff College course because of his refusal to listen to the arguments of others, he interjected himself into the matter and used his influence to get the grade improved. Yet it worked upon him that the highest possible grade had not been awarded, and he arranged for the Staff College to hear three lectures from the former student. It was quite unheard-of, a series of speeches from a junior officer whose sojourn at the school had been so controversial. But when the Marshal himself came to hear de Gaulle there was no choice for the faculty but to follow suit. When the hour for the first speech came, all expected Pétain to enter the hall first. He stood aside and gestured to his aide to precede him. "The honor is yours. It is the lecturer's privilege to lead the way."

They went in and the Marshal took the podium and said, "Gentlemen, Captain de Gaulle is going to express his ideas to you. Kindly listen to him attentively." In the speech de Gaulle mentioned Alexander the Great, Caesar, Napoleon, Frederick the Great—and Henri Philippe Pétain. He said that the Marshal had a genius for method and putting things in their right place. He looked to him, he told people, as guide, philosopher, and friend, and let it be known that the Marshal was the godfather of the boy named for him, young Philippe de Gaulle. The statement was untrue, for the actual godparents were the child's grandparents. But de Gaulle could be forgiven. Philippe played a central part in his father's life, for his sister, the only other child, could offer little to a man like their father. "Charles and I would give anything," Mme. de Gaulle wrote, "health, all our money, advancement, career, if only Anne could be an ordinary little girl like the rest." It could not be. She was hopelessly retarded, a victim of Down syndrome, unable to speak. Her parents would not put her in an institution but said that as she had not asked to come into the world they must do everything to make her happy. She loved her father's military cap. A gleam came into her dead eyes when he wore it. He would pick her up, rock her, clap his hands, slap his thighs, dance about singing songs for her, do pantomimes, swing her about. Something like a laugh emerged from her lips. Then she slept with her hand in that of her father—and his stern face would tighten and sometimes he would cry. It was forgivable that he gilded the lily in terming Marshal Pétain his son's godfather. Above the boy's bed was a photograph inscribed, "To my young friend Philippe de Gaulle, hoping that his life may show all his father's qualities and gifts."

The Marshal commanded the forces suppressing insurrectionary Arabs in Morocco, made a tour of America, where he dined with Daughters of the American Revolution and then held private meetings with, as he put it, some great-granddaughters. He carefully supervised de Gaulle and the other ghost writers who turned out his speeches, prefaces to books, articles, instructions, orders of the day. He was an expert editor, grafting on less than he pruned and cut: "If you tell a woman 'I love you,' that is enough. You don't need to say 'I love you very much.' "

The great figures of the war passed off the stage. Four of the six Marshals of Victory died, and a fifth, Franchet d'Esperey, became a wheelchair-bound invalid. The men who had served under them as junior officers and sergeants rose to high position military and civil. It was impossible that they avoid a deferential tone when they addressed the soldier who had saved the country and was still in place and in uniform, hardly changed in appearance from the days of glory. He pushed for upgrading the military air arm seen as a defensive weapon to ward off enemy attack planes, followed the building of the Maginot Line with great care, often visiting it, served a term as War Minister, ate well (he drank moderately and did not smoke and disliked others' doing so), supervised the production of wine at the Ermitage, sallied forth sometimes with Mme. la Maréchale on his arm—and sometimes other women.

France in those years was not a happy country. There had been a brief golden period when the world came to Paris and there was music, exhibitions, the brilliant talk of the artists and writers of the Left Bank, food, excitement, Coco Chanel, Mainbocher, Schiaparelli, Coty, a Riviera and Deauville and Loire Valley jammed with tourists, with happiness being defined by the Germans as being as happy as God would be if He could be in France, and others saying every man had two countries, his own and France. Then it all faded away as the War to End War receded into the past and it came to be seen that there could not be an eternally powerful France dictating the affairs of a Europe bowing to a new Napoleonic, imperial Paris. French culture and French wines and French glamour were at a discount. France began to doubt herself. She was not the first nation of the postwar world to do that. Out east in the wreckage of the Austro-Hungarian and German and Russian empires there had existed since 1918 a ramshackle structure of weak little countries ever suspicious of one another, puny and insecure heirs as they were of destroyed political systems whose death had given them life but whose disappearance in clouds of artillery fire and killing along the Eastern and Western Front had taken away stability, tradition, the ways of a millennium. What replaced the understood old polished ways and centralized governments and accepted rule was base and despicable.

Out there, out east, the uprooted had learned to cheat and lie and smuggle across the new borders, to intrigue against one another for petty advantage, to embargo one another's goods, to make propaganda and to assassinate, fight undeclared wars, depart completely from the path that a score of earlier generations had traveled, and find in the earthquake of 1914–18 and its aftermath justification for all that a previous code had disdained. Pauperized, overcrowded, poor, prejudiced, stratified, the Europeans on the other side of the Rhine learned to forgo the use of good solid silver coins in favor of shabby banknotes of monstrously high denomination, to live in surroundings mean, drab, chaotic, to live in armed bankruptcy with the wall hangings in shreds and the furniture covers filled with holes. In the 1930s the demons from the other side of the Maginot Line crossed over it and came with their curse to the very heart of civilization, a France caught in the Great Depression.

France turned ugly. Selfishness became the hallmark of the politicians of the Third Republic, of whom it was said that for them there was no such thing as a ministerial portfolio that was dirty—they would pick one up from the gutter. They traded a bridge here, a road there, a job, a terminus, an armory for votes, an enlargement of a military garrison; they negotiated by free and easy nods and winks and slaps on the back, deals, compromises, favors, accommodations, mutual concessions: the Republic of Pals. Over a period of years ministers lasted in office an average of three months.* Then they fell from office to reappear a ministry or two later. Almost always lawyer-politicians, they defended rich clients against the laws they themselves proposed or at least endorsed, and at the same time cried that they were for taxing the rich who bled France. A famous cartoon depicted a hostess telling her household staff that two deputies and a minister were expected for dinner that night: the servants must be sure to count the spoons carefully.

France held her politicians to be contemptible. Behind one anoth-

---

*Over a period of twenty-two years there were forty-four Premiers.

er's backs, overcharged and superheated, they made promises that could never be kept and were never believed. Their mistresses negotiated backstairs on their behalf. Schemes, plots, corruption, bribes filled the atmosphere of the round robin of men standing for nothing beyond their own personal advantage. No one trusted anyone, and those in office were buffeted by political enemies, unions, committees and commissions and syndicates and a public opinion framed by a press and radio universally believed to be for sale. The poor felt exploited, as they were, and the rich felt social reforms were used not to better conditions but as political weapons, as they were. From the decline in public morality and the personal quarrels of competing politicians there arose the most appalling hatreds. It was quite common and acceptable in many circles to hold that France would be far better off under Adolf Hitler than under the leftist Léon Blum; and Blum permitted himself to face those of the right in Parliament and shriek at the top of his lungs: "I hate you!"

In this fragmented and dislocated society, in disarray, stalled, the faithful of many faiths viewing their opponents as the representatives of the anti-Christ, those who hated the Republic referring to it as La Gueuse, "the Slut," Science and the Machine seen as the villains, or perhaps the bankers, capitalism, the foreigners, those who had made the Revolution of 1789, or those who had never accepted it, Marshal Pétain held a particular and special and unique position. Another world had passed away, the Indian summer of French greatness had come, and the last remnants of the France of glory and dominance and hope were dying or dead, the *grandes horizontales* and dandies of the Second Empire grown old, the silky and scented *belle époque* prewar courtesans given way to fake silver-foxed modernites, Clemenceau gone, Foch, Joffre, Ravel, Anatole France. Time was of course bound to take them all, but time brought something else to replace what they represented. It was the belief that the world committed suicide in 1914 but that the dying took long and that now the last breath was about to be drawn, that there was coming the reign of the hollow men in a world made sick by psychic tuberculosis and a syphilis of the soul. Pétain remained.

Of bribery, graft, corruption, preference, red tape, pettiness, disorganization, chiseling, he had no part. Of an earlier and better day, he represented uprightness mixed with kindness, a man who never kowtowed to Power and was always regarded as the soldiers' champion who alone of the great military chiefs understood what they had undergone so that France could win through in the Great War. The Third Republic had about it a tone that was mocking, skeptical, and cynical, but "our noblest and most humane soldier" was what Léon Blum termed Pétain. There was, said Premier Paul Reynaud, a feeling that he was something akin to divine, a warrior of all the ancient virtues, self-sacrificing, a stranger to self-interest and pettiness. In a France that was soulless and of no ideals and pursued only material satisfaction and self-indulgence, gambling on foreign exchanges and seeking lucrative friendships with financiers, he knew no such ambitions and no such transactions. He stood alone on a certain plane. There was no competition.

And yet for all the astonishing clearness of the pale blue eyes and smooth pale skin, the straight back and springy walk, he was seventy, seventy-five, eighty; and those who knew him well noted little memory blackouts, quickly covered and followed by perfect lucidity but disconcerting nevertheless. De Gaulle wrote a book based on the three Staff College lectures which Pétain had arranged, and dedicated it to his chief. "This essay, M. le Maréchal, could only be dedicated to you, for nothing shows better than your glory how clear thought can lead to correct action." But even as he did so de Gaulle said in private to younger officers that if in the next war—already they talked about the next war—he attained high rank he would not hang on too long, but would retire when the fighting was over. He was excited about the possibilities of organizing a small mechanized army, an elite force of tanks supported by attack aircraft. But Pétain and the Maginot Line represented the ideas produced by 1914–18: defense only, no *à l'outrance*, no charges. So a coolness grew between the two men once so close, and de Gaulle became what Pétain once had been, an innovative thinker whose ideas were disdained by those above him. French military thinking had come full circle. Before 1914, Pétain talked about firepower for defense and everybody else talked about a slashing attack; now France had no thought for anything but defense while de Gaulle talked of attacking with his tanks.

The two men came to a parting of the ways when de Gaulle, after leaving the Marshal's staff, finished by himself the book on the French soldier that they had begun together and together had abandoned. De Gaulle dedicated it to his former chief, but Pétain found both book and dedication an impertinence and wrote protestingly to the publisher. "This officer, without first applying for my authorization," had used for his book staff papers written under Pétain's direction. It was a breach of trust, he said. De Gaulle had proved ungrateful. "That turkey-cock!" De Gaulle was at first shocked and distressed. "The old man is losing his sense of proportion," he said. "He isn't himself anymore. He can no longer control the demons inside him, as he could when he gave us the example of a man of character." Then when Pétain's anger did not abate, de Gaulle grew angry also. "The poor Marshal died," he said. "His body is there, his mind is gone."

He was not the only man to say that. Pétain's memory was going, which he recognized and feared. Sometimes, one of his intimates wrote, you could have written on his forehead, "Closed owing to old age." But the next day, or even later on the same day, he would display the sharpest acuity. To the world he appeared unchanged, the only leading soldier of the war who still held a commanding position in the military thinking of his country. Universally respected, revered, he worked his land, went away for weekend trips with women he introduced as his "cousin," made speeches. Pétain grew old.

12

THE EDUCATED SOLDIER

One November day in 1918, Field Marshal Sir Douglas Haig had as guests in his railroad car two representatives of Britain's ally Japan, Prince Fushimi and the Marquis Inouye. "The Japs sat on each side of me at lunch. I thought them most interesting, and much more open and frank than any Japs I have hitherto come across."

It was the eleventh day of November 1918, Armistice Day, and the guns of the Great War had finally fallen silent. He recorded his reaction when he learned that the Kaiser had fled to Holland. Had things gone against England, he reflected, King George would have had to go and the British Army would have become as insubordinate and disorganized as the German one. He thought of John Bunyan's remark upon seeing a man on his way to be hanged: "But for the grace of God, John Bunyan would have been in this man's place." It was perhaps the sole literary allusion in his journal. No other particular sentiment seized him.

The war was over. He had done his job, fulfilling, his wife thought, the sense of duty to his day and his generation which he felt as the servant of his destiny. He had fought battles that went on for months before reaching the objectives of the first day; he had waited for years to launch the cavalry charge which never came. He had faced a dilemma the solution to which no one has ever discovered. He was caught in a technological impasse which found the defense, until the tank was perfected, infinitely stronger than the offense. To eliminate the defensive German wire and to pulverize the defensive German machine-gun posts he must unleash tremendous bombardments. They made the ground in front of him all but impassable so that even when at terrible cost he took the enemy front line he had no way to get guns up to hit the second or third, and so no way to get forward.

His every attack was frontal and hideously expensive, paid for with losses unknown to previous history. He had to do that because there were no flanks. The great decisive battles he planned became the wearing-out fights which crucified a generation of young men, and left wives-who-might-have-been and, of course, children who never were.

Perhaps the Great War was like a fire that must roar on until it burns itself out. England saw the fire through, not without changes. (When the German Count Harry Kessler visited London afterward and saw that half the men in the stalls of a London theater were in lounge suits, the rest in dinner jackets, and only five or six in white tie and tails, he felt "astonishment." This was, he wrote, "a real revolution or, more accurately, the symptom of such.") But England was still England. The morale of the British soldier and his companion the Dominions soldier pulled the Empire through. Haig was the leader of those soldiers. He had won. In Germany he was termed the Master of the Field. Perhaps the war was like a new epidemic most terrible for which the doctor must take time to find a cure.

Could the British have held together without Haig? Hating everything about him, Lloyd George had never seen fit to replace him. "There was no one to put in his place sufficiently good to make it worth while making a change." That spoke volumes. Had there been somebody, Lloyd George would have put him there in a minute. Of course Haig was remote, stiff, and inarticulate, and of course he utilized infantry formations akin to those of the eighteenth century, and of course he never seemed entirely to understand that he was no longer dealing with the crude slum and farm boys of before the war, but the war was won, and "I don't care a *damn* what anybody says," Capt. Anthony Eden wrote home, "the result is not due to Lloyd George—Foch—internal trouble in Germany—the intervention of America, or anything else—but it is due to the BRITISH ARMY."

Haig stayed in France until April of 1919. On his last night there he dined at Chantilly with Marshal Pétain, who told him that actually the state of the French Army in 1917 had been much worse than he had dared to say at the time. Haig visited Pershing to say farewell and then went to Boulogne, where on the piers and jetties bands played and officers saluted. He boarded the *Princess Victoria*. At the end of the pier four pipers of the Fife Yeomanry played as the boat passed and made for Dover. That night after his children went to bed he wrote the final pages of his diary. Typed up by Lady Haig, it comprised thirty-six volumes, three-quarters of a million words, the equivalent of seven books.

Churchill said when he came to write of the war:

> He presents to me in those red years the same mental picture of a great surgeon before the days of anesthetics, versed in every detail of such science as was known to him: sure of himself, steady of poise, knife in hand, intent upon the operation; entirely removed in his professional capacity from the agony of the patient, the anguish of relations, or the doctrines of rival schools, the devices of quacks, or the first-fruits of new learning. He would operate without excitement, or he would depart without being affronted; and if the patient died he would not reproach himself.
>
> He might be, he surely was, unequal to the prodigious scale of events, but no one else was discerned as his equal or his better.

By then Haig was nearly ten years dead, his reputation permanently set as a butcher. He would not have cared. When he had talked with Churchill his attitude was as if he discussed events of one hundred years previous, always in impersonal and detached fashion. He had no interest in making himself look good for history, but told Churchill just to get the facts right. Let people judge for themselves. They judged. When the Second War came no one referred to him with anything but horror. All the British commanders had him in their mind's eye as the example they must sedulously avoid. When the

United States commander Gen. George C. Marshall spoke about large-scale frontal attacks upon the Germans there was not a British officer who did not tell him it was no use talking to them about such projected endeavors, for Marshall was going up against the memory of those who had died in frontal attacks along the Somme and before Passchendaele's ridge. By then, it was said, the lions who had formed the British Army of 1914–18 had found out the asses who had led them.

But that was much later, when everything had fallen apart and the War to End War, the War to Make the World Safe for Democracy, had brought unrest and terrible disillusion, Communism to Russia, Fascism to Italy, Nazism to Germany, and made France weak and bitter and England the most pacifist country in the world, where at Oxford University the students voted through a resolution that under no circumstances would they ever go out to die for King and country. In the first days of Haig's return from France the British *had* to believe it had been for something, the dead boys forever young in their cemeteries, the endless In Memoriam notices in the newspapers for My Son, or Beloved Husband, or Father, or Our Brother that went on for decade after decade until those who placed them joined in final rest those for whom they were placed. (The girls they would have married turned graying spinsters.) So the former Field Marshal Commanding in Chief was given a title and became Earl Haig of Bemersyde. Other soldiers became Plumer of Ypres or Allenby of Megiddo, but Haig said he did not wish to distinguish one spot on the Western Front in preference to another and so took the name of his family's ancient seat in Scotland, purchased for him by popular subscription from another branch of that family. It stood high above the Tweed River with views of the Eildon Hills.

There he lived. Bemersyde was no great castle; the staff consisted of a butler, a footman, his former batman to act as his valet, a cook and three girls in the kitchen, a lady's maid for his wife. He had hoped to be named Governor-General of Canada or Viceroy of India, and particularly longed for a post in South Africa, but Lloyd George was still Prime Minister and he would get nothing. So he went about to receptions and parades and meetings of Old Comrades of the regiments of the army he had led, and unveiled memorials for the Fallen, the Honored Dead. He had a study in Bemersyde's old Peel Tower, and there he sat and wrote answers in his own hand to letters sent him. He devoted himself to unifying the various veterans' groups into one great organization, the British Legion. On train trips he went through the cars asking men if they had served under him, and where.

Often he had to make speeches, in the course of which he stammered and hesitated, making people wonder if he was going to be able to finish. Eventually he developed a routine of saying in his opening sentence that he was no orator. It made people smile. That was the only sign of a sense of humor he ever showed in public, although his daughter Victoria, named of course for the Queen, said in later years that it was only her father's dislike for off-color stories that gave rise to the belief that he was completely without any light touch. (Another daughter, Alexandra, named of course for the Queen, late in life married the renowned British historian Hugh Trevor-Roper.)

He traveled to Canada and South Africa with Lady Haig, learned to dance on shipboard. He assiduously studied golf and tennis with professionals, fished the Tweed, went on special diets of his own creation—oranges, health tonics, special breads.

He took no notice whatever of the flood of books brutally critical of him which came from the presses as the disillusionment of the postwar world overwhelmed Britain. That men threw their medals into the Thames brought from Haig no comment. In late January of 1928 he was invited to address a group of Boy Scouts. "When you grow up," he told them, "always remember that you belong to a great empire, and when people speak disrespectfully of England always stand up and defend your country." Two days later, visiting the London home of his much-beloved sister Henrietta Jameson, he was heard groaning in his sleep. It was a heart attack. He was sixty-six.

The body was borne through London to Westminster Abbey on an artillery carriage, the King's sons walking behind. Marshals Foch and

Pétain represented France at the ceremonies and together called on the widow. From Westminster Abbey the coffin was taken to Edinburgh and then through the bleak wintertime hills along the Tweed to Dryburgh Abbey for interment. "The Flowers of the Forest" sounded, the traditional dirge for the fallen soldier.

By then, 1928, the wooden markers along the Western Front had been replaced by stone Crosses of Sacrifice and Stones of Remembrance, and travel agencies organized tours of the former battlefields. Relatives came seeking particular graves upon which they had been allowed to designate the words under the name and unit and date of death: In Loving Memory of Our Dear Horace Aged 21. From Mother and Father and Family . . . God Be with You Dearest Tom Until We Meet Again. From Mother and All . . . Rest in Peace Sweetest Husband and Loving Father. Alice and the Girls. There was an immense Western Front silence that spoke of what had been lost. Many of the stones were Unknowns: A Soldier of the Great War. Worcestershire Regiment. Known unto God; A Sergeant of the Great War. Royal Irish Rifles. Known unto God.

Former Tommies came to seek the graves of friends, and then adjourned to little roadside taverns where they were expected and welcomed, and they kept those taverns going for fifty years and more. They got slightly potted and took out their old paybooks and pictures and showed them around. There was always a refrain repeated endlessly as they pointed to the old pictures of their pals: "He's dead . . . he's dead . . . he's dead." They stood up on the slight rises as no one could have done when they were there before and looked at the graveyards stretching everywhere, 150 of them outside Ypres.

Unexploded shells, deadly dangerous still, stood piled alongside the roads to be taken away and detonated by experts. They rose, and rise, to the surface of the land after heavy rainstorms, or plowing farmers turn them up. Bodies are still found. Often their uniforms are still in good shape. Letters in the pockets are sent to survivors or, now, descendants. (Years ago the rule was set up that letters to girls would be destroyed.) Each cemetery has a visitors' book in which one is invited to write what one will. The Commonwealth War Graves Commission has thousands of books stored away dating from the 1920s. People write, "Thanks, my pals are here" or "Beautifully kept—thank you" or "Respects of a little girl nine years old." Sometimes people write remarks about Douglas Haig, Field Marshal. The comments are not pleasant.

13

THE ETERNAL JEW

How do you do?" a visitor asked the German Foreign Minister.

"This is how I do!" Walther Rathenau replied, and took out a Browning pistol. From the day of his appointment threatening letters had poured in, sent by people for whom everything he did, or did not do, was an abomination. No German in history had ever been seen by so many of his fellow countrymen as the agent and symbol of so many evils. He inspired, wrote British Ambassador Lord d'Abernon, "hatred, almost horror."

The eradication of all central and traditional authority in vast areas east of Berlin had unleashed among other upheavals anti-Semitic riots of a type not seen since the Middle Ages, and when Jews fled west from the Ukraine and Poland and Rumania their coming to Germany was held to be Rathenau's doing. Jewish sex fiends, it was said, were defiling German virgins, as were France's black troops in areas under occupation—and it was the fault of the Jew who championed the treasonous Policy of Fulfillment. Germany was impoverished and Germans thin and haggard—it was the work of the enormously rich capitalist. He was at one and the same time denounced as the Stab in the Back pillar of the pirate Weimar Republic which had betrayed the army of A Thousand Victories, and as the warmonger who had called for a bloody levee en masse for a last-ditch stand. He was the greedy exploiter of the poor whose jail visit to Karl Radek was made to arrange the latter's marriage to the former Edith Rathenau.* If inflation was

---

*She was married to a banker.

rising it was because he was giving away Germany's money to the French, his aim being to make first Germany and then the world a Jewish proprietorship to crush the middle classes and bring poverty and universal misery.

To countless plotters, brotherhoods, tiny secret political action groups, little frustrated circles of German nationalism filled with hatred and violence, all their moorings gone, he was the symbol of all that had gone wrong with the times. He was Weimar, the Jew Republic, to all those whose props had been shot away by the war, who dwelt as rebellious strangers in a country where tradition, order, panoply, Yesterday, had been taken away, trampled upon and buried. For a time Rathenau permitted police to patrol before his home and escort him wherever he went, but then he said he could not bear to have them around and dismissed them. For years, he said, German foreign policy had lain fallow and now he must invigorate it. He could not do so as a prisoner hemmed in by armed guards. If something were to happen to him, that would be his destiny. He would not attempt to avoid it. "I am merely a stranger who has come to give of himself, and I shall live only so long as there is still something to give."

All who knew him were terrified. Chancellor Wirth implored him to permit the police to resume their guard duties. Rathenau said he would not, and Wirth told him there was a particular cause for alarm. A priest had been told by a penitent, in the confessional, that there was a definite plot to kill Rathenau. The priest had agonized over what to do and had gone to consult the Papal Nuncio, Eugenio Pacelli.* The Nuncio gave permission for the priest to tell Wirth. It was unheard-of that such a thing should be done, Wirth told his Foreign Minister. Did not he see how serious this step was? Rathenau stood silent for what Wirth estimated was two full minutes. He was motionless and pale. Wirth said nothing as it seemed to him Rathenau appeared to gaze upon some distant vision. Then his eyes took on a look of benevolence and gentleness and such calm as Wirth had never seen in him before. The Foreign Minister put both hands on the Chancellor's shoulders

---

*The future Pope Pius XII.

and said, "Dear friend, it is nothing. Who would do me any harm?" He left the room with what Wirth thought was a look of "incomprehensible serenity" on his face.

When he learned of what had happened, Lord d'Abernon decided that Rathenau was too proud and self-willed and self-confident to have policemen guard him. It came into Emil Ludwig's mind that perhaps Rathenau the prophet saw his fate in store and both welcomed and deeply dreaded it. One's life did not end in arbitrary fashion, Rathenau said in his mystic way. One died when there was a reason that one die. He worked on to relieve Germany of the crushing burden of war reparations and to win back the country's moral position. He seemed to be succeeding. But it was at a cost. "His most cordial relations," wrote Count Kessler, "are with the British, followed by the French, Italians, Japanese, and so on; his worst, with the Germans."

It was 1922. Nearly four years had passed since the guns were silenced, and three dozen nations met in Genoa, Italy, to see to the reconstruction of a shattered world. The stated purpose of the conference was to deal with international trade, but there was a higher aim. The Genoa Conference was compared to those councils the medieval church summoned for the salvation of Christendom. This conference was called finally to end the war. To it came prime ministers, bankers, industrialists, trade union representatives, even the leaders of a Soviet Union hitherto regarded as a wild-beast country gone mad. Failure at Genoa, it was said, would portend catastrophe for European civilization.

It was accounted as a reconciliation and muting of the world's fears and hatred that Germany and Russia, the first a pariah nation for having made the war, the second for having embraced Bolshevism, were even in attendance at Genoa. As the conference began there were rumors that the Soviets were going to arrange a deal with the former Allies at Germany's expense—Russia would pay back a portion of the Czarist regime's debts and return nationalized property belonging to foreigners. In return Germany would be forced to give Russia giant reparations.

Such an arrangement would have been catastrophic for the stability of the already shaky German currency, and for the country's position in the world. She would be surrounded by neighbors with a tremendous stake in keeping her down permanently. Rathenau tried to get to Lloyd George. In one day he telephoned and sent two notes. There was no response. His face turned haggard.

In the early morning hours of Easter Sunday, 1922, a Foreign Ministry official came into his hotel room. Rathenau was in mauve pajamas. "I suppose you bring me a death warrant?" he asked. He was told Soviet Foreign Minister Georgy Chicherin was on the phone. He told Rathenau he wished to see him later in the day.

The Germans had planned a picnic after Easter church services. They canceled it. The delegations of the two countries met for luncheon at Rapallo, a short distance from Genoa. By evening everything was arranged. The sensational news went out that Russia and Germany had agreed by the signatures of each country's Foreign Minister to forgo any claims upon one another for war damages and reparations, that they would offer one another most-favored trade agreements and economic cooperation. The two pariahs were now aligned. Germany was no longer isolated. Communist Russia had an ally. It was the greatest shock the world had experienced since 1914. France put her army on alert. Immediate invasion of Germany was discussed.

But Rathenau had them, the Allies. They could not know that secret arrangements between the contracting parties would permit German troops to train in secluded Russia, that German planes would be designed at and flown from Soviet airfields, that treaty-forbidden heavy guns and tanks would be tested. But the former Allies could not invade or even discipline the Germans without losing all hope of collecting reparations and creating an unpredictable chaos in the heart of the European continent. Rathenau rose to speak to the assembled representatives of the world. Germany could not permanently remain a debtor nation, he said; it could not be that the former Allies intended to collapse the Germany economy, would refuse to allow their debtor to earn that by which the debts might be paid. As he spoke the translation mechanisms broke down; he instantly in his flawless French and English translated for himself. He finished with an apposite quote from Petrarch, delivered in Italian: "I go crying, Peace, Peace, Peace!"

A great roar of applause came at him. The Germany of after-the-war had come of age. In Rome to the south the carabinieri stood passively by as Fascists rioted in front of the Italian Parliament—within the year Benito Mussolini would rule there—but Weimar Germany, the freest country in the world, seemed safe for democracy, openness, a new dawn. Rathenau prepared to return home. But he was worried, he told Count Kessler as they sat over coffee. Munich demonstrators had hauled down the Republic's flag from a pole at the city railroad station and burned it, and President Ebert as a result had canceled a visit to the city.

Rathenau returned to Berlin. There at his villa in the Grünewald a British colonel came to pay a call. When the officer got out of his car two men in civilian clothes halted him. Whom did he wish to see? Where were his papers? He identified himself and went in to find Rathenau playing the piano by candlelight. The colonel said he was glad to see that his host was taking safety precautions. At his words Rathenau became violently excited, rushed to a telephone, and made a call in which he demanded that the police leave; he forbade molestation of his guests. When the colonel left, the men were gone.

Sometimes it seemed to Ernst von Salomon, the young veteran of those Free Corps legions which were the ghosts of the Imperial German Army, that he could never be still again after what he had seen and done out east. It was like a disease, he reflected, this desire to do *something*. He had difficulty understanding those of his comrades who decided their wild soldiering days were over and returned to farming. It seemed to Salomon that the historic order of matters had been reversed. Other revolutions began with a rebellion of spirit and ended in hand-to-hand fighting on the barricades; in the case of the Free Corps, the men—boys, really—had first fought and now must make a revolution. It was called for. A spiritual uprising was called for by the blood that had been spilled. Suffering must be justified.

Like many others, von Salomon set himself to finding an answer. He read. He read Rathenau's works and noted what he had said in his *Reflections:* "Action is never contemptible, inaction always." Von Salomon wandered through that multitude of little groups who stood for doing *something*, anything, who said they stood for German spirit, genius, honor, who joined old ideas and beliefs to the latest catchwords and truths and half-truths. He saw a young man seize the crop of a French occupation forces officer, strike the officer, and break the whip. He sought out the young man, who was former German Navy Lt. Erwin Kern. They became friends.

Kern was twenty-four, of medium height, Nordic, blond, and with noticeable large eyes. He was the center of a little group of youths, a dozen or so in number, who like other little groups harassed the French occupiers and ran guns to Germans in former German territories ceded to other countries, and told one another they stood for their country's honor. They lived by thievery and extortion and forced contributions and spoke of the day when they would save Germany to the accompaniment of blood running the streets. They saw Bolshevism as a threat to the Western world and had talked of dynamiting Soviet Foreign Minister Chicherin's train as it had headed toward the Genoa Conference.

The mad rampaging of the Free Corps out east was the model for their behavior, and they regarded the older generation as having lost its authority because it had lost the war. They saw a Germany resisting the claims of its enemies by paper formulae, diplomatic notes, requests, protests, appeals, as a Germany that had forgotten its faith in the old Prussian verities and virtues which they would redeem. How exactly they would do this was not for them to say. "We must poke holes in the roof," Kern told Salomon, "so as to let the fresh air blow through." The way and the final goal were not clear, but the act of striving for something new justified the act. "We are not fighting to make the nation happy," Kern said. "We are fighting to force it to tread in the path of its destiny."

One day in the late spring of 1922 they sat on a bench in Berlin's Zoological Gardens, Kern, Salomon, and Hermann Fischer, a quiet and thoughtful young man from Saxony. Salomon's frantic reading aimed at helping him to make sense of what had become of Germany had not yet given him the answers. "We want to understand what it means to be a German," he told his friends. In Rathenau's books he had read that a moral, cultural, religious, social, political revival would one day bring back Germany to herself. Rathenau also had wanted to understand what it meant to be a German.

Everything was gone, washed away by the war. Kern had been in the navy during the war. How, Salomon asked as they sat on the bench, had Kern survived the defeat?

"I did not survive it," Kern answered. "As honor demanded, I blew out my brains. I am dead. What still survives is another thing. I will not be other than the two million who died. I died for the nation; and all that is surviving in me lives only for the nation."

They talked on. Something was on Kern's mind, although he did not immediately refer to it. In April a seventeen-year-old boy had remarked to a friend that he intended to assassinate Germany's Foreign Minister. *Shoot down Walther Rathenau, the goddam dirty Jew.* The friend put him in touch with Kern, the older leader of Salomon, Fischer, and the two Techow brothers, Ernst-Werner and Hans Gerd. He commanded the loyalty of these and a handful of others who had lost all loyalty to anything else. The intimacy in the group almost touched upon eroticism. They were all intelligent and of good family—Fischer had studied engineering and the Techow brothers' uncle was an architect who had designed buildings for Rathenau's General Electric Company. The war for which all save Kern had been too young had put them in rebellion against what is called civilization and all civilized values—they were not alone; the members of an insignificant Munich group centering around the lance corporal who had cried at the Armistice were identically of their ilk—but they retained something that could only be called pure idealism.

"Duty is no longer duty," Kern said on the park bench, "loyalty is no longer loyalty and honor no longer honor—what remains is action. Our task is attack, not government."

Then, "I intend to shoot the man who is greater than all those who surround him."

"Rathenau," said one of the listeners.

"Rathenau."

This would be a call to raise people to further action, Kern said. He could not predict the exact result of that action. That was not the point. "When the end is to come does not rest with me." Through circles which touched upon theirs they sought to obtain a British machine gun of the type used along the Western Front. A promised one did not arrive. They looked around and obtained another. When they tested it, it misfired. One day they looked at a picture in the window of a photographer's shop on the Unter den Linden. It was Rathenau. Salomon thought the eyes were eager and self-possessed and that they stared searchingly out of a narrow, aristocratic face. "He looks a decent sort," Fischer remarked.

They decided to forgo a machine gun, and practiced shooting with pistols in the Grünewald, quite near where Rathenau lived. The results were unsatisfactory to Kern. The level of accuracy was too low. He obtained a submachine gun and grenades. On the night of June 23, 1922, they went to a tavern and drank beer, cognac, and wine. They spoke of the necessity to strive, to go on, to do, to be. All that they said could have been taken from Rathenau's works: they were the Men of Purpose whose virtues he had so often praised as opposed to the Men of Thought he had so often damned. Here were the blond Teutons whose type he had extolled for so many years, so warmly, his friends had thought, that some had wondered if there was something of the suppressed homosexual in him.

At their table the young men drank the night away. Rathenau at their age had tried to do the same thing, unsuccessfully. He had found himself unable to become intoxicated, and said sadly that he must remain only an observer at student drinking bouts, the perpetual observer and never the participant. He had also said that the Jew lies who says he enjoys hunting. The young men were hunters of a sort, with the hunter's lack of hatred for the quarry. They did not see their plan as destructive, but constructive, aimed at the establishment of the People's State which Rathenau had envisioned, the enthronement of Soul in Germany and in the world. Materialism did not interest them, but ideals. No group of people could more typify those for whom he had written his book *To the German Youth*.

That night, as Kern and his group drank, Rathenau dined at the United States Embassy with Ambassador Alanson Houghton. They talked of the substitution of coal for cash reparations. Rathenau remarked that Hugo Stinnes knew everything about coal and suggested that they telephone him and ask if he would join the discussion. A call was placed. Stinnes said he was finishing dinner. He would come in a little while. When he arrived the talk went on until midnight. After some conclusions had been reached they put aside the coal matter, and Stinnes offered the opinion that Rathenau had made a mistake in taking on the Foreign Ministry and should get out. Rathenau laughed and said that someone had to hold the job. It was 1:30 in the morning. The two Germans had overstayed their visit to the ambassador and decided to adjourn to the Hotel Esplanade, which Stinnes owned. They went there and talked until 4:00 A.M..

Rathenau slept late the following morning, June 24, and did not leave for the Foreign Ministry until 11:00. He traveled as always in a rather old dark-red car driven by a chauffeur, using his usual route. The top of the car was down. Rathenau sat in the rear seat. On the previous day the head of the Commissary of State for Public Order, the chief of the Prussian police, had told him that no police in the world could guarantee the safety of someone who traveled in such fashion without an escort.

The weather was pleasant. Rathenau was fifty-five, of an age to dwell upon, Count Kessler thought, the figure he would cut with posterity, and perhaps permitting the thought of it to weigh down his mind. It would not have been his nature to believe he would be remembered kindly. Just before going to Genoa in the spring he had received from Emil Ludwig a sprig of thorn Ludwig had taken from

Rathenau's garden; joined to it was a laurel from his own. Rathenau had gracefully written that here were buds of promise, but that to his own mind the thorns predominated. Just days previous to his night-time meeting with Ambassador Houghton and Hugo Stinnes he had written Lili Deutsch: "What a wretched life that is which follows its even course undisturbed! The wonderful thing is that all real suffering has its beauty. . . . Certainly there is not much more left for me to do.

"My flame of life is burning low."

His car went down the Königsallee from his Grünewald home. In a side street a group of young men stood by a large, dark-gray, open car, borrowed. Its hood was up. One of the Techow brothers worked on the motor. The oil feed was broken, he told Kern, but the vehicle was capable of making a short, quick run. "What motive should we give if we're caught?" Salomon asked.

"Throw all the blame on me," Kern answered. "Say anything— Lord, it doesn't matter what you say. Say he's one of the Wise Men of Zion or that his sister is married to Radek, or any rot you like. Don't get caught!"

They waited. Fischer came. He had been standing on the Königsallee looking in the direction from which Rathenau must arrive. Fischer got into the car without saying anything. Kern shook hands with the others on the sidewalk and followed Fischer. He stood upright for a moment in the open car, his coat billowing in the wind. He sat.

Rathenau's car came down the middle of the Königsallee and Fischer got in line behind. Where the Wallot Strasse met the König-sallee the road curved and Rathenau's car slowed. Some laborers were working on a building. A bricklayer, one Krischin, looked over and recognized the Foreign Minister. He would probably not have noticed the second car save for the apparel of the two men in it. They were wearing long leather coats and leather driving helmets. "Magnificent leather coats," the bricklayer said. Rathenau was about a half mile from his house.

The little dark-red car was going slowly because of the curve and for the care that the chauffeur was taking that the tires not get caught in the tram lines running along the Königsallee. Fischer pressed down on the accelerator and, as he came parallel, went ahead and then over so that the red car was cut off. They were almost directly opposite the workmen. Rathenau looked over to see if there would be a collision. Kern lifted up his submachine gun. The bricklayer Krischin, in the direct line of fire if Kern missed Rathenau, looked Kern almost straight in the eye. He had time to think, "A healthy, open face, what we call 'an officer's face.' " He flung himself on the ground.

Rathenau was hardly more than the length of a man's body from one of his blond Men of Action, from the German Youth. The butt of the gun was tucked under ex-Lieutenant Kern's arm. He pressed the trigger. Nine shots spat from the gun's muzzle. The shells bounced into the street.

Rathenau's car slid to a stop, trapped against the curb. The chauffeur was screaming for help. The gray car's driver, Fischer, stood up, pulled out the pin, and flung a hand grenade. Rathenau was lying on his side in the rear seat. The grenade made his car bounce in the air. Fischer sat down at the controls of the dark-gray car and drove off.

A nurse, Helene Kaiser, slim, pale, no longer young, was walking on the sidewalk. She jumped into the car and lifted Rathenau's head. He looked up at her. Their eyes met. He was bleeding heavily and unable to speak. Miraculously, his car was still operative. The chauffeur made for a police station not thirty yards away. He explained what had happened. Police motorcycles in a moment went pouring into the street. They passed a halted open car, the oil feed out of action, two men standing quietly by. Fischer and Kern had flung their magnificent leather coats and helmets and weapons over a wall into a garden full of spring flowers. The police roared on.

The chauffeur, Nurse Kaiser, and the wounded man went the half-mile to 65 Königsallee, home. Rathenau was carried into his study. A doctor came. Rathenau had been hit by five bullets. His spine and lower jaw were smashed. The grenade had almost severed his legs from his trunk.

By noon, hardly more than an hour after he had left for the Foreign Ministry, Rathenau lay in his study, his head leaning back and to the right, the lower part of his face covered with a linen cloth so that only his close-cropped mustache showed. His hands were folded over his breast. All over Germany work came to a halt as people poured into the streets. They carried no signs, only Weimar's black-red-gold flag, and were entirely silent. Their masses halted traffic and blocked squares. Nothing like it had ever been seen before, millions of people simply marching solemnly and irresistibly up and down. The Parliament met at three, Rathenau's seat veiled in crepe and with a bouquet of white roses on the table in front of it. Half the chamber arose and in unison three times shouted, "Long live the Republic!"

Count Kessler wrote in his diary: "A new chapter of German history begins as a result of this murderous act." He looked at the unheard-of masses of silent people and told himself that in marching for Rathenau they were expressing a more deeply rooted emotion than prewar monarchial affiliation had held. He was granted, Kessler wrote, a striking and unforgettable vision. This death, he thought, was the real birth of Weimar, of the German Republic.

In Parliament, Chancellor Wirth said the killers were mere deluded boys in the service of a great and terrible evil. "The real enemies of our country are those who distill this poison into our people!" In the streets the playwright Carl Zuckmayer heard an amended version of the song about the dead man:

> *Rathenau's croaked, that's fine,*
> *The goddam Jewish swine.*

It was not homicide, Lloyd George said in London. It was a suicide—for Germany.

Two days later the funeral was held in the Parliament. Before the body was taken from Rathenau's home, Kessler went to look for the last time upon the dead man's face. From the furrowed countenance there emanated, Kessler thought, immeasurable tragedy. In Munich Adolf Hitler told his followers that the assassins, their identities revealed to the police for money by a member of the group, were German heroes.

At noon work ceased all over the country. All German trains halted and remained unmoving for ten minutes. More than one million people stood in the streets leading to the Parliament building. The coffin, palms standing at each corner, was behind the Speaker's rostrum shrouded in black and with a wreath of black, red, and gold. The coffin was covered with a gigantic national flag. A black canopy hung from the ceiling. Long black ribbons hung from the overhead lights. There were branches of the fir tree, the emblem of fidelity. Wirth led Mathilde Rathenau to the Imperial box still crowned with a W. She sat with her daughter and some friends, including Albert Einstein. Her face behind a heavy veil was deadly pale, stonelike. An orchestra out of sight played the *Egmont* Overture.

President Ebert spoke. "This atrocious crime has struck not only at Rathenau the man, but at the whole German people." One hundred and fifty thousand silent marchers went through Munich, a similar number in Chemnitz, 100,000 each in Hamburg, Breslau, Essen. Never before had a German been so honored. The Republic was burying its symbol as the Romans buried their emperors. "You have slain one man," the *Vossische Zeitung* said, "but have wounded sixty million. The whole world turns in horror and loathing from a country in which a spirit such as yours could grow and ripen. In this man you have betrayed the fate of our people. You have struck at the future of Germany."

The services ended. The "Funeral March" from *Götterdämmerung* sounded. The coffin was carried through the lobby to the entrance stairway at the foot of which stood an army company under steel helmets. Drums rolled. The sound of the music swelled. It was raining. The coffin bearing the Republic's flag was put on a hearse swathed in red roses and to throbbing drums moved off toward the family vault at Oberschöneweide in Berlin's western outskirts.

It was over. Rathenau was gone. For the French opponents of Germany the great obstacle had been suddenly removed, and with it all trust won for the former enemy. So bloody-handed a method of doing things stamped the country as an outlaw nation whose conduct justified any measure of foreign intervention; and soon French troops marched into the Ruhr, there to do what they would with whom they might. The German mark, already weak, fell catastrophically upon the news of Rathenau's death, and it would continue to do so. Within weeks it was down from four hundred to the dollar—before the war it had been four to the dollar—to seven hundred, to twelve hundred. By the first day of the year 1923 it was fifty thousand to the dollar and from there went to a million, a trillion, four trillion. The savings of a lifetime would not buy a postage stamp. One was paid with wheelbarrows of currency. What would have bought all the real estate of Berlin in 1914 would no longer buy a fresh egg, or a spoiled one, for that matter. The death of the founder of the Policy of Fulfillment found Germany's nationalistic spirit expressing itself ever more stridently and loudly, and soon enough the world would learn what the end would be and at what cost.

The murderers Kern and Fischer fled to where they planned to meet a motorboat on the Wannsee which would give them transport, eventually, to Sweden. They missed connections. The boat was not there. Their pictures plastered on every kiosk, Kern in his navy whites, they got bicycles and went into the forests of Mecklenburg and the Mark of Brandenburg. They spent nights in farmhouses and gatekeepers' huts. They begged food and ate berries and fruits. They stole corn. Once a gamekeeper fired at them.

They went into eastern Hanover, the police following. Newspapers raised rewards for their apprehension. They came into Thuringia, where they tossed their bikes into the Saal and broke into the empty and abandoned Saaleck Castle. It had two massive gray weatherbeaten towers. They lived in the top of one. The Rudelsberg rose sharply out of a valley; the Saal flowed past between wooded banks. Their lights were spotted by local folk who knew the brooding castle was supposed to be empty. Police arrived to investigate. Kern drove them away with his pistol. Now their lair was known. One hundred police came. Sightseers came. On July 17, 1922, twenty-three days after they killed Rathenau, a storm lashed their castle, a gale. Giant crowds gathered to look up at their frowning tower shrouded in mist. Rathenau had left Parliament to the music which accompanied Siegfried to Valhalla, but nothing could have been more Wagnerian than the last hiding place and last acts of his murderers. They stood in the wind and rain on the battlements of the tower and together shouted down, "We live and die for ideals!" Gashes of lightning lit up the sky. "Others will follow us!"

They were in the west tower. The police went into the east tower. They tried to throw down written notes explaining what it was they had attempted to accomplish by killing Rathenau. The shrieking wind blew the notes away and into the Saal. The police opened fire. A shot took Kern between his right temple and his ear. Fischer carried him to a bed and tried to bandage him with strips of linen. He saw it was hopeless. Fischer laid the dead man on a bed, folded his hands, closed his eyes. He put paper under his shoes so that they would not dirty the blankets. Fisher sat on the other bed and put a revolver to the same point on his own head where Kern had been hit.

The other conspirators, Salomon, the Techow brothers, and half a dozen others, received sentences of from five to fifteen years. Time went by. A tenth-anniversary commemoration of the assassination drew sparse attendance. Months later Hitler took power. He was Chancellor. A group of German jurists applauded a declaration that the killers were justified in their act. Their graves were decorated, the chief speaker on the occasion being Ernst Röhm, the only person in the world save for family members who addressed the Leader with the familiar *du*. By then Röhm was living in 65 Königsallee, Rathenau's home which he had left in his little dark-red car on June 24, 1922. A plaque was put up at the castle where Kern and Fischer had been: *Do What You Must, Conquer or Die.*

Below, center: Field-Marshal Sir Douglas Haig as painted by Sir William Orpen. For some, "An ignorant Colonel Blimp of colossal scale who mindlessly sent legions to die"; for others, the Educated Soldier and Master of the Field. (*New York Public Library*)

Above: Haig in his private train, "Advanced G.H.Q.," in France; aide Sir Philip Sassoon at right. (*New York Public Library*)

Above: The Commander In Chief of the British Forces in France and Flanders: General Sir Douglas Haig, G.C.B., K.C.I.E., K.C.V.O. (*New York Public Library*)

Right: Field-Marshal Sir Douglas Haig. Victory parade, London. (*New York Public Library*)

The Somme. Troops fix bayonets before going over the top. (*Imperial War Museum*)

Passchendaele. "Good God!" cried Field-Marshal Haig's chief of staff. "Did we really ask our men to fight in that?" (*Imperial War Museum*)

Walther Rathenau. One of the richest men in the world, a recognized artist, scientist, musician, architect, designer, one of Germany's two greatest businessmen, [and] at one time its best-selling author. "This chap will one day accomplish more and know more than we all," said Thomas A. Edison. (*New York Public Library*)

Walther Rathenau at various stages of his life (*Die Ziet* [*The Times* in German])

Walther Rathenau, the only man in the German War Ministry who did not wear a uniform, the civilian and the Jew. "We must march to St. Petersburg and Moscow and occupy a larger part of Russia for a prolonged time. The discipline and restraint of the German soldier, the justice and incorruptibility of the German administration, will become legendary in a short time." (*New York Public Library*)

The French at war
(*New York Public Library*)

The Sacred Way up to Verdun. For 10 months an average of 90,000 men a week, 50,000 tons of material. "They shall not pass." (*Imperial War Museum*)

Metz, 1919. Pétain is made Marshal of France. Looking on are, from left to right, Joffre, Foch, Haig, Pershing; Weygand is behind. (*Imperial War Museum*)

The Head of the French State, "We, Philippe Pétain...If we leave France, we may never find her again." (*Wide World Photos*)

Pétain with Pierre Laval. "You're no more than a marionette, a puppet, a figurehead and weathercock twirling in every breeze!" one shouted at the other; "M. Laval is the man I most despise in the whole world," said the other. (*Wide World Photos*)

The trial of Marshal Pétain (*Wide World Photos*)

Eden as Prime Minister, with Queen Elizabeth II (*Wide World Photos*)

Above: His Majesty's Secretary of State for Foreign Affairs, aged 38 years (*New York Public Library*)

With Lady Eden, the daughter of Churchill's brother (*New York Public Library*)

Le Premier ministre et sa femme. Lorsqu'ils se connurent, il était déjà député, elle était petite fille.

This was the war to end all wars. (*Imperial War Museum*)

14

CAPTAIN EDEN, M.C.

Not very enthusiastically, the young ex-officer decided in October of 1919 to go up to Oxford. It was largely his mother's idea. In Christ Church Hall there was a portrait of one of his ancestors. He enrolled there.

He studied Oriental languages, Persian, and Arabic, founded an art society, and did research on artists. He traveled on the Continent, had love affairs. He took away his degree and a heightened interest in literature and history. In 1923, twenty-six years old, well connected, the possessor of an excellent military record, his qualifications quite in order for the England of after-the-war, he stood for Parliament as a Conservative candidate. His speeches were dry, well researched, dispassionate. He appeared to have, and did have, integrity and honesty, and an air of sincerity. He was elected.

He married. His bride was Beatrice Beckett, the daughter of a fellow MP whose first wife had died and whose second was the widow of that Colonel the Earl of Faversham buried in the mud along the Somme. Beatrice was eighteen, very pretty—as pretty as Eden was handsome. They proved to be unsuited for one another. She was flighty and did not share his interests. He was not easy to live with. Beneath the perfect manners and politeness and extreme good looks there was a tightly nervous personality given to displays reminiscent of those of the late Sir William Eden. He could explode without warning over nothing. He was terribly high-strung, prone to moments of self-doubt. He suffered from ulcers. Yet then and always he was the soul of honor, a gentleman. He was incapable of a mean act, very serious about his work as an MP. He tended toward the study of foreign affairs and became the protégé of Sir Austen Chamberlain, the Conservatives' expert in the field and the country's Foreign Secretary for five years beginning in 1924. All that Chamberlain was charged to work for, all that Great Britain cared about, was that there should never be another war. No one could hold that conviction with more feeling than Eden, who had seen the war and known the Western Front. At Chamberlain's side he went to international conferences where no one failed to recognize in him a representative of and voice for the generation of whose number so many would remain forever young in their little corners of a foreign field forever England. He felt himself consecrated to speak for those who would never speak again. Many of the young men of the war getting active in public life felt that way. "The survivors of that terrible holocaust often felt under a special obligation," wrote the future Prime Minister Harold Macmillan, "like men under a vow of duty."

It was in that spirit, Macmillan said, that he and Eden and the others entered politics. It seemed to Macmillan that Eden stood out. He was, Macmillan thought, "the best of the youth that had served in the 1914–18 war, that band of men who had faced the horrors of that fearful struggle with something of an Elizabethan gallantry." To Winston Churchill, Eden was the living symbol and testament of those who never came back.

He dedicated himself to the League of Nations. Here was, he thought, the answer. He never alluded to his own record, never mentioned his Military Cross or that he had held military positions few other of his age had, but spoke only of the losses suffered by the England of his generation, always in words and phrases lacking epigrams or memorable sentences but shining with sincerity, idealism, and a good faith that could not be mistaken for anything else. He became Minister for League Affairs and spent years campaigning for universal disarmament. A hard worker attentive to detail, politically skilled, sensitive to people and to atmosphere, he stood out from the dreary men who ruled postwar England because those who should have been in their place were resting beneath the stones and the rose bushes set to blooming in the cemeteries along the Western Front. The homburg became known as the Anthony Eden because he regularly wore one, and he was compared to Noel Coward and the debonair actor Ronald Colman. His marriage was in disarray, he and his wife united only in devotion to their sons, Simon and Nicholas, and both he and she had numerous discreet romances, and he inflicted his appalling rages upon those who knew him well, but it had nothing to do with his work, which was to bring peace. As early as 1931, Prime Minister Stanley Baldwin told him that in ten years he would be where Baldwin was.

An excellent tennis player and welcome guest anywhere, he was received everywhere. "Dinner," he wrote in his diary of a stay at the royal residence of Sandringham. "We are clocked off beforehand. Boys one side (average age 80), girls the other (average age Aunt Blanche). I stray into the wrong pen, by accident (not lechery). Confusion. Equerries rush. I am rescued from temptation." In 1934 he became the first foreigner of note to be received by the Leader of Germany. He wrote Beatrice—they had remained friendly; there was no bitterness—of his reception: "Miles of passages, heavily guarded, and everybody saluting, even the typists, so that I had difficulty not to giggle." Hitler he found quieter than expected, shy. "No doubt somebody had told him that Englishmen do not like being shouted at. Dare I confess it? I rather liked him." A year later, in 1935, he again met with the German dictator and at luncheon discussed their experiences in the war. They discovered that in July of 1916 they had faced one another across a few hundred yards of no-man's-land along the Somme, Hitler tracing their positions on a menu card which the visitor carried away. When Churchill found out, he inquired why in God's name Eden hadn't "shot the bastard" when he'd had the chance. By then Eden's promising first impression had changed and he shared Churchill's estimate of the chief of the Third Reich.

From the meal he went on to Moscow to be the first high-ranking Western statesman who had ever met Joseph Stalin. He visited art museums in the Russian capital and went to the ballet, where in his honor the orchestra played "God Save the King" for the first time since the Revolution. Eden became the best-known member of the British government. "Anthony was the Golden Boy," wrote Sir John Wheeler-Bennett, "slim and handsome and charming." In December of 1935, at the age of thirty-eight, he became Foreign Secretary, the youngest man to hold that post in a century and a half. The foreign policy of Great Britain was entirely in his hands, for Prime Minister Baldwin had an almost pathological distaste for considering anything that occurred outside the British Isles. He bestirred himself once to remark to Eden that perhaps Britain should do something about getting on good relations with Hitler Germany.

"How?"

"I have no idea. That is your job."

But Germany was not the main issue of the early days of Eden's ministership. Italy was. Using the slimmest of pretexts for their mission, Mussolini's forces invaded a primitive and completely unindustrialized Ethiopia against whose barefoot soldiers armed with spears they used machine guns and mustard gas dropped from airplanes. Driven from his country, Emperor Haile Selassie, the Lion of Judah, descendant of the Queen of Sheba, went to the League of Nations in his imperial robes. "God and history will remember," he said. The League did not act. It was not for lack of trying on the part of Foreign Minister Eden, who put his heart and soul into an attempt to discipline the Italians, to send battleships to block their sea lanes, cut off their oil, and so display that the world must respect the rule of law and abandon the use of force. For a long time he battled on, but it was hopeless. England would not go fight for King and country. Europe would not risk another war. Eden turned from the sad Palace of Nations by the lake at Geneva and toward the view that the peace could be maintained only by pressure upon those who threatened it by Italian aggression, German rearmament and reoccupation of the Rhineland and forced union with Austria and claims upon Czechoslovakia, Poland, and perhaps the world.

He held a minority view. In a Cabinet meeting he could not help reading a note atop a pile of papers written by Coordinator of Defense

Sir Thomas Inskip: "Eden's policy to line up the U.S.A., Great Britain and France, result war." "I swear to you, Tom," he said, "that if we can really get this lineup there will be no question of war. You will then see how the dictators behave themselves." Inskip shook his head sadly.

Baldwin's successor as Prime Minister, the half brother of Eden's mentor Sir Austen Chamberlain, was more forceful than his predecessor with the Foreign Secretary he inherited. Neville Chamberlain as Chancellor of the Exchequer had been Eden's closest personal friend in the Cabinet and had held views similar to his in most respects. Chamberlain's cousin Norman, the person he had been closest to in his life, played the role for him that the dead brothers Jack and Nicholas did for Eden. When Norman Chamberlain had gone into the Grenadier Guards his cousin Neville had said he did not see how he could get along without him always at his side, and his death in France was a blow from which he did not ever fully recover. The only book he ever wrote was a privately printed memoir of his cousin. He had gone into politics in 1919 to make good on what Norman had written home in one of his last letters: "Nothing but immeasurable improvements will ever justify the damnable waste and unfairness of this war. I only hope that those who are left will never, never, forget at what sacrifice those improvements have been won."

But the Prime Minister's view on how to make good Norman's death was utterly opposed to Eden's belief that a solid front, a tough and determined look, must be presented to Hitler and Mussolini. For above all things, Neville Chamberlain was a logical, direct, cool-headed, and successful businessman whose world consisted of arrangements, compromise, reasonable agreements. Perhaps it was a lack of imagination that permitted him to view Hitler and Mussolini as world leaders whose claims, if overblown and stated in crude and un-English fashion, merited respectful and sympathetic attention. He was not alone. Lloyd George called upon Hitler at Berchtesgaden to be greeted as the real victor of the war and to return from the visit praising the German. "He is a great and wonderful leader. He is a man who cannot only plan, but can put his plans into execution. He is the savior of Germany." Hitler was no such thing to Eden, but along with his ally Mussolini an appalling danger to Britain and the world. He excitedly told Chamberlain that the last thing England must do was "court" the two, "pursue" and run after them. Chamberlain replied: "Go home and take an aspirin."

The final break between Prime Minister and Foreign Secretary came when President Roosevelt sent a message saying that he had it in mind to call an international conference in Washington where disarmament, access to raw materials, and possible territorial adjustments would be discussed. That he raised the possibility meant that isolationist America might join the solid front Eden had prayed for. Eden was vacationing on the French Riviera when the message arrived. Without consulting him, Chamberlain wrote Roosevelt brushing off his suggestion. He had always thought the Americans were good for nothing but talk. Eden found out when he returned from his trip, and rushed into the office of Sir Horace Wilson, Chamberlain's closest adviser, who had recommended to the Prime Minister that Roosevelt be rebuffed.

"You damn fool!" Eden burst out.

"I beg your pardon, Minister," Wilson returned. "Is something amiss?"

"Roosevelt's message! Don't you see how vital it was for us to accept?"

"Oh, that. Surely you wouldn't have taken that seriously, would you, Minister? Woolly nonsense, you know, just woolly nonsense."

It was the end. Eden resigned. A telephone call to the out-of-office Churchill gave him the news. It was February 20, 1938, and for the single time in his life Churchill lay awake all night. "On this occasion only, sleep deserted me. From midnight till dawn I lay in my bed consumed by emotions of sorrow and fear. There seemed one strong young figure standing up against long, dismal, drawling tides of drift and surrender, of wrong measurements and feeble impulse. He seemed to me at this moment to embody the life-hope of the British nation. Now he was gone. I watched the daylight slowly creep in through the window, and saw before me in mental gaze the vision of Death."

Eden went to America to speak out against Chamberlain's policy of appeasement and to be received as Prince Charming, described by newspapers as "the handsomest man in politics" with his classic features, long dark eyelashes, limpid eyes, clear skin, and wavy hair. He was treated like a movie star by the American press and got countless letters from women. When he visited the State Department, secretaries peeped out of their doors "in a high state of excitement." He returned to England and with Churchill was one of the very few members of Parliament who failed to stand and cheer when Chamberlain announced he would be going to Munich to meet with Hitler, there to present to Germany that portion of Czechoslovakia which contained the country's equivalent of the Maginot Line. It was, Chamberlain said, peace with honor, peace for our time; but in the House of Commons Eden said, "You may gain temporary appeasement by a policy of concession to violence, but you do not gain lasting peace that way. We must clearly make a stand when not to do so would forfeit our self-respect and the respect of others. Successive surrenders bring only successive humiliations, and they, in their turn, more humiliating demands."

Within a year the new humiliations and demands were quite clear. Hitler bloodlessly helped himself to what was left of defenseless and mutilated Czechoslovakia, and the country became a part of the Third Reich. He must now have the Free City of Danzig. There must be territorial adjustments over that part of Poland which had once been German.

The blinders fell from Chamberlain's eyes. He extended to Poland, and to Rumania and Greece, an ironclad guarantee that Britain would come to their aid if they were attacked by a foreign power. He set in motion the first peacetime conscription in British history—the Great War had been two years old before the British began drafting men—and had Parliament vote vast sums for armaments. Eden joined the reserves of the King's Royal Rifle Corps with the rank of major.

Through the summer of 1939 the French and British desultorily bargained with the Russians in Moscow about forming a united front against Hitler, and when they failed to come to an agreement, Eden asked Chamberlain if he might fly out and lend a hand. Chamberlain rebuffed him. He drilled with the KRRC, and once on a route march came under the thoughtful eye of the German military attaché in London, and then with all the rest of the world learned of the German assault on Poland. He walked with other MPs to Parliament Square to hear Chamberlain's declaration of war. Sirens began to sound. "They ought not to do that," said Leo Amery. "People will think it's an air-raid warning."

"My God," Sir Harold Nicholson said, "it *is* an air-raid warning."

"We better make for the House," Eden said. "We still have time." They went on. "We're walking pretty fast, aren't we?" Derek Gunston said; and then a car driven by Sir Edward Spears stopped for them and they all piled in, Nicholson sitting on Amery's knees and Eden on his. Chamberlain brought Churchill into the Cabinet to be First Sea Lord and Eden to be Secretary for the Dominions, in which capacity he supervised the alignment of the Empire countries with the war effort of the mother country. For more than half a year nothing happened on what had been the Western Front of what had been the Great War now become the First War, the previous conflict, the 1914–18 war, the last war. Then the Germans struck. Churchill became Prime Minister and Eden Secretary of State for War.

The German advance was of a speed and force undreamed of and undreamable. The tanks supported by dive-bombers took in minutes what had held for years in the previous war. Verdun and the battle-fields in front of it fell in less than half an hour. The Belgians surrendered. France's army flooded back, melting away as it went. Britain's army on the Continent, taking with it all the guns and tanks and armored cars Britain owned, fell back toward the sea. A ring of Germans formed up.

Down the coast twenty-five miles away, a British garrison at Calais held the Germans so that ships could take away the men wading into the waters off Dunkirk. The defenders of Calais included a battalion of the KRRC. On the evening of May 26, 1940, Churchill dined with Chief of the Imperial General Staff Sir Edmund Ironside and Secretary of State for War Eden. They had to decide whether to take away the Calais garrison or to order that it fight to the last man and last round so that Dunkirk could be safe a little while longer.

Eden had come of age wearing the uniform of the KRRC. He knew many of the officers of the battalion at Calais. In his presence, knowing what would have to be done, Churchill felt physically ill. In Eden's name as Secretary of War a message was sent to the Calais commander saying there could be no evacuation. Of the three thousand British soldiers, fewer than fifty survived. By then Marshal Pétain had joined the French government.

15

VICTOR OF VERDUN

It seemed to the British novelist Mary Borden, Lady Spears in private life, that the France she had known so long and so intimately was no longer recognizable. Fleeing crowds, hideous, surged down roads white with dust under the merciless sun of the cloudless May of 1940. Their faces were frenzied, mad with fear. It seemed to her that the torrent of people in a river of cars six abreast without an inch to spare between bumpers was the outward indicator of a nation gone out of its mind.

Mary Spears had known bad days for France during the Great War, but it had been different then. She had gone out to the Western Front with a mobile hospital endowed with her money, the nurses paid from her private funds and the orderlies and doctors supplied by the French Medical Service, and had seen death, wounds, disfigurement, lice, mud, but also a willingness to serve France and if necessary die for France that she thought sublime, almost holy. Now she was back again with a mobile hospital to see the French running from the Germans in limousines with smart chauffeurs wearing livery, in trucks, in Citroëns, in decrepit Fords, each with a mattress on the roof and pots and pans and kettles swinging from the running boards and hoods, baby carriages, bird cages. People pushed bicycles loaded with possessions, horses and oxen pulled carts, fire engines with the crews came down the roads. Motorists leaned out their windows to punch at pedestrians—"Get off, keep clear!" By the side of the road sat vehicles broken down or out of gas.

People looked up into the blinding sun seeking the German Stukas outfitted with a device which emitted a terrifying screaming sound when the plane went into a dive so that its pilot could machine-gun the refugees. The ghastly shriek hung in the air when the guns had stopped as the plane flew on and those below faced the immediate awful decision of whether they should get their dead back into the car or leave them where they lay beside the road. The German tanks, always said to be just behind, assumed the identity of dragon-monsters in medieval myths.

Mary Spears paid a flying visit to Paris. Her husband, Maj. Gen. Sir Edward Spears, had been Captain Spears when in 1916 he walked into her hospital along the Somme. He had stopped his car to take aboard Anthony Eden and other members of Parliament headed toward the House on September 3, 1939, the day Neville Chamberlain asked for a war declaration, and then with the appointment of Churchill had gone to be the Prime Minister's liaison to the French government. Sir Edward and Lady Spears met in the general's suite at the Ritz. His wife before seeing him had seemed to assume that all that she had witnessed was a temporary local phenomena, horrible but ultimately controllable. One look at his face told her otherwise. The eyes were bloodshot, there were lines inches deep, and she saw a smile which did not belong creep on for an instant and then flow away leaving a look ravaged, exhausted, savage. At once she saw what was happening and what was going to happen. She was terrified. She went away to rejoin her fleeing hospital unit running past houses jammed with refugees or locked tight, their yards and parks filled with French infantry without rifles but drunk and waving bottles, artillerymen who had abandoned their guns and left them in ditches, generals talking without conviction out of white faces. Their troops had vanished and their staffs cowered in the dust and gasoline fumes.

The Marshal of France Henri Philippe Pétain had been in Madrid when the Germans struck, sent there as ambassador in an attempt to secure the neutrality of the dictator Francisco Franco. (Paris did not need another enemy to the south.) But when the German infantry effortlessly poured through Belgium and their tanks roared out of the

Ardennes Forest, he had been asked to return and join the government as Vice-Premier. Like General Spears in Paris he saw from Madrid what was coming. If the Maginot Line, outflanked by the Germans at both ends, could not save France, the game was up.

"My country has been beaten," he told Franco. One week had passed since the German onslaught began. "I have come to say good-bye to you."

"Do not go, Marshal," Franco said. "Use your advanced age as an excuse. You are the victorious soldier of Verdun. Do not lend your name to what others have lost."

"I know; but my country calls and I owe myself to her." On May 18, Premier Paul Reynaud told the nation over the radio, "The victor of Verdun, the man thanks to whom the attackers of 1916 did not pass, thanks to whom the morale of the French Army was reaffirmed in 1917, returned this morning from Madrid. From now on Marshal Pétain is at my side devoting his wisdom and his strength to the service of the country."

When he went to greet the Senate the members rose to their feet. By then the streets of Paris were jammed with cars bearing license plates from the frontiers to the east where the Germans were coming through, and to the journalist Alexander Werth there seemed something funereal about the sound of the last bars of "La Marseillaise" which preceded radio announcements about the situation, their cautious wording unable to conceal what was happening. If the radio reported fighting "around" towns which had held rocklike in 1914–18, it meant those towns were surrounded by Germans and could be expected to fall at any moment. If the radio said a particular place was in French hands, it meant everything east of it was lost. *Abreuve nos sillons* came from the radio, the familiar notes, and then more terrible news, always terrible. There were bank runs in Paris, no buses in the streets, no taxis. Werth went to the Parliament. The Speaker of the Senate, Jules Jeanneney, was deadly pale. President Edouard Herriot of the Chamber was weeping. Paris began to empty out, people driving off to sleep and wash in fields or in inns or in castles whose rooms hung with medieval armor, halberds, trophies, now were filled with the sense of panic. The Paris newspapers by May 21 were reduced to a single sheet of paper. The electricity was uncertain, and the water. Soon there was no telephone service. A column of smoke, visible all over the city, rose from the lawn of the Ministry for Foreign Affairs. State papers were being burned there. Clerks threw packets of them from windows.

Off to the east the soldiers whose fathers had withstood days of bombardment bolted at the approach of a German tank. A hideous rot had seized the French Army, produced partly by the wasted months of the Phony War, *la guerre de drôle,* which found the men sitting in the Maginot Line from August to May doing nothing, partly by the superior German tactics of massed tank attacks and air strikes, but mainly by something that had been wrong with France ever since the mutinies of '17 which Pétain had managed to contain but the source of which neither he nor anyone else could entirely remove. Across the border and the miles, Adolf Hitler had sensed it, had said and known they'd never fight.

They simply melted away, the French. It was hard to take it in. Promoted from colonel to brigadier general on May 15, Charles de Gaulle received details of new retreats from a captain over the telephone and raged, "It's not true!" "But this is my information, my general. I am afraid it *is* true." "Be quiet, do you hear?" Reynaud brought him away from his command and into the government as Under Secretary of War, for he was one Frenchman who was known to be willing to fight. There were not many. It might have been expected that among their number would be found the man who upon his installation in the Academy had been described in Paul Valéry's speech of introduction as the "spirit of the Resistance" of 1914–18; of whom the nobleman René de Chambrun, son-in-law of the politician Pierre Laval, said, "To every Frenchman Pétain's life stood as a symbol of resistance at any cost." But the Marshal gave no indication of what was going through his mind. He sat in his office in the Boulevard des Invalides behind a large mahogany Empire desk, calm, quiet, peaceful. The huge Aubusson carpets and Gobelin tapestries in the offices of the President of the Republic were rolled and strapped up for shipment out of Paris so that if the Germans came they could not have them; but Marshal Pétain when asked his opinion of matters at council meetings replied that he had nothing to say.

His features were as noble and regular as ever, and his pale skin almost unmarked by the passage of his eighty-four years, and the eyes for which he only occasionally used reading glasses were as clear as they had always been, but sometimes it seemed he was in another world from that of the Paris of May 1940 when all about him was panic, despair, impotent rage, terrible fear. Premier Reynaud's voice became more and more frayed as he disputed those around him saying France was lost, and his mistress the Countess de Portes, odious in the eyes of all who knew her save Reynaud, raged at him that he must give up; but when Maj. Gen. Sir Edward Spears looked to the Marshal for guidance—for he had always admired him enormously—he found him expressionless, somber, seemingly unaffected, always in plain-clothes instead of uniform, and usually with his eyes apparently study-ing the carpets of the rooms in which he sat. Spears wondered if the old man had become senile. But when he remarked that it seemed to him that the French and British had once together won a great victory at Dunkirk hundreds of years before—the Battle of the Dunes, was it not?—Pétain's rejoinder could not have been more lucid. "Yes. June 14, 1658. There Turenne beat Condé and Don Juan of Austria, a very important battle; it led to the end of the war with Spain. It is curious that Cromwell should have sent a contingent to help Louis IV. French history pays homage to the bravery of the Puritans."

Spears stood open-mouthed as this display of memory, and he wondered as he drove away if the Marshal did not assume a mask of age and disinterest for his own convenience. The two met again privately when the Dunkirk evacuation was complete and the British were back on their island with their military equipment broken on the beach or in German hands and the men of the King's Royal Rifle Corps in Calais graves. The deafness Pétain had shown at a meeting with others that morning had vanished, Spears noted, and he was friendly and almost paternal to his English visitor. But when they looked at a map together his words were chilling. Having driven the British into the sea, the Germans were now unstoppable. One had only to see the lines of their stunning advance and to estimate the strength of their forces. "It is hopeless," Pétain said. His voice was cold. He spoke of the Republic's politicians, and the glacial tone became infused with fury. With their machinations, he said, the politicians had between the wars thrown a veil over the face of France. "As you know, a matricide is led to the guillotine with a veil over his face. It is that sort of veil, but it is over the face of the mother. The murderer has thrown his veil over his mother's face."

He turned to the appointment of Charles de Gaulle as Under Secretary of War and then to the book which he felt de Gaulle had wrongly published after he himself, Pétain, had conceived and outlined it. His former protégé was vain and ungrateful, he told Spears, monstrously conceited. Spears turned back to the question at hand. France must continue in the war. She must. Why were officials running away and leaving behind undestroyed stocks of gasoline to be poured into German tanks? Why weren't trees cut down to block the roads against the invader? Could France forget her ill-armed armies of the Revolution who defeated the world, and be less than her heroes of 1914–18? The British general had been brought up in France. It was truly his second country. He was almost weeping as he spoke, hoping that Pétain, Pétain of all people, would rally the country. Britain would fight on, Spears promised. The troops rescued from Dunkirk would return. America would help. They would win through yet. Adolf Hitler could not rule the world. It was up to the Marshal. He would seize the trumpet from the Angel of Victory at the Arc de Triomphe and sound a call to arms, he the leader who like Joan of Arc would save the French.

The mention of the name lit up the Marshal's face. "Joan of Arc!" he cried. "Joan of Arc! Have you read my speech on Joan of Arc?"

"No, Monsieur le Maréchal."

"Now that is too bad. I made it at Rouen; now when was it, in 1937, '38. It was an extremely fine speech, I must say. I shall read it to you."

He conducted a lengthy search of bound volumes of typescript taken from a bookshelf, failed to find what he sought, had an aide look, and when it was found, settled into an armchair. In a monotone he began to read. The speech was very long. They sat, the emotionless voice droning on. There was not a man or woman in the country, Spears thought to himself, who several times a day did not say, "Things certainly look bad, but they are bound to turn out all right in the end, for Pétain is in the government, he is at the head of affairs, he will save us as he did at Verdun."

The Marshal finished. Hardly a word had registered on Spears. It came to him how old the Marshal was, how very old. He was thinking that it was as if tears were falling on his heart, slowly, one by one, audibly. "Joan of Arc was a peasant of France," the Marshal was saying. "Our peasants are part of the soil of France. I made a very fine speech on the peasants of France—now let me see, it was some time back; you must see it, I shall read it to you." He rang for his aide, who brought the speech on the peasants. Desperately Spears said he would spare the Marshal fatigue by reading it to himself, and then made as if he were doing so, stealing a glance at the Marshal now and then for fear he might think the pages were being turned too quickly. He ended. Both men arose and the Marshal saw him to the door, Spears speaking of the bonds between Britain and France. The Marshal's expression indicated he was having trouble with his hearing but that politeness required that as Spears had listened to his Joan of Arc speech for so long, and had kindly read his speech on the peasants, he was entitled to have his say.

When Spears finished, Pétain made no reference to anything he had said, but led him to another room, saying there was something he wished to show his visitor. They looked at a shoulder-high pedestal upon which stood a sculpture showing the Marshal looking from his horse toward two *poilus* looking up at him. Affection and solicitude showed on the face of the rider, fond and trusting respect on the faces of the men on foot. Spears had never seen and was never to see any work of art more perfectly showing the finest idealized representation of the relationship between officer and soldier.

"I wish that group to commemorate me to the French people," the Marshal said. It came to Spears that the Frenchmen running from the Germans were the sons of the soldiers of the army of Pétain's time who today were the heads of households and who, trusting their old leader, often referred to him as the father or grandfather of their country. Their bond with him was indissoluble, Spears told himself. Nothing would permit the Marshal to break it, to neglect the elemental necessity which imposes on the old the duty of protecting the young.

The career politician Pierre Laval had never wanted the war. Laval was shrewd, thrifty, greedy, conniving, ambitious, a peasant of the Auvergne in central France. War to him, any war, was a monstrous waste. Before the Great War, at thirty-one the youngest member of the Chamber of Deputies, he had been listed with the army intelligence service as one of a number of "dangerous agitators and pacifists" to be interned if war came. When the armies marched he was not interned but put under surveillance. All through the years of fighting he supported attempts to negotiate peace, meeting with the Bolshevist Leon Trotsky and attempting to meet with representatives of the left in Germany. When in 1917 Pétain dealt with the mutineers, Laval campaigned for their lenient treatment. By then he had lost a brother at Verdun and Mme. Laval had lost a brother in one of the battles along the Meuse. When the Armistice came, Laval's political star rose, and in 1931, when Pétain went to America to join in the 150th anniversary celebration of the battle of Yorktown, Premier Laval went to confer with President Hoover on France's war debts.

Laval was physically unimpressive, with a pudgy body and splotchy complexion and perennial tobacco stains on his teeth. His trademark was a white tie. ("I do wish your father would reverse things: wear a black tie and white teeth," a woman told his daughter Josée.) He drifted in and out of ministerships, as the politicians of the Republic of Pals did in the years between the wars, making deals and trading arrangements. He became rich, as politicians of the Pals did. When it seemed that Hitler might one day make war on France he tried to arrange treaties of mutual aid with Mussolini's Italy and Franco's

Spain, unconcerned with the ideology of those countries and quite removed in his thinking from the Socialist and labor lawyer he had been when he began his career. (But then, people asked, did not his name read the same from left to right?) When in 1939 France declared war on Germany, Laval felt a colossal mistake had been made. The rights of Poland and the defense of democracy meant nothing to him. He cared for the soil of France, the absence of which on his boots he said he could not endure. He liked to walk around his hometown talking crops with the farmer and dickering over the price of things. He held that the new war should be called off as soon as possible.

In the second week of June 1940, as the Germans closed in, the French government left Paris, senators and deputies and ministers pushing their way through the mobs of refugees. They wandered toward Tours, sleeping where they could and meeting where they might. No one knew exactly where the Germans were, and the state of French Army intelligence was such that the favored method of dis-covering their progress was to call the telephone exchange of a town in their path and ask the operator if they had arrived. Laval was among those feeling their way along the roads, his wife saying he should not join any new government that might be formed and his daughter saying they should go to the United States. Also in the fleeing masses was the Marshal of France Henri Philippe Pétain, spending his nights in a railroad station at Gien, a prefecture in Nevers, a castle in Puisaye. On June 11 he retraced a part of his journey to attend a conference in the castle of Muguet near Briare for which Churchill would fly over from London. In a corridor he came face to face with the recently promoted Charles de Gaulle. "You're a general," Pétain said. "I don't congratulate you. What good is rank during a defeat?"

It was not yet a defeat for his former protégé, who pointed out that Pétain himself had first become a general during the 1914 Great Retreat, which then turned into a stand along the Marne and, even-tually, victory. "No comparison," Pétain said. They met with the other French leaders and Churchill and his party. Anthony Eden sat next to the Marshal and found him "mockingly incredulous" when Churchill said that if necessary Britain would go on alone in the war. Everything the French said was so appalling that General Spears found perspiration starting from the pores of his face. The French said there was nothing at all left to stop the Germans. "We are fighting on our last line and it has been breached," said Commander in Chief Maxime Weygand. "I am helpless, I cannot intervene, for I have no reserves, there are no reserves. It is the breakup." Spears's mouth went so dry he could not swallow. He looked at Pétain. The Marshal's face was as expressionless, Spears thought, as a slab of marble. "We are at the last quarter of an hour," Weygand said.

The next day Spears talked at length alone with Pétain, with both men on their feet, the Marshal leaning against a wall. "An armistice is inevitable," he said. "Soldiers are being killed and the land of France is being ruined."

"You cannot leave us to fight on alone," Spears said.

"What do you want?" asked the Marshal. "You have no army. What could you achieve where the French Army has failed?"

"You will see, Monsieur le Maréchal, you will see. I know in my soul we shall win. If not, England will be a heap of rubble. This will not be the case if you go on fighting with us."

The Marshal was not listening. "It is a catastrophe, a rout," he said. Spears saluted him but did not shake hands. They were never to speak again. The French government came to Tours, Pétain saying to the council members who spoke of setting up a redoubt in Brittany that it was militarily impossible and to those who spoke of fleeing to the African possessions to continue the war from there that to do so, to emigrate, to desert, to abandon the territory of France, would be to deprive the homeland of its natural defenders and deliver it naked to the enemy. Others might do what would kill the soul of the country and make of it another Poland ravaged and torn. He would not. He would never leave but would remain among the French people to share its sorrows and its miseries.

Thousands of French soldiers, tens of thousands, fully armed, were surrendering to the Germans, who took their weapons and piled them by the roadsides, where they lay undisturbed or were mashed into uselessness by the tanks. The French Air Force pilots kept their planes on the ground, and when upon occasion they decided to take to the air they found the airfields blocked by the carts of peasants fearful of Luftwaffe revenge. The flamethrowing German tanks came on, and the parachutists and the screaming Stukas. The high skies were eternally clear; it was a sun-lit nightmare. *Rally on my white plume*, shouted Henry IV in his armor, and in 1871 Paris fought the invader at its gates, and Ferdinand Foch cried in 1918 when Ludendorff came on, "Let's die with our boots on, let Pétain die, let Haig die, then we'll stop the Boche!" But all that had been long ago: different worlds.

The government of the Republic wandered on fearful that German paratroopers might fall upon them from the skies or a mechanized German column suddenly appear, and came to Bordeaux to meet in schools and theaters and to sleep jammed together in every available room and sometimes in their cars, and where at the Chapon Fin, a restaurant with grottoes, huge artificial boulders, waterfalls, and a brilliant wine list, one saw Pierre Laval sitting at a table endlessly conferring with his cronies. The debacle did not stun him as it did others, and he saw clearly to whom in a little while the French would turn: Marshal Pétain, of whom what Minister of Finance Yves Bouthillier said was what they all felt: "His prestige was such that his words seemed to me to be those of an oracle."

A journalist friend told Laval that the look of extreme old age was in the Marshal's eyes, that they wandered away when he did not make an effort to keep his mind on a conversation, and Laval replied, "That doesn't matter. What will be asked of him? To be a statue on a pedestal. His name! His prestige! Nothing more." He did not know, perhaps, and probably would not have cared, that the Marshal was having great trouble sleeping and that sometimes he wept when he spoke of the horror surrounding them. Above all things Laval was down-to-earth, businesslike, concerned with practical matters.

The French appealed to President Roosevelt to bring America into the war at once, which was constitutionally and politically impossible, and rejected an offer by Churchill that France and Britain join in union of the two countries, with dual citizenship, for that would mean they must continue with the fighting. Premier Reynaud was almost alone in the government in wishing to go on. He said he would not ask for an armistice even when the Germans arrived in undefended Paris and set swastikas to flying over the great buildings. But he began to shrink under the pressure. His paramour the Countess de Portes shrieked at him that they must have done, there must be an end to the fighting. Hysterical, weeping, she became unrecognizable, and to the American journalist Vincent Sheean it seemed that her face actually turned a pale-green color.

There was no longer any question of continuing to fight in France itself, but there remained the concept of a departure for the African outposts. Or there could be a government-in-exile in Britain. But that, what would it mean? It meant abdication of responsibility for metropolitan, mainland, France. Could one serve one's country by fleeing her in her distress and leaving her people to face the domination and spoliation of the cruel conqueror? Allowing the gates of a prison to close so others could be buried alive while one took to one's heels? To be a runaway where by staying one could share sufferings and try to alleviate them?

To Pétain there was only one answer. "If we leave France we may never find her again." To the Cabinet Minister Paul Baudouin it was as if the Marshal were the last column still standing of the temple of eternal France. Reynaud resigned. President of the Republic Albert Lebrun sent for Pétain. To the President's surprise he took from his pocket a list of proposed Cabinet men, most of whom he hardly knew and the most prominent of whom was Pierre Laval. Learning what was happening, General Spears found the meal he was eating at the Chapon Fin suddenly tasted like cardboard served in sauces of sand. An old friend, Gen. Pierre Hering, asked the new Premier if one might congratulate him and was told, "Only as a martyr." Within one hour of taking office he sent for the Spanish Ambassador to France and asked him to act as an intermediary who would carry to the Germans a request for an armistice.

At noon of the next day, June 17, the Marshal went to the Bordeaux radio station to address the nation. Flashbulbs were popping. "You see," he whispered, "these affairs start with flashlights firing at you and end with machine guns doing it."

There was some difficulty about the way the microphone was positioned. He waited for it to be adjusted by a young studio employee. "It's appalling," the new Premier had moaned to Paul Baudouin, his new Foreign Minister. "I who commanded the French armies to final victory . . . ah, where is that final order of the day to the troops, 'You have covered your flags with immortal glory'?" All German units marching in formation through towns from which the defenders had fled respectfully presented arms to the monument to those of 1914–18 in the central square; and in a moment he must speak to those of that host who yet lived. The young studio hand was slow in his work with the microphone. The Marshal lashed out and kicked him.

Over the radio he said that it was with a broken heart that he must tell the people that it was necessary to cease all resistance to the Germans. There was something else he could offer. "I make France the gift of my person."

In a clearing in the forest of Compiègne stood enshrined the railway car in which Foch had received the Germans in 1918 when they came seeking an armistice. Outside stood his statue. It was covered with a swastika flag. Adolf Hitler stuck out his arms, threw back his head, and danced a few steps up and down. In the car the French were given Germany's terms. Three-fifths of the country would be occupied though theoretically remaining under French rule. The remainder would be left to the leadership of Marshal Pétain, as would be the overseas possessions. He would not be permitted to govern from Paris.

His government removed to Vichy in the south, a resort town set in a valley surrounded by foothills. For decades it had lived on the reputed therapeutic value of its thermal springs, among which the ill or overly self-indulged moved with graduated cups taken from wicker baskets as they sought relief from the waters for liver problems or other ailments. The overseas French possessions had neither munitions nor factories, and even if they had had these things, so what? France had fallen to the enemy. What was the sense of fighting from Saigon or Tombouctou? So reasoned the Marshal and the men and women who surged into Vichy's elegant hotels, the officials and hangers-on and their mistresses, the adventurers, spies, journalists, functionaries, industrialists, recipients of secret funds from the ministries, military officers, bankers, and the diplomats of thirty-two nations. Every room in town was crowded, and there were people who slept on straw in the stalls of the Vichy racetrack.

The Marshal put up at the Hôtel du Parc overlooking the Old Park with its mineral-water springs, galleries, promenades, casino, and took his meals in a private dining room. All rose when he passed, his dignity and bearing and sovereign presence most striking. He was, after all, Pétain. There was whispering. He walked with a majestic slow gait, nodding at people and receiving salutations with a slight gesture of his hand or a brief pause to say a few words. He was always in civilian clothes. The sight of him reassured all who saw him. Holland, Belgium, Czechoslovakia, and Poland, it was true, had established governments-in-exile based in London, but what, asked the French, did that signify? In three weeks time, Commander in Chief Weygand had predicted, "England will have its neck wrung like a chicken's." France in its history had been occupied by Romans, Arabs, Vikings, Spaniards, the Flemish, the British, and yet always emerged as eternal France. Here in Vichy where glory met disaster, power the powerless, grandeur decadence and nobility weakness, the pettiest of aims the highest of purposes, was an old man majestic in his acceptance of misfortune who would carry France through and in God's good time make it France again.

One voice was raised in dissent. Charles de Gaulle had gone to London in a plane with General Spears, there to be set up in a suite of rooms bare when he entered them but eventually outfitted with some furniture of a sort, and from there to write for printing up: FRANCE HAS LOST A BATTLE. BUT FRANCE HAS NOT LOST THE WAR! His posters seemed ridiculous. Straying animals and dead soldiers and abandoned equipment marked the emptied towns of the French rout, and in Paris each day German motorcyclists, wearing on rainy days iron-gray slickers draped in folds over their machines, cleared the Champs Elysées of the few vehicles traveling there as a military band came shrilling music that pierced the ears. There were snare drums and whistling fifes and a glockenspiel of red and black with plumes at its top. There was an officer on horseback with drawn saber and a company in ranks of three, studded boot heels banging on the pavement. Two million French soldiers, out of a nation of forty million, sat in German prison camps. In the First War little groups under corporals had held out; in this one armies under generals ran away. Then movement was measured in feet over years; now it had been hundreds of kilometers in a week. No one rallied to de Gaulle. It took six months before his followers numbered even three thousand, most of them sailors of French ships caught in British ports, and with his most notable adherent being the French leader of Somaliland.

He seemed mad. General Spears thought him characterized by vindictiveness and prejudice, and Lady Spears, back from France and her scattered mobile hospital, looked upon him as a monster of ingratitude. Head weaving back and forth in a mannerism which people said resembled the movements of a cobra, his hooded eyes glaring from his long face, he asked that Spears be appointed "ambassador" to him, for, he said, after comparing himself to Joan of Arc, "I am France." He proclaimed that no one was a good Frenchman who did not rally to his cause. In time Churchill moaned that of all the crosses he had to carry, the heaviest was the symbol de Gaulle adopted: the Cross of Lorraine.*

The France de Gaulle had fled, the land of great military victories and waving banners, had one asset left: its fleet. Many of the ships were in North African harbors. If joined to the ships of the Germans, they would outgun the Royal Navy, and so on July 3 a British task force steamed to Mers-el-Kibir to ask that the French ships sail with them to continue the war, or submit to detention in England, or make for

---

*De Gaulle was also sometimes compared to Dr. Frankenstein's creation, the monster who got out of control and ran amuck.

French possessions in the West Indies. The French Admiral Commanding was not in a position to assent to any of the requests of the recent ally. It was horrible for the British naval officers on the scene, and only a direct order from Churchill forced them to open fire. The French were badly deployed, anchored too close to one another to use their guns and blocked by a rocky spur from effectively replying to the British bombardment. The trapped squadron consisted of four cruisers, six destroyers, an aircraft carrier, four submarines, four torpedo boats, and several dispatch boats. After thirteen minutes the French commander signaled, "All my ships are disabled. I ask you to cease fire." More than a thousand French sailors were dead. In Vichy there was an immediate demand from many of those around the Marshal that he take France into the war on Germany's side. That he would not do. In London de Gaulle said the British had been justified in their act.

A week later, in the Grand Casino at Vichy, Laval told the assembled senators and deputies of the Third Republic that the time had come for a change in the way France was governed. "We have the good fortune and the happiness to have," he said, "despite the misery in which we live, a victorious soldier, a Marshal of France. The entire universe respects this man." Speaker of the Chamber of Deputies Herriot: "About the person of Marshal Pétain, in the veneration that his name inspires in us all, our nation is gathered in its distress." President of the Senate Jeanneney: "I assure Marshal Pétain of our veneration and of the great debt he is owed for this new gift of his person. We know the nobility of his spirit. May it have the effect in these days of terrible trial of guarding us against all discord." They conferred upon him the rights of the President of the Republic, those of the two houses of Parliament, and those of the Premier and all the ministers. The Chamber of Deputies voted to do so 593–80, the Senate 229–1. Louis XIV had not known such powers. He was Head of the State, a puppet dictator selling his country for a tinsel crown, a leader whose only love was France giving his people someone about whom they might gather.

The Third Republic was over and the French State replaced it, substituting for *Liberté-Equalité-Fraternité* Work, the Family, the Country. The busts of Marianne, symbol of the Republic, were removed from the town halls of both Occupied and Unoccupied France, to be replaced by pictures of the Head of the State and the state's symbol, a battleax whose shaft was the baton of a Marshal of France. The nation that summer was like a dazed accident victim, Paris silent and empty, decanted alike of much of its population and all of its former spirit, the other cities gloomy and with the inhabitants speaking in quiet tones and seeming never to laugh, and the farms going to weeds because there were no young men to work them. The conviction that surrender was justifiable because the war was soon going to be over dwindled as Britain fought on, but the national song of the French was "Marshal, We Are Here" and an oft-repeated prayer was: "Give us each day our daily bread, give France back her life; let us not fall back into vain dreams and falsehood, but deliver us from all evils, O Marshal!"

"You have suffered," he said over the radio. "You will have more to suffer yet. Your life will be hard. I shall not endeavor to soothe you with false words. I hate the lies which have done you so much harm." He said that France would go on, that there would be truth for falsehood, good for evil, health for sickness, order for disorder, France for anti-France. Renascent France would yet see another springtime. He praised religion, discipline, the ancient virtues. He was against international capitalism and international socialism, both of which in the former society had made money the servant and the instrument of falsehood. He attacked unemployment by authorizing great public-works projects, canals, railroads, harbors, the clearing of the ruins made by the German bombs and shells. Controlling all legislative powers, making all laws, holding in his hands appointments to all civil and military posts, the magistrates and functionaries, he began on July 11 to refer to himself in the manner of King and Emperor, all his decrees commencing, "We, Philippe Pétain, Marshal of France . . ."

His government he ran in the fashion of a despot. The ministers were treated as head clerks, as in the days of Louis XIV. "Here, sign this," he told them, handing them new laws. When a minister once ventured to say he felt himself unable to approve a new decree, the Marshal snapped, "That's quite enough. Your only duty is to obey. If someone were to tell me tomorrow to wash the dishes, I should wash them. Go and sit down in your place." Anyone who displeased him was simply told to leave. In the first year of his rule there were four ministers for Foreign Affairs, five for Interior, five for Education, six for Industrial Production. People jockeyed unceasingly to get to the man in whom was vested all power. He bore on his shoulders a heavier responsibility than anyone in the history of France and presided over a Court of the sort of the Principality of Gerolstein or Ruritania or Graustark.

Only de Gaulle stood against him, broadcasting from London that this pathetic shadow of a glorious soldier had sold his honor and his country for the sake of his senile vanity. Pétain in turn condemned his onetime aide to death as a traitor, a runaway, an émigré who lingered safe in foreign places and lived on England's gold. "Ingrate," he said. "A serpent I nourished in my bosom." But in the margin of the death sentence he wrote that it was a judgment rendered for principle and meant never to be put in effect. In strictest confidence he ordered an underling to discover if Mme. de Gaulle and the children had gotten out of France. If they had not, the father's military allowance were to be remitted to them.* De Gaulle from his exile, on his own authority which existed solely in his own mind, announced that he condemned Marshal Pétain to death. His radio broadcasts paralleled the Marshal's "We" with "I, de Gaulle" pronounced so that it came out one word— Moidegaulle. "Work?" he asked in reference to the slogan of the French State. "He lost the habit long ago. Family? He never wanted children, he's an old libertine. Country? The man who saved Verdun has become a traitor." But in private: "It is terribly sad. Old age is like a shipwreck. Poor old Marshal! Pathetic outer shell of a past glory, he has been hoisted on the shield of defeat. 'I weep for you and for myself, but it had to come to this,' said Corneille's Curiace. You see, Pétain is

---

*They had joined General de Gaulle in London.

a great man—who died." He quoted Racine: " 'Oh, I have loved him too well not to feel hate for him now.' "

In Vichy Pétain put through measures limiting the sale of liquor to cut down on alcoholism, and encouraged women to bear children so as to raise the notoriously low birth rate. By fiat he instituted reforms in old-age pensions and civil service regulations—the bickering politicians of the Republic had not been able to do anything comparable. Technicians and professional administrators and academicians free of the political place-trading of the past swarmed to Vichy and what came to be called the National Revolution took place. (The Marshal would have preferred Recovery or Resurgence, but the name stuck.) The German menace was always in his mind, "Polandization"—concentration camps, mass shootings, deportations, the destruction of a country's soul. When in violation of the Armistice the Germans annexed Alsace-Lorraine he protested only privately and said when urged by some of his entourage to speak out more openly that he could not do that. "The Germans are sadists. If I displease them they'll pulverize the Alsatians, you don't know them!" But when he met the self-exiled mayor of Metz, where now a German *Gauleiter* ruled and where long ago he had received his Marshal's baton as Haig and Pershing looked on, he wept.

There were some, not many, of his advisers who thought he went too far in his efforts to appease the Germans—"You think too much about the French and not enough about France," said the faithful Serrigny—but to the nation he said over the radio, "I was with you in the glorious days. I am and shall stay with you in the dark days. Rally to me." ("You tell me that Frenchmen go hungry and cold," de Gaulle said to a man who questioned his merciless attacks on the Marshal's placating manner to the Germans. "But what counts is *la Patrie.*")

Their two opposite viewpoints met on the fringes of the French Empire, control of which by the Armistice remained in Vichy's hands. In Syria and Africa little groups of de Gaulle's Free French supported British invaders. Vichy's men there fought for fear of what the Germans would do to metropolitan France if they did not. In the cemeteries Pétain's men and de Gaulle's men were buried under the same markers: *Mort pour la France.*

More pictures of the Marshal were sold in Paris than the city had inhabitants, including children and infants, and every day people came asking to shake his hand or touch him, and when each Sunday he made little tours of the unoccupied region, crowds and children with flags, avenues lined with flags, greeted him. He had stopped the fighting and stood between them and the Germans and was the leader, father, legal holder of power. "This is the people," he said. "We understand each other well." But sometimes he seemed crushed at what had become of the man who held Verdun. They shall not pass. "Pity me," he said to the departing Foreign Minister Paul Baudouin. "You are going, but I, at eighty-four, must stay and lead this sort of life." Tears came into his eyes.

He swung to and fro, saying one moment that de Gaulle deserved execution and the next moment that his place was by his former protégé's side. "I am building a raft so that France may keep afloat and survive," he said, and "God is at work through you, Monsieur le Maréchal, to save France," clergymen told him; but in private he invariably used the word *Boche* for "German" and sometimes the warrior in him rose and he damned them and said, "The swine aren't going to win the war, all the same. We got them before, we'll get them again." Sometimes, wearing his old-style horizon-blue uniform of 1918 and surrounded by his Garde du Maréchal as he visited Vichy's forestry work camps, land-reclamation and road-construction projects, photographed with children, farmers, artisans presenting gifts, he appeared remarkably youthful, his bearing splendidly soldier-straight. Those who saw him were disconcerted by the lineless skin and firm walk of a much younger man. But in an instant he could change and become suddenly disconnected and terribly old, as when at a meeting he recognized an acquaintance from long ago and said, "My dear man, I'm very happy to see you. I don't think we have seen each other since Verdun." Five minutes later he fell asleep in his chair, to awake a quarter of an hour later and say, "My dear man, I'm very happy to see you. Do you know we haven't seen each other since Verdun?"

In the mornings he was generally himself, stimulated by the electrical massages and drugs his doctor, Bernard Ménétrel, gave him, but in the afternoons a vague and lost look overcame him and whatever was suggested he would approve and whatever was put before him he would sign. Yet the French, clinging to him and putting his picture in every home, bank, office, schoolroom, in both occupied and unoccupied zones, said his defense of them against the sinister Germans through Vichy was as glorious as his defense of them at Verdun. People attributed to him whatever they believed or saw in the images of their fantasies. An Englishwoman married to a Frenchman dared to wear a Union Jack on her blouse and when Pétain passed and did not order her arrested nor the flag ripped off it was said, "That goes to show he is secretly for the British." Others felt he had been insulted but had looked straight ahead as if he had seen nothing. "How noble he is."

It was, of course, Pierre Laval, one floor below him in Vichy's Hôtel du Parc with its connecting doors taken off their hinges, and typewriters wedged between wardrobe and washstand, who was running the day-to-day matters of the French State. Pétain detested Laval with his perpetual dangling cigarette, his white tie often none too clean, his untidy, sloppy manner. Laval in return with his brutally practical manner held the Marshal to be a figurehead of decorative function. To Laval the National Revolution centered at Vichy on the banks of the Allier with its romantic and medieval ideas of purifying the country, scouring it to replace selfishness and pettiness with virility, comradery, a tribal community, the glorification of the artisan and peasant and family, the village and the soil—it was all bosh, something only a booby would take seriously. He was involved in tricking the Germans, meeting every demand for supplies for their war factories with deception, lies, evasions, empty promises. Slipperiness itself, he told people even in public meetings that he was willing to run every risk, expose himself to anything, in order to save France for itself, receiver in bankruptcy as he was. "Another man would have saved his honor," he said. "Yes, perhaps, if he had looked at things in a different light. And in so doing he would surely have crucified France."

It was all very well for de Gaulle in London to thunder defiance, Laval said, and he said he admired him and that if he had not been Laval he would have wished to be de Gaulle—but he was in France under the German heel, not in England; he was holding the handle of a frying pan in Vichy, not a microphone in London. Did the Germans want Jews? He would give them Jews. He had the French gendarmerie round them up, and people thought to themselves that it wasn't enough that he dealt with the Germans, he had to do their work for them. But the Jews were foreigners, Poles, refugees from Berlin or Vienna. Ninety percent of French Jews survived the war, while the same percent of those in other countries under German rule died.

"I know my business and what I have to do," Laval said, and when one of the Marshal's people came down from the third floor of the Hôtel du Parc to indicate that the Marshal was reconsidering something Laval had badgered him into signing, the emissary would be greeted with, "For God's sake, don't bother me!" or, mockingly, "Oh, so he's changed his mind again!" Politically as skilled as Pétain was clueless, energetic and quick-minded, he ran rings around him and his desires, and over his head did as he pleased. Laval sweet-talked the Germans into freeing prisoners of war by the hundreds of thousands, got them to return railroad locomotives they had taken away. A favorite device was to churn up what he called "administrative chaos" to convince the Germans he was doing everything they asked, and would soon make good on his promises. It was wrong to give them a direct refusal, he said. That irritated them. But it was wrong also to accept all demands. He told the occupiers that while Germany could torture France, she could not eradicate her, and so it behooved the Germans to go easy. He acted not as if asking favors when he spoke of gentler treatment, but as if offering benefits.

Vichy in theory controlled all of the country, occupied and unoccupied, but the Germans could supersede Vichy's laws, and so Laval instituted their practices upon occasion, including the wearing of yellow stars by Jews in the unoccupied zone. The Marshal had said he would never permit that. Laval asked if it was better to arouse the Nazis so that they would do far worse things to the Jews, unimaginable things such as they were doing in Poland. He would give them the minimum so that they would not do the maximum. But there were those who said that he was willing in his coarse manner to barter away France's soul to save her body. "You're the biggest stinker!" screamed Minister of the Interior Adrien Marquet at Laval in the Restaurant Ricou. "Stinker! Do you hear?" "Shut up!" Laval shouted back. "You're a—!"

"Monsieur Laval," the Marshal told an agent smuggled in from London who would soon be returning there, "is the man I most despise in the whole world, but I still have need of him. Later, I shall get rid of him. You can tell the English that."

In October of 1940, four months after the Armistice, Laval was told an important German personage wished to confer with him. A convey of Wehrmacht cars took him to Montoire near Tours. He assumed he was to meet with Foreign Minister Joachim von Ribbentrop, but as he traveled he was told it was Hitler he would see. "*Sans blague!*" the world was told he cried—"No kidding."* In the little town hundreds of Germans patrolled with submachine guns in their hands. The telephone and electric lines had been cut and the people ordered to keep indoors with their shutters closed. All roads were blocked. Planes circled overhead. Potted plants brought from Tours were at the railroad station, and a red carpet taken from a church. Antiaircraft guns were everywhere. In his excitable way the Leader told Laval the French were not doing enough for their conqueror. Laval put him off with his combination of evasion, bluff, promises, even small jests. Two days later Laval was back with the Head of the State, his cheeks pink from Dr. Ménétrel's morning electrical massage and wearing a raincoat over his horizon-blue uniform upon which was pinned only the Medaille Militaire, which only privates and general officers could wear.

All along the way to Montoire the car, surrounded by motorcycle outriders with white gloves, had been halted every fifty or sixty kilo-

---

*What he actually said was "*Merde alors!*"

stuck firm. He would not go. Laval went up to the capital and returned saying the German authorities there said Hitler would take nonattendance by the Marshal as a personal insult, that he must be at the solemn ceremony which would see the Emperor's son brought to his father's side in an atmosphere of torchlights and massed artillery pieces.

Something of the old command presence rose in the Marshal, or perhaps it was the machinations of the Cabinet officers and ex-Cabinet officers conspiring to pick up what power there was in the Court of a sovereign weak in actuality but possessed of appearance. He told Laval he was discharged. "You do not have the confidence of the French people. You do not have my own."

"I have never thought of anything but the interest of France. I hope, Monsieur le Maréchal, that your decision will not bring too much misfortune to my country." He always said "my," never "the" country, or "our" country, Laval. "You will not refuse to take my hand?" The Marshal shook it. Police came. Laval was placed under arrest. "The bastards!" he cried. By removing him, the dunghills, the long streaks of nothing, they had put France at risk to the Germans, "the people who can wring our necks if they want to, who can reduce our villages to ashes." Laval was correct. The occupier became alarmed, and German Ambassador to France Otto Abetz rushed from Paris to Vichy surrounded by heavily armed members of the SS, Heinrich Himmler's Elite Guards. Freed, Laval confronted Pétain. It was horrible. "You chucked me out like a lackey," Laval shouted, his voice audible to listeners with their ears pressed to the door, Vichy's palace politicians on the make. "The interest of France is to be on good terms with her conquerors in all honor and dignity, but you trifle with honor and dignity!" Laval shouted at the hero of Verdun. "You're no more than a marionette, a puppet, a figurehead and weathercock twirling in every breeze!" There was no answer.

The freed Laval went off to his estate and was replaced by Admiral Jean Darlan. It was said that with Laval if you asked for a chicken he gave you an egg and a smile; Darlan when asked for an egg would give you a chicken. He loved medals, decorations, and orders, and in his meters so that Wehrmacht officers in full dress could order their men to the Present Arms before getting into vehicles to fall in at the rear of the rapidly swelling procession. Laval was dying for a cigarette. The long line of cars halted. Hitler was waiting with von Ribbentrop and Field Marshal Wilhelm Keitel at the station platform. Pétain crossed over the church's red carpet, and Hitler stepped forward and offered his hand. The Marshal took it—only the fingertips, he told his people later, although the photographs taken as flashbulbs popped did not show that. "I am happy to make the acquaintance of a Frenchman who is not responsible for the war," Hitler said.

"Quite well, thank you; quite well," Pétain said. To the French looking on he appeared majestic and commanding when compared to the German with his thick and vulgar nose, his skipping gait. They went into Hitler's train, and the Marshal offered good intentions and vague talk to Hitler's demands, avoiding the issue of French entrance into the war on Germany's side and asking about the return of prisoners of war still held by Berlin. At Hitler's insistence he said he would make a radio broadcast urging his countrymen to all cooperation with the conqueror.

As a reward for the broadcast Hitler announced that on the hundredth anniversary of the return of Napoleon's body to Paris from his death site on St. Helena, the body of his son, born in Paris and buried in Vienna, would be returned to lie by the Emperor's side in Les Invalides. It was December of 1940, and France suffered shortages of everything as the Germans looted and robbed, and in Paris people in unheated homes said of the return of Napoleon's long-dead son, "We need coal and they make us a present of ashes." The symbolism of Germany offering France a favor, any favor, appealed to a Pierre Laval who believed he could build on that, and he worked on the Marshal to be in the capital to receive the offering.

The idea did not appeal to Pétain. He said he would not go to Paris with its swastikas. "I don't want pictures of me surrounded by German soldiers." Laval insisted, and in the Elysée Palace, the residence of the President of the Republic in times past, German engineers replaced the outmoded heating system in preparation for the visit. The Marshal new capacity never went anywhere without his own twenty-four-piece band. He was utterly ineffective in dealing with the Germans.

It was apparent that the British were not going to cave in and that a long war was in prospect. Depression and hopelessness overcame France. To each of the forty thousand heads of townships the war became a nightmare of rationing and deprivations, hunger and cold and the black market. Yet almost all stayed at their posts. "But think a moment," they had been told. "There is one man who bears upon his head the sum of all the heartbreaks which you feel, of all the exhaustion from which you suffer, and that man remains at his post." As the viziers and subviziers maneuvered for advantage, Marshal Pétain lived amid ceremony and the symbols of glory, uniforms and flags everywhere, people coming to see him, elaborately formal reviews of the Armistice Army of 100,000 men restricted by German orders to bicycles and horses and with no tanks or armored cars or motorized artillery but with plumed headgear and echoing bugles and throbbing drums. Vichy evoked the atmosphere of dress parade and color guard and the mystique of medieval offering of oaths of fealty to the Marshal as officials, teachers, peasants, intoned, "Passionately attached to the nation, the soil, the family, convinced that Marshal Pétain is protecting the primordial interests of the country, I swear obedience to his person."

The Minister of Education reported that for Christmas of 1940 the Marshal had received from children 2,200,000 drawings. As part of their schoolwork they read that he was one with the undefeated hero Vercingetorix, who surrendered to Caesar to save his soldiers. Superior students received "Marshal's Commendations," as did artisans and mothers. Loyalty oaths, speeches, and ceremony constituted official life along the Allier. Marshal Pétain represented order, discipline, authority, morality, the newspapers constantly said. "Be worthy of him!"

Perhaps the vanity of an old man unseen when he was young came to surface, and he seemed content, eating and drinking well and saying that all that was lacking to make him completely happy was ability to make love several times a week. Yet sometimes he vanished for a couple of hours with one woman or another. He still had, he told his people, his "moments of inspiration."

But a sense of what de Gaulle meant grew in France. The Resistance came into being. A German Navy officer was shot at a Paris Métro station. A German lieutenant colonel was shot near the cathedral at Nantes. For the first death the Germans said they would shoot fifty Frenchmen unless Vichy shot any six Communists already in prison. Their wishes were followed. For the second death the Germans shot fifty hostages, some in Nantes, others in Paris, others in Châteaubriant. They announced another fifty would be shot in twenty-four hours unless the slayer of the lieutenant colonel was found.

"They have shot fifty hostages," the Marshal cried, ashen-faced. "We cannot remain here. We are dishonored. All this blood will fall on us." His advisers said they must of course protest. "Protest, protest, that's easy," the Marshal said. "Yes, we shall protest. But that is not enough. We must oppose it. We must stop this killing!" He had not slept all night. "I must go to Paris and hand myself over as a prisoner. I shall be a hostage. Prepare the car. The men shot were Frenchmen, and the bullets which killed them were enemy bullets."

To go and offer himself might have meant grandeur unimaginable and made him a personage of noble legend. But the majority of his aides said that if he left Vichy and his office a German would reign in his stead. He did not go. He met instead with Hermann Göring to utter the usual and accustomed protests about prisoners of war, railroad cars, coal, raw materials, Germany's requisitions of France's food crops. "I should like to know who is the conqueror and who the conquered," Göring said in answer; and sometimes to his circle Pétain said that he had become a lost soul, that he who had hoped to be the rampart of the French was a prisoner. "I have made a gift of everything, even my honor." On the radio he told the people, "In the partial exile to which I am subjected, in the semiliberty which remains to me, I try to do all my duty. Every day I try to rescue this country from what threatens it, from the troubles which lie in wait for it. Help me!"

At the end of a year's service, the incompetence of Admiral Darlan was clear to all. He must go. Laval's son-in-law René de Chambrun, who had known the Marshal since childhood—his father was an old friend—came for a visit and the Marshal asked, "How's your embarrassing father-in-law?" De Chambrun, "Bunny" to the Marshal as he was to all his friends, said Laval was worried about developments. "I intend to see him shortly," Pétain said. He met with Laval. Word of it got around, as things did in the hothouse gossip-about-royalty atmosphere of Vichy, and, informed by American Ambassador William Leahy, President Roosevelt sent Pétain a note saying the United States would not look kindly upon Laval's return to power. Darlan showed the note around. Its contents reached Hitler, who flew into one of his accustomed rages and declared that Pétain must choose between Germany and America, and that Germany wanted Laval. Frenzied maneuverings followed. Laval came back. "Do you think I want the job?" he asked his friends. "It's my duty to take it."

By then the Germans were deep in Russia, but what appeared another lightning victory looked like turning into bloody stalemate. The murderous SS chieftain Reinhardt Heydrich, "the man with the heart of iron," Hitler called him, he of whom even Heinrich Himmler was afraid, arrived in Paris to say he was not there to negotiate but to give orders which the French must obey. To please the occupier, Laval prepared a radio speech in which he would say, "I believe in and wish for a German victory." He showed the speech to the Marshal, who said, "You have no right to say 'I believe in a German victory.' No, you have no right, you're not a soldier, you can't make prophecies about the result of the war." Laval on the radio said, "I hope for a German victory, for without it Communism will take over all of Europe." He ended, "Frenchmen, a great soldier whose whole life is an example of sacrifice and discipline presides over the destiny of our country. I am speaking to you in his name."

To his friends Laval said of the Germans and of his speech, "I prefer to pay them in words instead of acts, because the price is less high, the cost is less high for France. A phrase like that can be worth the return of a hundred thousand prisoners, a politeness can permit me to refuse the workers demanded for Germany by the hundreds of thousands." The following day, he pointed out, he must meet in Paris with

German officials. "As always, they'll talk to me of their sword. My own sword will be these words. I have no other."

That was in June of 1942. In November the Allies, the British, the Americans, de Gaulle's Free French, invaded North Africa. The German Army immediately began crossing from the occupied zone to the unoccupied, there to take up positions guarding against an Allied thrust across the Mediterranean. It was the end of what independence Vichy had enjoyed, and people urged the Marshal to fly south and join de Gaulle and return with him for the forthcoming liberation of their country. A plane was made ready. But he would not go. "A pilot must stay at the helm during a storm," he said. "If I left, France would suffer the same regime as Poland. France would die of it. I will not leave, even if I were to lose all my glory. I have made the gift of my person to France."

Laval also would not leave. "I beg you, resign!" cried his daughter Josée de Chambrun, but he said, "You don't understand! Resigning means desertion. I must remain here to protect the prisoners on furlough, the refugees, the people of Alsace-Lorraine, the Jews, the Communists, the Freemasons. If I were to quit, France would be transformed into a vast underground. How many thousands of French people would pay for my cowardice with their lives? Look at what is happening in Poland, the Balkans, everywhere!" Hitler demanded that the French join with him in an alliance against the Allies to last through "thick and thin," but Pétain and Laval would not do it. Laval went to brave the Leader's rage, saying to a group of visiting prefects at Vichy's town hall, "They blame me for going to see Hitler as if he were the devil. I want you to know that I would see the devil himself to save French lives!"

But French lives were being lost in abundance as the growing Resistance, encouraged by de Gaulle and equipped by air drops from London, derailed German troop trains and shot German soldiers. The occupier took fearful reprisals, burning houses, torturing and killing. The Marshal in broadcasts spoke against "dissidents," and the Resistance in reply began moving against Vichy's officials, those who in later days would be termed "collaborationists" but who during the period were known as those who waited to see—*attentistes*. Private scores and criminal assaults mixed with the voiced concern over the fate of the nation, and the Marshal under the Germans presided over a country almost in a state of civil war. It was the supreme nightmare, Frenchman slaying Frenchman. He withered under his burden. When a friend asked for his picture, he said he would give him one, but not of the man of the present day. "It's the picture of the Pétain of 1919 that I would like you to keep as a memento," he said, and handed over himself on horseback at the head of his troops now become the Generation of the Fifty-Year-Olds, taken on Bastille Day, 1919, beneath the Arc de Triomphe long ago.

Laval lied to the Germans, falsified figures, jousted with the German economic and industrial coordinator Albert Speer, who in welding his country into the most efficient possible fighting machine said that he followed the model created by Walther Rathenau in the previous conflict. Laval traded him war goods in exchange for his relieving France of the imposition of forced labor drafts. But other German officials rounded up people coming out of the Métro or the theater and shipped them over the Rhine as slave laborers. The percentage of the population taken was far lower than in any other occupied country, but still it was "Polandization" on a lesser scale, and it was done in connivance with Vichy's authorities—Polandizers, the Resistance said.

The war went on all around, but not in, France; and Laval exalted that its years-long duration destroying Europe had cost his country but a few days of combat under 1940's sunny spring skies. The Germans ordered the dissolution of the 100,000-man Armistice Army, fearing it might be used against them, and the French scuttled the remaining ships of what had been their navy for fear the Germans would use them against the Allies. So Marshal Pétain had left only what amounted to a personal guard grandly named the First Regiment of France, extolled by Vichy's press as the depository of the country's military memories, upholder of its traditions and guardian of its honor. The First Regiment of France consisted of three thousand men parading for a soldier who had once commanded three million. His country once had been the first military power of the world. Now it had nothing left for glory but its idealization of himself and of his pitiful little crew of tin soldiers made giants by the newspapers: "A brilliant march-past followed. First came the motorcyclists with their machine guns aligned, their commander standing up in a sidecar, then the cyclists. The band followed, playing 'Sambre-et-Meuse': the infantry came last, marching in perfect order, their heads held high, their bearing proud, proving by their appearance that they were worthy to maintain the glorious traditions of the French Army."

The Resistance grew, and in opposition Vichy set up the Milice, an antiterrorist group hardly less ferocious than the German SS squads shooting people by the thousands. The French equation demanded the creation of the Milice. If the Resistance was right, then all of Vichy's acts since June of 1940 were wrong. They could not face that. The Milice butchered and slaughtered, as did the Resistance, and the Marshal bemoaned its actions sometimes, and sometimes told its leaders, "You are acting as I did with the mutineers in 1917." Ever more brutal, the Milice set up mobile courts-martial which arrived at prisons where suspected Resistance fighters were held, received the accused unaccompanied by defense lawyers, called no witnesses, saw no exhibits, and decreed an inevitable sentence: death by shooting, no appeal, sentence to be carried out immediately. As the war turned against Hitler, the Germans with Vichy's connivance raised a division of French volunteers for the SS. The Charlemagne Division was committed against the Russians. Pétain sent it greetings, saying it represented a part of French heroism. People wondered if his hidden meaning was that de Gaulle and the Resistance constituted other parts.

De Gaulle was much on his mind. Sometimes he spoke of working with him when he came to France with the victorious Allies, as could be expected. At other times he wondered if de Gaulle would have him shot, or if the Resistance would do so. It would have been simple to get him, for each day he strolled through Vichy's city park with only a handful of guards idling along, yards distant. No attempt at assassination was ever made.

In the spring of 1944, Paris was heavily bombed, the Allies aiming at armament plants. There were many civilian casualties. It was decided to hold a mass for them at Notre Dame. Marshal Pétain was invited to attend. He decided to make his first visit to the capital since leaving it four years earlier with the fleeing government of the Republic. His only proviso was that no uniformed Germans be at Notre Dame. The Germans agreed. In his automobile surrounded by a motorcycle escort he headed north, pausing at Melun. At the prefecture enclosed by an iron railing he saw a group of schoolchildren. "You look as if you were in a cage," he said, smiling. He had always liked children. His greatest pleasure at Vichy was to play with the little daughters of his doctor, Ménétrel.

"Yes!" cried the children from behind the bars.

"Well, my children, I want you to know we are all in a cage!" The next morning he was at Notre Dame for the mass, to come out and face an absolute sea of humanity. The people screamed wild acclaim. He took lunch at the Hôtel de Ville after moving through streets jammed with cheering people. The Rue de Rivoli and the Avenue Victoria and the quais were thronged and the rooftops filled. People shouted for him to address them, so he spoke from the Hôtel de Ville. The enormous enthusiasm, entirely spontaneous, for there had been no attempt to drum it up, was of a nature hardly ever heard before in Paris. It was contagious. Mayor Pierre Taittinger heard a fat woman say, "We don't need that old monkey," but when in a moment she saw him she began screaming, "Long live Pétain, long live Pétain." She was, the mayor saw, "transfixed, almost in ecstasy." "La Marseillaise" was sung over and over again in defiance of German regulations that it was not to be heard.

When the roaring applause quieted he said from the balcony, "Today is my first visit to you. I hope to come later, and then I will not have to notify our keepers. I shall be without them, and we shall all be at ease. See you soon, I hope." He returned to Vichy and was there as the Allies pressed on into France. Of their invasion he said nothing beyond urging the nation not to react in such fashion as would bring tragic consequences. By August of 1944 it was apparent that France was lost to the Germans, and the Marshal was told they were pulling out of Vichy and taking him with them. He said he would not go. He had not deserted France in 1940, he had not left her when the Germans took over the unoccupied zone, he would not leave her now. On August 19 the German area commander, General von Neubronn, came to tell the Marshal that Berlin had ordered his departure and to warn him that he must obey. He seemed embarrassed to have to speak to Pétain so. If the Marshal did not voluntarily leave, he said, force would have to be used, and if there were popular uprisings the Germans had artillery available.

"I'm sorry for Neubronn," the Marshal said. Then, "I have no right to let Vichy be bombarded merely to enter history with more glory." Laval and some of the other ministers had already gone to Belfort near the Swiss border. It was 8:30 in the evening. Neubronn said they would be leaving in one and a half hours. The Marshal said that was too little notice. "Five-thirty tomorrow morning." "That's too early." "Six o'clock." Silence. "Seven o'clock."

In the night the Marshal wrote out a statement which was pasted up on Vichy's walls and distributed through unofficial channels: "For more than four years, resolved to remain in your midst, I tried every day to serve the permanent interests of France. I had only one goal: to protect you from the worst. If I could not be your sword, I tried to be your shield. Sometimes my words or acts must have surprised you.

"Know that they hurt me more than you yourselves realized. I held off from you certain dangers; there were others, alas, which I could not spare you. I adjure you to be united.

"It is not difficult to do one's duty, even if it is sometimes difficult to know what it is."

It was his last word as Head of the French State. In the morning, helmeted Germans came wearing raincoats to ward off driving precipitation. They cordoned off the Hôtel du Parc with heavily armed vehicles along the Boulevard des Etats-Unis. There were one hundred men, army field police and Gestapo, carrying rifles and submachine guns. General von Neubronn went up to the Marshal's room. Aides stood in the hallway. The door was locked. Very politely, the German asked everyone to stand aside while he had the door broken in. There was a second locked door. He had it taken off its hinges and went in. Marshal Pétain was sitting in a chair tying up the laces on his boots. Dr. Ménétrel pointed out that he had not had breakfast. It was brought. When he finished, Pétain came out of the room, pale, sad. He silently shook hands with his aides and with Mme. Pétain went down in the elevator.

His personal guard was drawn up in the square before the hotel. "Present arms!" He slowly walked down the ranks and shook hands with the officer commanding. It was 8:15 in the morning, August 20, 1944. In five days de Gaulle would enter Paris to be tumultuously welcomed and to reflect that many of the cheering people had cheered Pétain when he had been there. He recognized them from pictures taken at the time, he remarked.

Several hundred people had gathered in the rain before the Hôtel du Parc to see the Marshal go, and as he got into an automobile which no longer flew his official flag, they sang "La Marseillaise." He drove off surrounded by German vehicles to wander from château to castle to château as the Allies and Free French came on, and finally to be taken across the Rhine for a flight through the Black Forest ending in Sigmaringen, a romantic old town in Württemberg some thirty miles from the Swiss frontier where generations of the Prussian royal family had added on adornments to a colossal edifice built on a crag of rock at a bend in the Danube, gables, turrets, ramps, courtyards reminiscent of a gingerbread creation or a fairy tale. For seven months he remained there in the Provisional Seat of the French State as French opportunists, adventurers, and outright adherents of Nazism made unauthorized use of his name in broadcasts over Radio Stuttgart calling for war to the death against the Allies and for volunteers for the SS. His protests at their actions availed him nothing.

Some four thousand of Vichy's people were settled into the castle and the town, their number closely approximating the total de Gaulle had gathered in the first days of his own exile in foreign parts. Some of them compared their case to his, saying they would yet return in triumph to Paris. Members of the Gestapo were everywhere. Mme. Laval became seriously depressed and once during a walk began screaming over and over the names of dogs left behind in France. Pétain lived on the seventh floor of the great castle with its Ancestors' Hall, King's room, Green, Black, and French drawing rooms, and Portuguese Gallery. He kept largely to himself and spoke with few people.

In April of 1945 he learned that de Gaulle was going to try him *in absentia* on charges of treason. He wrote to Hitler that he must return to France, for he could not permit it to be believed that he sought refuge in a foreign country. His honor was at stake, he told Hitler. "At my age, there is only one thing one still fears: it is not to have done one's duty, and I wish to do mine." There was no answer. Hitler himself was days away from his self-inflicted death in his bunker beneath ruined Berlin, where the heavily decimated Charlemagne Division, regrouped some sixty miles north of the city after being split in three sections by a Russian drive, now arrived by truck. No less desperately than their predecessors had fought at Verdun, they battled to deny the Führer-bunker to the Russians. There were some five hundred of them. In the end they died almost to the last man in their German uniforms with a shield on the sleeve in the colors of France.

In Castle Sigmaringen the Marshal was told he must go to southeastern Germany. When he said he would not he was told by an SS officer that if necessary he would be handcuffed. He drove away surrounded by German cars filled with fleeing and disorganized troops and went along roads being strafed from the air by Allied planes. Communications with Berlin were cut off, and finally the German escorts took him to the Swiss frontier. He crossed it on April 24, his eighty-ninth birthday, to be told that the French government requested him to be at Vallorbe on the frontier on April 26 at 7:00 P.M. When at that time he got out of a car and stepped over into France, a Swiss contingent commanded by a lieutenant presented arms. He saluted the Free French Gen. Pierre Koenig, who was waiting with a small group of soldiers. No one responded to the salute. There was no removing of hats by civilians present. The Marshal held out his hand. Koenig declined to take it.

They got into an automobile and drove to the railroad station, where a special train was waiting. It paused at Pontarlier, where some fifteen hundred people were gathered yelling, "To the stake!" "Traitor!" "Death!" The train departed amid shouts and curses. People spat at his coach as it moved off. Others struck it. In Paris de Gaulle said to his aides, "The guilty men of Vichy must be arrested, but I wish I could have left the Marshal out of it. What a terrible pity!"

He was imprisoned in the Fort of Montrouge south of Paris. The charges against him were plotting against the internal security of the state and collusion with an enemy. His trial began on July 23, 1945. "Bring in the accused." He came into where the High Court met in the first chamber of the Court of Appeal in the Palace of Justice. He wore khaki uniform, his Medaille Militaire, a silk sash, and white gloves. His lawyers had wanted him to carry his baton as a Marshal of France. He declined to do so. He halted and offered the court a majestic slow salute. As one, as if obeying a magnetic impulse, every person in the room rose. (That evening a man who had been present somewhat shamefacedly told de Gaulle that he could not forbear getting to his feet. "I have always said the Marshal is a remarkable individual," de Gaulle said.)

The charges were read. He was asked if he wished to reply. "A Marshal of France does not ask for mercy," he said, reading without glasses from a piece of paper. "Your judgment will have to face God's judgment and posterity's. They will suffice for my conscience and my memory. I leave it to France." For the remainder of his trial he sat in almost total silence.

It was quite different for Pierre Laval. He argued, contradicted, gave long explanations. "I love my country," he shouted, "and it is only my country that I have served!" "A little more modesty, scoundrel," shouted back a member of the jury. "Shut up, traitor!" called another juryman. "Skunk!" yelled a third. "Pig! A rope for his neck! No, a dozen bullets in his hide!"

"This is incredible!" Laval shouted. "The jury, before even judging me—"

"We've judged you already! And France has judged you too!" In the waiting room Mme. Laval said, "Finish, Pierre. But finish big! Later, the world will know what you were." From then on he was silent. On the morning of the day he was to be shot he took cyanide. He did not wish an execution squad of France's soldiers to be accomplices to what he called a judicial crime. He was revived with stomach pumps and water forced down his throat, and then assisted to the firing stake. He wore his usual tie. He stood before the soldiers and cried, "I wish to say one thing before I die: my love for my country was as great as yours. *Vive la France!*"

For the Marshal there was a death sentence which the jury said it hoped would never be carried out. De Gaulle commuted the sentence to detention for life, and the prisoner was sent to the island of Yeu in the Bay of Biscay, where in increasingly infrequent moments of lucidity he talked with his jailers of women he had had in the long ago and with the priest of the Great War almost forty years in the past. He drifted into the vagueness of extreme old age, wandering away in his mind but returning upon occasion to say he had only one last wish, that one day he might lie with the soldiers sleeping forever in the vast cemeteries along the heights of the Meuse, at Verdun.

16

CAPTAIN EDEN, M.C.

As early as 1940 it was obvious that if anything happened to Winston Churchill it would be Anthony Eden who would succeed to the Prime Ministership. In 1942, leaving for a possibly dangerous trip by air, Churchill put it in writing in a letter to the King. Eden was at the Prime Minister's side throughout the war, or off on important missions. In Cairo in 1940 he worked with the British field commanders on the campaign which took Sidi Barrani, Tobruk, and Benghazi; a year later, back in Cairo and moved from the War Office to the Foreign Secretaryship, he put into order a Balkan front which held up the German Army in such fashion that the invasion of Russia was put forward several weeks. That perhaps cost Hitler a quick and decisive conquest in the east.

As the war went on, Eden was with Churchill at meetings with Roosevelt and Stalin, in Washington as the British government's representative at the President's funeral, at San Francisco for the conference drawing up the Charter of the United Nations. He was Churchill's emissary to Charles de Gaulle, the only British leader able to get on with the difficult Frenchman. By the time peace arrived, Eden had been to Russia, Algiers, Quebec, Tehran, Italy, and Greece, and he had lost in the skies over Burma the older of his two sons. Simon Eden was twenty-one. Where Eden's brothers Nicholas and Jack, the dead Simon's dead uncles, had been joined in death by a million Britons in 1914–18, Simon was one of only a third of that number to perish in 1939–45 despite the greater length and geographical spread of the Second War. Field Marshal Sir Douglas Haig had no successor as the presenter of giant bills to the British people for the purchase of tiny pieces of real estate in France and Belgium. Memories of his offensives haunted Churchill. He was not going to throw away once again, the Prime Minister said, the "seed" of the Empire.

Eden's health had suffered badly during the war. He was overwrought and tense. Relieved of the pressures of high office when the voters went for Labour in 1945, he gained back his strength during the six years the Conservatives were out. In that period he became the party's crown prince in waiting. For Churchill wanted one more moment in the sun. Having attained it as a vindication and final salute, Churchill said, he would not hold it long. Then it would be Eden's turn to move to 10 Downing Street. The moment came in 1951, and Churchill was Prime Minister again as Eden returned to the Foreign Secretary's rooms looking to the west across St. James's Park and to the north across the Horse Guards to the Admiralty. His golden Labrador, Bess, walked him there from the Foreign Secretary's official residence in Carlton Gardens.

All the great buildings were in place, and the names of the ministries and departments, and Great Britain was one of the Big Three that had won the war, but from the windows one looked out at a different world. England was tired and shabby, and there were many new things to see. Perhaps Churchill did not wish to look. Seventy-seven years old, a victim of several small strokes, sometimes foolish, irritable, and overtalkative, he was yet upon occasion the Churchill of great dreams and plans. He thought of glorious and sweeping summit meetings which would adjust the world, then dropped his line of thought in favor of playing bezique and resting. He read little but the newspapers, few government papers or telegrams, and it was an effort for him even to sign letters. He talked of resignation, and then of great conferences and great deeds. "Winston is trying to relive the days of World War Two," Dwight Eisenhower said sadly.

Yet Eden seemed to see that Britain was threadbare and gray and bomb-damaged and haunted by the economic and spiritual decline brought by the deaths of the Jacks at Ypres and Nicholases at Jutland and Simons in far-off Asia, a decline which now led to what was called the Great Withdrawal: England's departure from all those crimson-colored places on the map which had marked the Empire. With what Winston called an occasional "splutter of musketry" and a flotilla of gunboats upriver, and with traders and bankers and ironmongers and their great ships of the line, the British had ruled the world. Now they were stretched far too thin. A royal would go out to don tropical white uniform and a band would play as the Union Jack sank down for the last time on the polestaff at Government House. Then a new nation's flag would go up as the former subjects of Queen-Empress and King-Emperor became their own masters. The natives would dance far into Independence Night.

India, Ceylon, places in Africa, Burma—they went. The British had made and unmade kings and princes and maharajahs thousands of miles from London, and the word of their viceroys and counsels had been obeyed without question. They had used bribery, threats, seduction, browbeating, flattering this ruling circle, flattening this clique. Now it was over. The tide receded. They had brought the Book and the Law, the Pax Britannia. They had brought their ways. The ruling circles and cliques had adopted those ways of the mother country. The new President had been educated at Oxford, the new Commander in Chief had been at Sandhurst. But they were going—they were gone. It was not easy for the British.

The other two of the Big Three were bigger by far than Britain, Russia for its vast military power and new influence all across Eastern Europe, America for its military power and enormous financial pre-eminence and its overriding brash cultural appeal. The Americanization of the world was under way. It was not pleasant for the British.

Inflation and the austerity program and rationing still in force a decade after its wartime beginnings, and the terrible balance-of-payments problem, and the Commonwealth which was the successor to the Empire looking elsewhere for its lead and inspirations . . . Britain came to be seen as an island off the European mainland which bereft of its leadership of a larger international entity did not seem to amount to much. Britain seemed out of step, out of place, out of time with its great houses, the vast stone piles, the Halls and Places and

Manors freezing for lack of coal, and the large homes in Belgravia or
out Bayswater Road subdivided because no one could afford the servants needed to keep them up. Even had there been money enough,
no one wanted to be a servant anyway. There were only a handful in
service where once there had been more than a million.

The governing classes were hostages to history, after the wars. Yet
the country acted like a Great Power. It was a sort of fraud, a confidence trick acceptable so long as the British acted in accordance with
what the genuine Great Powers, the superpowers, desired. Sometimes
it came to the British that their country was filled with people living in
the past, many of whom were men in power who should never have
been there, replacements as they were for those Field Marshal Haig
had left out on the Western Front. Then the British would reason that
they were to the United States as Greece was to Rome, talented,
experienced, physically weaker yet somehow stronger. But there was
always the thought that the game would work only by the sufferance of
those who only yesterday they had equaled and surpassed.

Meanwhile, they conducted the Great Withdrawal, harried as they
went by the Irgun in Tel Aviv, the Mau Mau in Kenya, EOKA in
Cyprus, leftist insurgents in the Malay States, riots and disturbances
and slaughter in India and Pakistan. The Colour Trooping ceremony
went off as flawlessly as ever before Buck House, although the staff
inside no longer wore livery as in pre-1939 days; the names of the
Second War's Glorious Dead were chiseled onto the church memorial
plaque or village monument below those of their predecessors of
1914–18, although the phrases put there for Haig's men somehow
seemed a little out of place when seen above those who fell under
Montgomery; and they went on. Winston was growing terribly old,
people said, but Anthony as Foreign Secretary was splendid. He did
great work in getting a cease-fire in French Indochina and a division
into North and South Vietnam, shuttling back and forth between
China's Chou En-lai and America's John Foster Dulles, whose
countries did not recognize one another and whose representatives
therefore did not speak. He was the guiding light to get Germany into
the North Atlantic Treaty Organization and back into the family of

nations, speaking once as he did so of the memories of one who as a young subaltern had at a Battle of the Somme casualty clearing station searched among literally heaps of bodies for the wounded of the riflemen of his company. Eden soothed the intense feeling the Chinese Communists had about Formosa's offshore islands. He mediated disputes in the Middle East, Iran, Iraq, and Egypt, and was given the Order of the Garter, becoming thereby Sir Anthony.

His marriage, shaky for decades, finally ended, and he married Clarissa Churchill, the daughter of Winston's brother John. She was thirty-two years old to his fifty-five, but the match was a very happy one. The Churchills gave the reception in the garden of number 10. He helped set up the Southeast Asia Treaty Organization. There was always a reason why Churchill felt the moment had not yet come for the retirement—the Queen was away and not due back for a while; he would wait until the anniversary of the end of the war in Europe—but perhaps it was the cranky stubbornness of old age despite his saying he would not hang on too long as Lloyd George did, or perhaps the illusion or delusion that a new Elizabethan age impended and that he would be there to see and superintend it. Finally after staying four and a half years when he had said he would stay a few months, he gave up office. Sir Anthony was Prime Minister after being the dauphin for fifteen years. It was April 1955.

The war had been over ten years. Nostalgia for its great days possessed every segment of British society . . . Dunkirk and the long lines of men boarding the inland steamers and private yachts and fishermen's dinghies sent to get them safely away, the Blitz, Winston with his V-for-victory sign and his cigar, Monty in the desert, indomitable England always winning the last battle by seeing it through. Something else mixed with the memories of glory. Of England in the summer of 1955 the American diplomat and intelligence officer Chester Cooper wrote, "Something seemed amiss. There was a wispy, enveloping *tristesse de vivre* among all I met—from our benighted charwoman to our knighted neighbor. It took the form of bitter little jokes about 'Merrie Olde . . .' or of half-finished sentences that ended with a bleak 'Well, anyway . . .' and a rolling of the eyes, or trailed off drearily with a barely audible 'However . . .' and a shrug. For many, rich and poor, Chelsea and Cheapside alike, the Battle of Britain had given London a massive dose of adrenaline, a moment of high purpose and common glory. Everything after that seemed anticlimactic."

Only in the previous year had all rationing ended. Cooper gave his charwoman thirty-five cents an hour. A high Foreign Office official got eight thousand dollars a year before taxes, and taxes were murderous. For a century and more the British gentleman represented the highest social position the world knew. Now the gentleman's tweeds were shiny in the seat and elbows and his collar frayed. Britain had always been a small country, Cooper reflected, but it had taken victory over Germany, Italy, and Japan to put in on its way to becoming a small power.

That thought could not be absent from Sir Anthony Eden's mind. And he was taking over from Winston Churchill, who had once declared in his grand way, meaning it at the moment he said it, that he had not become His Majesty's First Minister in order to preside over the liquidation of the British Empire. Churchill was not easy to follow nor the concept easy to live up to. Eden seemed nervous, appointing people who appeared oddly suited to the positions he gave them, and then being far too ready to call them up at all hours to ask if they had seen this article in the papers or responded to that charge in the House. He was touchy, jumpy, tried to keep his finger in every pie, was liable to change his mind about trifles as well as important matters, was tense, oversensitive, and unpredictable. Everything began to fall apart on March 1, 1956. Eden had been Prime Minister for eighteen months when King Hussein of Jordan, twenty years old, gave the British Gen. Sir John Bagot Glubb, for years the gray eminence of Anglo Arabia, two hours to get out of his country.

In 1917, with the Somme battle over and the battle for the Passchendaele ridge getting under way, a British cavalry officer Field Marshal Haig had never cared for was sent from the Western Front to Cairo to see what could be done about the threat offered by Germany's ally Turkey to the Suez Canal. There Gen. Edmund Allenby received a young man attired *à l'Arabe* who performed miracles with Turkey's rebellious desert subjects. Between them, Lawrence of Arabia riding with tribesmen and Allenby conducting the last great cavalry campaign in history, the two destroyed the Ottoman Empire in the Near East.

Their exploits with horse and camel were to set back the clock of mechanization for twenty years in the British Army, the disbanding of the last mounted regiments being put off until 1938 and the approach of another great world war, but the main result of their work was to set the flag of a Christian nation flying over the Holy Land for the first time in a millennium. When the Great War was over the British and French took over what the Ottomans had lost, ruling in name and fact through Protected States, States in Treaty Relationship, Mandated Territories, chiefs, emirs, Kings, Crown Princes, satraps, and politicians, the sons of whom went to Harrow and Sandhurst. Mostly the area was a British, not French, fiefdom. The British ran the enterprises and transportation, furnished the military drill and officers, sent out Colonial Office water and agriculture experts, controlled the vast oil fields. The Royal Air Force built airfields; the route to India was safer than ever before. British banks set up shop. The Near East became the last great area painted crimson.

Then came the Second War, and the realization of the subject peoples of how frayed was the overlord's coat, how raveled his sleeve. In 1917 the British had enlisted Jewish support for their fight against the Kaiser by promising a Jewish national home in Palestine, and thousands of Jews had gone there, with thousands more anxious to do so. After the end of the Second War serious fighting broke out between Arab and Jew. Once the British would have been able to stop such disputes with a waved finger, but by 1948 the spirit and the ability to do much was gone. They threw up their hands. The Union Jack came down and the flag of the State of Israel went up as armies battled even in the hour of parting from England.

The British hung on precariously elsewhere in the region. In Egypt their corrupt puppet King Farouk was chased away and the vibrant Lt. Col. Gamal Abdel Nasser came to reign in his stead. Nasser was a great trial to the British. In the Second War, Churchill had accounted the defense of Egypt and its Suez Canal, the lifeline of the Empire, as second in importance only to the defense of the home islands. Even during the daunting moment when a landing by Hitler on the Dover shore was expected almost hourly he had refused to weaken Britain's forces there. Across the deserts, Montgomery had battled Rommel and won the single purely British victory of the war. To Lieutenant Colonel Nasser all that was meaningless ancient history. His stock in trade was pulling the tail of the so clearly and sadly shopworn British lion. He called for an Arab Empire with himself at the head and extending across thousands of miles, including the French possessions in North Africa where for long Paris and then Vichy had ruled. Nasser became for France a terrible menace. Ousted from Indochina in a defeat smaller but almost equal in humiliating nature to their rout by the Germans in 1940, the French said they would never leave North Africa. It would be the last straw.

To Prime Minister Sir Anthony Eden, Nasser was a personal enemy. He knew the Egyptian leader had been behind the decision of young King Hussein to kick Glubb Pasha out of Jordan on two hours' notice. Nasser's allies in Jordan had inspired the King to do so. With that action Britain's oil sources had suddenly come into peril, and her communications through the Suez Canal. Nasser was pledging the Egyptian cotton crop in exchange for arms from Russia, that Russia with whom for centuries Britain had contested what was called the Great Game of influence throughout Asia. Russia had finally won that game. Now Russia with Nasser's connivance looked like winning in the Middle East. Radio Cairo jubilantly praised Hussein and poured out abuse of the British, any Arab friends they still had, and Israel. It was maddening, infuriating. Had Britain won through in 1945 for this?

There was something else. Nasser had dark skin. The Nassers of the Empire for all of Eden's life until the end of the Second War would never have been permitted to enter the front door of any officers' mess or gentlemen's club of any country Britain ruled or controlled. There is nothing in the record to suggest that Eden ever referred to this, but others did. To the British man in the street and meagerly pensioned-off colonial district agent or proconsul living in modest country cottage or city digs, Nasser was a wog, a nigger, a Fuzzy-Wuzzy—a native. Now he was bidding to throw into the dustbin of history the England that had in Eden's youth ruled the world and the seas and so spread its flag that the sun never set upon it.

Something snapped in Eden. For thirty years his every House of Commons speech had been unemotionally logical and so diplomatically phrased as to resemble a Foreign Office position paper. Now when he spoke of Glubb's ouster he lost his temper in public for the first time ever. The listening members of Parliament were appalled. Some of them knew of his private rages reminiscent of his father, and that always before they had centered on trifles, a mix-up in hotel accommodations or a late train or something of the sort. This was different. He raged on in a bumbling fashion and got in return roars of disapproval such as no Prime Minister had heard in years, not since the days of Neville Chamberlain when the House feared he was going to kowtow one time too many to Adolf Hitler. Measurelessly frustrated now as they sat in the seats which had once held the elect of the world, the Champions of the Empire, Britain's elected representatives took it out on Eden. "Really, the House *must* listen to the Prime Minister!" he shouted. Lady Eden wrote in her diary that the events in Jordan had "shattered" him. His nervous fatigue was "sapping his powers of thought." When the Foreign Office official Anthony Nutting spoke with the Prime Minister he felt as if he were having a nightmare and dealing with a stranger.

Spring of 1956 came, and summer. Radio Cairo exalted and boasted. Perhaps all countries new to nationhood are bumptious. A part of Nasser's promised magic was that soon he would build the Aswan High Dam, a construction so large it would be remindful of the works of his Pharaoh predecessors. The dam would mobilize the waters of the Nile as never before and bring under cultivation two million new acres of land and so prove the salvation of Egypt. Then he would destroy Israel and rule the Arab world. The Russians were helping with cash, arms, advanced airplanes flown by Russian and Czech pilots.

But to build the Aswan High Dam, Nasser needed money, of which he had none to spare. Negotiations had been going on with the World Bank, which had declared it would largely finance the project if the United States contributed $56 million and Britain $15 million. (The disparity in figures revealed all too clearly the disparity between the two members of 1945's Big Three.) The United States had indicated it would agree to make its contribution. Then President Eisenhower and Secretary of State Dulles had second thoughts. The President was up for reelection in November. Helping Egypt build the dam would not earn him the votes of southern states competing in the world market with the cotton producers of the Nile Valley. It would not help him with Jewish voters protective of Egypt's archenemy Israel. It would not earn him votes among anti-Communists who saw Egypt on its way to becoming a Soviet satellite that might lead the entire Arab world into the Russian orbit. In mid-July, Secretary Dulles, releasing the information to the press before informing the Egyptians, announced the United States would not advance any money for the dam.

Dulles had not told the British of the American decision in advance. Eden had to learn it from newspaper reports. He also had to trail along after the Americans and follow their lead. The next morning, Egypt's ambassador to Great Britain was told that that country's offer of $15 million was being withdrawn. That evening the World Bank announced it was no longer in a position to advance money toward the building of the dam.

Four days later at Alexandria, Nasser delivered a speech to a vast outdoor crowd. It was notable that in the first few minutes of what became a three-hour oration he mentioned the name of Ferdinand de Lesseps, creator of the Suez Canal nearly a century earlier, more than half a dozen times. Radio carried his address all over Egypt and the Arab world. He ended, "The Suez Canal belongs to us. The Canal will be run by Egyptians! Egyptians! Egyptians!" Even as he spoke the soldiers of his army were reacting to the code word "de Lesseps." They seized the Suez Canal. Through it had sailed the Curzons and Kitcheners and the troopships with the men to conquer Mandalay and Kabul and Kuala Lumpur and the Kiplings to chronicle their move-

ments along the path of Empire which secured the way to India and
the treasures of the East.

Britain owned 45 percent of the shares of the Suez Canal Company,
bought for her by Benjamin Disraeli, Eden's predecessor, Victoria's
favorite Prime Minister. For generations British navigators and pilots
had come up rope ladders trim and neat in their white shorts and knee
socks to guide the world's ships along the hundred-mile-long lane of
water in the desert—only they were said to know how to do it. W.
Somerset Maugham, copies of all of whose works Eden owned, had
gone through the Canal to write in the 1920s of all those Britishers
who in their dress-for-dinner fashion in the jungle ruled millions,
sahibs with their memsahibs having their gin sundowners on the
sweeping verandahs of their high-ceilinged Edwardian and Victorian
houses as natives pulled punkah ropes to fan them in the tropical heat.
Now the natives had taken the Canal.

In France, Nasser's action was seen as a catastrophe. The Empress
Eugénie had opened the Canal. One and a half million North Afri-
can–born Frenchmen lived in the area stretching from Casablanca to
Tunis. Their position and even their lives were now at risk. If Nasser
could seize the Suez Canal he might also inspire the natives of
France's holdings to rise in rebellion even as he might inspire Iraq and
Kuwait to nationalize British-owned oil companies in those places.
The men in Paris holding high position were largely former Resistance
fighters or early followers of Charles de Gaulle. They had endured the
hideous sun-drenched May and June of 1940, years of German
occupation of their country, years of bitterness and division between
themselves and those who had followed Marshal Pétain. They had
seen their forces kicked out of Indochina. De Gaulle had left office,
saying to his intimates that he was not made to be a constitutional
leader and adding that if Joan of Arc had lived to rule, to marry and
have children, perhaps to be deceived by her husband, she would not
be remembered as she was. So, he said, it was necessary for one who
had saved his country to depart. His followers now leaders could not
view themselves in that light—who could, save de Gaulle?—but they
were the government of *la Patrie* of great past if of recent and present

doubtful eminence. Nasser and the millions who saw themselves reflected by his skin and his rise could take away what glory still attached to the word "France."

The French and the British consulted. They told each other that Nasser was not another Hitler, for his country was not powerful enough for that. He was a Mussolini acting as stalking horse for the Russian colossus that had replaced Germany as menace to the West. Mussolini had gone into Ethiopia and the former Allies of the Great War had stood by and done nothing, and from their inaction Hitler deduced that it was quite safe for him to reoccupy the Rhineland and take Austria and the Sudetenland and the rest of Czechoslovakia and then the Free City of Danzig—and from that had come the Second War. "It is all quite familiar," the British Labour Party leader Hugh Gaitskell said of Nasser's action.

Once it would have all been very simple for London and Paris. In their pasts they had conquered islands, countries, whole continents. Colonial adventures and punitive expeditions had been the meaning of their soldiers' lives. One white regiment could shatter legions of tribesmen. A flotilla of gunboats could subdue a regime. But now the natives had tasted blood, seen the white man's back as he lowered his flag and then turned and ran. And they had Russian arms and Russian backing. The British and French thought of the United Nations. It was they who had created the League of Nations—Eden had been England's Secretary for League Affairs—and they who with America set up the United Nations, with Eden signing the Charter in his country's name. But the United Nations delegates now very often had skin black or yellow or brown, and were ex-subjects of the same Britain and France. It was impossible that they would back the former colonial overlords against Gamal Abdel Nasser sitting in his capital city and freely going to and coming from Cairo's Gezira Club, where among other places Sir Anthony Eden had played his tennis after sleeping well and dining splendidly at the British Embassy, with its lawns down to the Nile and terraces, gazebos, flowers, Chinese lanterns, candelabras of Bohemian crystal, tall Turkish harem glass shades, coils of incense, and hordes of Arab servants in red and gold.

Then there was the question of the United States. The Americans needed the new nations set up from the wreckage of the old empires, needed them for backing in the struggle with the Soviets. To John Foster Dulles the former rulers of the world were secondary players in the game he played against Russia. There were no more Great Powers. There were two superpowers, and the French and British merely fitted into a basket along with everybody else.

Anthony Eden had been born within days of Victoria's Diamond Jubilee, when the world gathered to honor the Queen of Earthly Queens. He was the son of a hereditary baronet twice over. When his brother Nicholas died at Jutland, King George V had sent a letter of consolation. He had once said in the House that England could never be a second- or third-rate power. She must be a first-rate one or, he said, she was nothing. On August 2, a week after Nasser took the Canal, Queen Elizabeth at her Prime Minister's request signed an order recalling twenty thousand British reservists to active duty.

The French fleet began gathering at Toulon. There were palavers back and forth, suggestions that an international consortium should own but not operate the Canal, that a Users' Association should run it. Nothing looked like working out. In the first two weeks of August the British took from mothballs landing craft, tank carriers, destroyers, and minesweepers. They painted the tanks and trucks which had rolled through conquered Germany desert camouflage colors. An armada gathered at Malta, an infantry division was flown into Cyprus. In Algiers, elements of three French divisions assembled; six battalions encamped near troopships docked at Marseille. The world began to take alarm. Secretary Dulles was asked in a news conference if the United States would join in an attempt to shoot a way through what Nasser now called the Arabs' Canal, should that become necessary. He answered the United States would not. Asked in the House if the same was true for Britain, Eden refused to reply. Lord Beaverbrook's jingoistic newspapers headlined: KEEP GREAT BRITAIN GREAT. Others said that to take direct action would be a mad attempt to turn back the clock of time. The British government received a note from Soviet Premier Nikolai Bulganin pointing out that "small wars can turn into big wars."

In a press conference Secretary Dulles referred to "colonial powers," and President Eisenhower asked his intimates if as in 1914 and 1939 the British and French might go to war thinking the Americans must come in and support them. Such a war, he said, might "array the world from Dakar to the Philippine Islands against us." The United States election day was weeks away.

To Eden, Nasser's action was "a thumb on our windpipe." He told his military planners to go to work. They did so in London underground tunnels constructed in the early days of the Second War, mapping targets and seeing to logistics in the deepest secrecy, with friends and acquaintances informed they were out of town, on vacation, away. The planning was more intensive than anything seen in 1939–45. All this against an enemy contemptuously referred to as Johnny Gyppo. Throughout the work the Prime Minister, although overseeing everything, questioning, hectoring, endlessly involved, seemed strangely restrained emotionally, almost hypnotically calm after his earlier rages against the Egyptians. It was very strange. His health acted up: he suffered liver troubles, jaundice, was briefly hospitalized when his temperature rose to 106. He wrote Eisenhower that Nasser was holding Europe and Britain for ransom, that there impended a possible "ignoble end to our long history." He swung from extreme confidence to moments of horrible doubt. Sometimes he seemed unaware of the possible consequences of a military attack upon Egypt, sometimes he seemed obsessed with them. The dead of the Somme and Passchendaele came before his vision. He had learned years earlier that when making a radio address from a studio it was wise to direct his words to a single listener, and had in a man from his old platoon in the King's Royal Rifle Corps who had in the long ago served as a sergeant under the subaltern Mr. Eden. Perhaps the ex-sergeant now turned gray as himself was in his mind, and the boys they had been, when he thought of the boys who would die if he sent British troops into action. Perhaps it was Nicholas as he had been when last he saw him, sixteen years old, or Jack swank with his monocle and mustache fresh from South Africa with the regiment. He told his officers that above all else they must concentrate on keeping casualties down if they went into Suez.

But how could they go up against Johnny Gyppo? What would occasion such a move? There was nothing they could point to that would justify it to the world. They had hoped the Egyptians would prove incapable of running the Canal, for that would have provided an excuse, but Nasser had gotten pilots and navigators from Communist countries and Scandinavia, and the Canal traffic moved as smoothly as in the past. Eden had thought that perhaps in contravention of international law Nasser might ban British ships, and so provide an excuse for action. He had not. Only Israeli shipping was banned, as it had been for years. And aflame now with his desire to be Pharaoh of a new and greater Egyptian Empire, Nasser was actively supporting fellahin commando raids from Gaza into Israel. The British and French opened talks with men from Tel Aviv.

Meanwhile they held discussions with others, but the discussions were fruitless. It could well be said that the whole matter was symbolic in any event, for the construction of giant cargo tankers that did not use the Canal was eroding its importance year by year. But the former colonial powers, their position in the world at stake, could not see matters that way. It was particularly so for those who had seen London win two world wars within living memory. A Yugoslav diplomat counseling a high Foreign Office official against the use of force was told, "Britain is not used to getting advice from small Balkan powers." To a Swede: "And what did your country do in the last war?"

Three months had passed since the seizure of the Canal when in a secluded house in the French countryside to which men drove up in unmarked and modest cars, the British and French came to an agreement with the Israelis. Everything was under the seal of deepest secrecy, the Israelis never officially to admit there had been an "arrangement." There was. Under the pretext of destroying the commando bases in Gaza, the Israelis would invade. The Egyptian Army would certainly fight back. Nasser could not do otherwise. The Israelis would raise the level of the fighting. Then the French and British, professing concern that the Canal would be damaged in the dispute, would step in assuming the guise of impartial peacemakers coming to put out the fire, and would also invade Egypt. The result would be that Nasser would be driven from power and the Canal restored to its former situation. The men left the house in the French countryside.

On October 29, 1956, Israeli armored columns pushed into Gaza and into Egyptian territory, preceded by parachute drops and followed by infantry in the method perfected by the Germans in France in the spring of 1940. The Egyptian Army went into action. The Israelis outflanked them and kept coming, heading toward the Canal a hundred miles away. It was not the only heavy gunfire the world knew in the following days, for in a wholly unrelated manner a kind of revolution broke out in Russia's Eastern European satellites. It stemmed from Nikita Khrushchev's denunciation of the late Joseph Stalin at a Communist Party congress. He had called Stalin a coward and a stupid terror expert. This puff of fresh air shook the Communist world. Outbreaks everywhere commenced. They reached a climax in Hungary. Budapest rose against the Russians. There was fighting all throughout the city. Russian tanks came in throwing phosphorus shells into street after street. Even as Eastern Europe looked like erupting with consequences unforeseeable, the British and French issued an ultimatum ostensibly directed at both Israel and Egypt. It called for an immediate end to their fighting and withdrawal to a distance of ten miles from the Canal by both—which actually meant an Israeli advance, for they were still some eighty or ninety miles from there.

The fighting went on in accordance with the Israeli-French-British secret agreement. Paris and London prepared to intervene. They needed to do so, particularly London. For the men mobilized in August had been sitting around doing nothing for three months, and it was said that *He had ten thousand men/He marched them up to the top of the hill/And marched them down again* could well have been composed with Eden in mind. Then a hitch developed. Word was received that the Israelis agreed to a cease-fire. Prime Minister Eden, nerves like stretched rubber bands, snapped. He broke down in front of his Cabinet, weeping unashamedly. Then word came that the Israelis had attached conditions to their alleged compliance. So they were not accepting the cease-fire. The twelve hours of the Anglo-French ultimatum ran out. At once their air fleets lifted from Mediterranean bases and headed for the airports of the Egyptian Air Force. They were in midflight when their commanders were radioed that the fields were filled with Americans boarding planes to get out of the danger zone. The planes reversed course, returned to base, waited until word came that the Americans were gone, and then returned effectively to destroy all Egyptian air power on the ground. At a cost of seven British and French planes, 260 of Nasser's were put out of action.

There had been few civilian casualties, for by design neither central Cairo nor Alexandria were hit, but the world was deeply shocked. The people of Britain, with the Blitz always in mind, were left ill at ease. President Eisenhower, mightily concerned about the developing situation in Eastern Europe and one week away from election day, was flung into a titanic rage. When word of the ultimatum to the Egyptians and Israelis reached Washington he had departed for the first time in his presidency from addressing a letter to Eden with anything other than "My dear Anthony" and substituted "Dear Mr. Prime Minister." Now he exploded in such fashion that the *New York Times* Washington bureau chief James Reston wrote that "the White House crackled with barrack-room language the like of which had not been heard since the days of General Grant."[*] Raging, the President ordered that Eden be gotten on the phone. "Bombs, by God!" he cried to his aides. "What does Anthony think he's doing?" The call went through. The President grabbed the receiver and demanded to know if he was speaking to the Prime Minister. "No," said one of Eden's aides at 10 Downing Street, but his answer was drowned out as Eisenhower rasped, "What the hell is going on? Anthony, I can only assume you have gone out of your mind."

The bombs rained down on Egyptian targets as British and French invasion fleets departed berths at Cyprus and the North African coast.

---

[*]He apparently did not know that General Grant was notable for the extreme mildness of his language.

Hundreds of ships steamed through the Mediterranean in an elephan-
tine, ponderous, and minutely detailed movement that appeared more
suited to a major war against a European power than for Johnny
Gyppo, with timings, loading tables, strategic appreciations being
constantly changed from London at the order of the Prime Minister.

Through the streets of Budapest went the Russian tanks, but it was
Britain and France who were denounced by practically every nation in
the world. Secretary Dulles in private referred to Eden as "the nut" and
"the playboy." United States Ambassador to the United Nations Henry
Cabot Lodge introduced a Security Council resolution demanding
that Israel withdraw its forces from Egyptian territory. The vote on the
measure was seven to two in favor, but Britain cast its first veto since
the international organization's founding. The Security Council was
thus neutralized, but the General Assembly voted by the largest majority in its history, 64–5, for an immediate cease-fire. Commonwealth
countries voted against England with a mixture of incredulity, rage,
and sorrow. When in the House of Commons Eden said he would not
accept the UN's views, members were in an uproar, screaming, "Resign! Resign!" He had thrown away in one fatal moment of folly, they
said, solidarity with the former colonies of the Empire, the Anglo-
American alliance which had won two wars, and adherence to the UN
Charter. The scene became so disorderly, so almost physically violent,
that for the first time in decades the Speaker suspended a meeting.

There was a rigorously enforced blackout on all news from the
Middle East, and therefore alarmed Britons gathering in more than
two thousand protest meetings and sending so many protesting telegrams to Downing Street that the Post Office announced there would
be a nine-hour delay in delivery could not know that the British
armada had requested that ships of the United States Sixth Fleet stay
clear to avoid any possibility of unfortunate incidents. The American
admiral commanding the fleet declined to do so in chilling words: "I
must dispose my forces and take all steps necessary." At one point a
United States submarine shadowing the British was taken to be proceeding with hostile intent. The British prepared to drop depth charges
and only a hurried rise to the surface by the submarine prevented that.

Military censorship more stringent than imposed in the Second War prevented all dissemination of the ghastly almost-disaster, but rumors spread that the Americans were going to intercept the British and shoot it out with them. It was said the United States was about to break off diplomatic relations. Ambassador Winthrop Aldrich was called to Washington for what were termed "consultations."

In the United Nations, deserted even by such as Canada, British Ambassador Pierson Dixon felt he was wandering the halls like a lost spirit and that others averted their eyes when he passed. In London the Prime Minister endlessly telephoned people, revised plans, changed and rechanged his mind. He could not sleep. He suddenly looked remarkably older. The world was calling his bombers and ships a venture a hundred years out of time. President Eisenhower said the whole thing belonged to an earlier century—not even the nineteenth.

It seemed to Lady Eden, she said, that the Suez Canal was running through her drawing room. When a Cabinet minister came to Downing Street for a late-hour conference he heard the Prime Minister pacing the floor above him. "Up and down, up and down, talking incessantly," he remembered. "That worried me."

The tumult in the House of Commons was unexampled. The ships plowed on through the Mediterranean. Cartoons in the world's newspapers showed an empty-eyed Eden holding a steering wheel detached from a wrecked automobile, showed him as a buccaneer, as a Victorian pirate. In the corridors of the House they whispered what Eisenhower had shouted over the phone: he had lost his mind.

By Sunday, November 4, the Israelis had driven south to take and hold Sharm-el-Sheikh at the mouth of the Gulf of Aqaba and so open the port there for their shipping. They had no wish to extend on westward toward the Canal and Cairo and held up their forces. The pushed-back Egyptians did not fire on them, and so the fighting was effectively concluded even as the French and British sailed on, the largest assemblage of ships in European waters since the end of the war now coming to stop fighting which had already ended. The thin screen of pretense was ripped into pieces, and the French candidly told the Americans it had all been a sham from the beginning. Eden did not, holding to his original position that he was only interested in acting as a peacemaker. At first light on November 5, transport planes came in over the northern entrance to the Canal. They held Anglo-French paratroopers. The ships would be arriving in a day. The skies over Suez filled with men floating down.

Even as he jumped, the British medical officer Sandy Cavenagh told himself that this was an atrocity. This overwhelming force used against a small and weak and already beaten opponent, this hammer against an ant, Cavenagh reflected, was aimed at preventing large casualty lists for the attackers. It was a legacy of the Somme and Ypres, he decided, because the generals were haunted by the memory of what had happened in those places. "Yet, paradoxically, if a generation had not vanished as in a dream in 1914–18 we might not have attacked Port Said at all. Eden was a survivor of the Lost Generation himself." The paratroopers came down and wiped out what Egyptian resistance met them.

The armadas arrived, the British coming at Port Said, the French at Port Fuad. By then gold was flowing out of Britain and a monstrous run on the pound was bidding to devastate the country's economic life. Chancellor of the Exchequer Harold Macmillan applied to Washington for a loan and was refused. He turned to the International Monetary Fund and was refused. The ships took up position. Even as they did so Eden was harrying his commanders with new plans and orders. (At one point he had thought to order the ships to change course and make for Haifa.) The night before they arrived in Egyptian waters he ordered that guns of no more than 4.5 inches be used. That would leave cruiser armament unfired. The entire bombardment schedule would have to be reworked so that destroyers could engage the targets marked for the cruisers. Then Eden ordered that the troops should land on the defended beaches with no artillery preparation at all. There should be no bombardment. (It was decided by appalled and rebellious admirals that the word "bombardment" would not be used. "Gunfire support" would be substituted to describe what was done.)

The first shell came over the water and hit a casino, which burst into flames. The cruisers opened fire, saying later they fired blanks intended only to scare the enemy. Gray-and-brown smoke came from targets. The troops went ashore, the British Broadcasting Corporation reporting they had done so without a preliminary bombardment. Britain and France joined together in a military walkover, two nations only yesterday the foremost military and naval powers of the world attacking a trifling opponent already dazed by the Israeli push. But the uncertainty of Eden the ex-soldier made the officers at Suez speak of him as once he had spoken of the politicians of Asquith's and Lloyd George's Cabinets. Why had he given a twelve-hour ultimatum and then let a week pass before the ships could arrive? He should have just bombed to bits the Egyptian Air Force and sent in the paratroopers immediately as the Israelis tied up Egyptian ground forces—never mind the ponderous naval movement. And the bombings that went on for days in a tentative and one-arm-behind-the-back fashion? Far better to have hit Cairo and Alexandria hard as soon as the ultimatum ran out. And the constant changes and arrangements! It became a favorite quip in the officers' mess of the Royal Scots to say that of twelve different prepared invasion plans, Eden chose the thirteenth. *

The officers of the Royal Scots, and those of the other regiments, were professional soldiers with no say in political matters. It was different for London's officials. As thirty thousand people met in Trafalger Square to chant "Eden must go!" and nearly a thousand police on foot and horseback massed to hold them back for four hours when they surged down Whitehall toward Downing Street, Eden's men fell away from him. Each day there were resignations. He threw an inkpot at his departing press secretary, who said he could not continue to be the conduit for appalling lies.

Beyond the street disturbances clearly audible in his office at Downing Street and the resignations of his men, a terrible vision came into being. The Russian news agency Tass issued a reminder to Britain and France that the Russians possessed rockets easily capable of reaching Paris and London, and that those rockets were loaded with nuclear bombs. It was hideous. Tass was an official voice for the Soviet

---

*Actually there were seventeen different plans devised.

government. The American diplomat and intelligence officer Chester Cooper saw British officials read the words and turn away "gray with exhaustion, ashen." The ringing of Sunday church bells made people wonder if this was an air-raid alarm. In Washington President Eisenhower said that if the rockets went off America would have no choice but to hit back "with everything in the bucket."

The rockets did not fly, but the events in Egypt permitted the Soviets to do as they wished in Hungary with little fear of recrimination from a West two of whose leading representatives were likewise engaged in warring upon a small and almost defenseless nation. There were ghastly cries from Radio Budapest—"This is Hungary calling. Early this morning Soviet troops launched a general attack against Hungary. For the sake of God and freedom, help Hungary!"—but what could the West say or do? The radio fell silent.

Eden was up all night as the British and French troops easily pushed on down the Suez Canal along the roads on its banks, covering a quarter of the hundred-mile length before halting for rest. The world united in denouncing the venture. It was said that United States–British relations had been brought to the lowest point since the American Civil War; Britain's *Economist* said one had to go back to the year 1783 to find the country so universally condemned. All through the Mideast, pipelines and pumping stations were blown up, flames rising in the desert night. All through the night a tortured Sir Anthony Eden was on the telephone with the French.

When daylight came he went to the House of Commons. He took his seat. He looked aged and ill, defeated and broken. "The Prime Minister sprawled on the front bench," wrote the Parliament correspondent of the *New Statesman*, "head thrown back and mouth agape. His eyes, inflamed with sleeplessness, stared into vacancies beyond the roof. His hands twitched at his spectacles or mopped themselves in a handkerchief, but were never still. The face was gray except where black-ringed caverns surrounded the dying embers of his eyes. The whole personality, if not prostrated, seemed completely withdrawn."

He spoke. Great Britain was throwing in its hand. The troops would remain halted in place in a dead-end enterprise partway down a causeway in Egypt far away. For the Isthmus of Suez the British had defeated Napoleon, Kaiser Wilhelm, Adolf Hitler. To Nasser they lost. To history.

In a little while a minister would look into Sir Anthony's eyes across the Cabinet table. A meeting was ending. "Is there anything more?" the Prime Minister asked. "For a moment," the minister remembered, "he was looking directly at me and I saw in his eyes a man pursued by every demon.

"I have never seen a look like it in any man's eyes, and I hope I never do again."

Within two days Chester Cooper would see long lines composed of young men and women on the north side of Grosvenor Square at the Canadian emigration office, and at the emigration offices of Australia and New Zealand. He saw them on succeeding days and believed he knew why they were there. "When you grow up," the Field Marshal Earl Haig of Bemersyde who once had commanded the Captain Edens told the Boy Scouts of 1928 in the last words he ever said in public, "always remember that you belong to a great Empire, and when people speak disrespectfully of England always stand up and defend your country." In a little while the British and French would trail home from Suez, and as they left the Egyptians would blow up the statue of Ferdinand de Lesseps on his tall pillar of stone. The pieces would tumble down into the waters of the Canal.

Eden finished his speech in the House. In a matter of weeks his career would be concluded. Prime Minister Eden, late Captain the King's Royal Rifle Corps, would give way to Prime Minister Macmillan, late Captain the Grenadier Guards. In the last moments before one succeeded the other they would talk of days gone by. It was in a drawing room at Downing Street on a late afternoon where a west window overlooking a garden let through a little sunlight. "We sat for some little time together," Macmillan remembered. "We spoke a few words about the First War, in which we had both served and suffered. I can still see him now on that sad winter afternoon."

Britain had on that day 700,000 men under arms. That was far too many for a place that had journeyed from an island nation to a world

Empire to a small country located off the European continent. Prime Minister Macmillan cut the figure in half. Regiments were disbanded and the banners, silver salvers, gold goblets, souvenirs of old campaigns were sent to new combined messes of the shrunken force of what Kipling used to call the Soldiers of the Queen.

His speech ended, Eden left the House of Commons. It was November 6, 1956, just forty years short six days of the official end of what Sir Douglas Haig had begun on July 1, 1916, the Battle of the Somme.

A F T E R W O R D

"The roots of their fate lay so deep in the past." So wrote B. H. Liddell Hart when he thought of those who endured the Great War. He had in mind millions of people, but to none of those millions could the words be more applicable than to the four men considered in this book. Like Fitzgerald's Gatsby, they were as boats fighting against a current pulling them back into the past.

One imagines they must have known that this was so. Even Haig. Haig's tragedy, his son said, was that he was unable to give voice to what he felt. While thinking, perhaps, that there were other aspects to Haig's life and doings that were at least as tragic as that he was inarticulate, one can accept that he had trouble voicing emotions and concepts. Perhaps this prevented him from ever saying anything about the war when it was over. But why did he cease, the day he returned from France in 1919, to keep up the diaries he had begun as a teenager and whose length approximated that of seven full-sized books? He had produced some 750,000 words over the years; then he simply stopped. We have Lady Haig's word for it. Perhaps he felt an era had ended and he did not wish to record anything of the era that would succeed it. But perhaps it was that he knew that the minute the war ended he and his thinking were entirely passé, that he was now a vision of the past. There is something plaintive in the words he directed to the Boy Scouts which told them to stand up for the British Empire and England should people "speak disrespectfully" of those places and concepts. Haig, Liddell Hart said, was the distilled essence of Great Britain, of a Great Britain whose military chiefs after 1918 turned their backs on the tanks—those "smelly things," those "petrol things" made for garagemen, not officers; "Thank God it's over and we can get back to *real* soldiering," one man said of the war—and Haig must have known in his heart of hearts that it was the unanswerable pull of England's great past which had in the end destroyed that England.

Of Pétain it can be said that he looked backward continually after the war, showing by his military thinking that he was completely wedded to defensive strategy—the Maginot Line—and, after the Germans flanked the Line in 1940, that he could not bear to sacrifice French lives to add to those lost in 1914–18. When he became Head of the French State he seemed to hope that he could bring back the France he had known as a child, the France of Napoleon III, with farmers working smallholdings, with workshops and craftsmen instead of factories and industrial combines, with religion dominant and the family paramount. A lost hope, of course. He loved not wisely but too well, some said of him when the occupation was over, but what he loved was of lost yesterdays.

Rathenau, prophet or not, was utterly the prisoner of his past and that of the Germany which produced him; and it was that Germany which so frightfully turned into what it did after 1933. The roots which produced Rathenau's death and made it a premonition of the appalling future were always there. Now, today, that Germany seems almost unintelligible and untranslatable—really it is hard to conceive that what happened *did* happen, despite all the books we have read and the television documentaries we have seen—and in parallel fashion Rathenau seems part of an entirely vanished and entirely remote world.

Anthony Eden was perhaps most of all the victim of the past, in himself almost a complete picture of the British governing class, elegant, wise, but fatally unable in the end to divorce himself from nostalgia for days that were gone. It was very sad. But they were all sad, these men. "Show me a hero and I will write you a tragedy," Fitzgerald said.

One thinks, with hindsight vision, that they should have better grasped what was occurring once the war began, should have known that the world they lived in, seemingly stable and settled, with place allotted to each country and class, each situation, was in fact over with forever once the guns began to fire and the soldiers to march. There is a theory that under the right conditions the physical motion of a butterfly's wings in the Sea of Japan can in time create conditions leading to a tidal wave in the North Atlantic—the "butterfly effect" discussed these days in Wall Street in terms of international finances. We think to ourselves that they should have seen that the firing of a pistol in a dusty Balkan town unknown and almost meaningless to the rest of the universe would bring the firestorm, the Day of Judgment, the revolutionary end to so many things and to so much. But who could have guessed. An Austrian archduke dies? There were "innumerable archdukes," Queen Victoria once remarked. Yet the death of this one puts the world asunder—children will in time starve in the hills of Budapest and the German Crown Prince will write the King of England from his place of exile to complain that he does not even have a bathroom in his house. And the millions of young men will sleep, forever young.

But of course the world did not foresee what was coming, did not know that it had come even when it was over and the peace came. The world for two decades more sought only to restore what had been, the security of before-the-war. The Communists fighting the Nazis in the streets of the Berlin of the 1920s sought that, whether they knew it or not. Then the Second War came and nothing was recognizable. For a brief time, eleven years after the end of the Second War, Eden permitted himself to forget the hard facts, to forget History itself, and to fall into a fantasy that the England of Rule Britannia yet lived, the England of men of his class in the summer of 1914, himself then in white flannels, blue blazer, straw boater. At the height of the Suez crisis he drove to Eton to sit at the feet of his favorite old teacher, then in his eighties, "to bare his soul and to seek approval and reassurance," wrote Chester Cooper. "It was a subconscious quest for the security of his boyhood, a pathetic voyage back to the womb." There was nothing the old man could offer. In a flash Eden and England and the world learned all was over that once had seemed so immutable. France had learned in 1940 it was no longer a Great Power, Germany in 1945. It took England until 1956 and the Suez affair to join the other two in

appreciation of the world that had come into being, the new order of
things. Humpty Dumpty had fallen off the wall and his pieces could
never be put back together again.

In fighting for what had been, the four men considered in this book
helped to destroy, or render meaningless, what it was they most held
dear. We understand that. What we do not understand is what our
world is to be. For forty years and more we knew the world to consist of
two superpowers facing off, supported to one extent or another by their
minions, the bit players who were the nominally Communist countries and the nominally free-enterprise countries. Then of a sudden, in
late 1989, came new things unforeseeable, with startling events succeeding one another practically by the hour—tomorrow there will be
new shocks—and the once-familiar universe became suddenly alien
and unpredictable. The world of 1914 did not fail, in time, to take
note of the fact that the first name of the fevered youth who shot
Archduke Franz Ferdinand was Gabriel, and that he did it on St.
Vitus's Day, an important date in the Serbia which armed him. The
trumpet signaling the death of many things had sounded, it was said,
and the world entered into a dance uncontrolled. Our trumpet and our
dance? Will a future which we can never know mark the instant the
music sounds and the mad cavorting begins as a moment we did not
notice, or will it come to us with resounding force that the climatic
event of our times is flitting across our television screens? Who knows?

Anthony Nutting called his book on Suez *No End of a Lesson*. Yes.
One ought to know one's lessons. We learn that in kindergarten. We
believe we know the lessons taught by the past. The ones we are taught
today? Someday someone will know if we learned them.

Douglas Haig, says Paul Fussell in *The Great War and Modern
Memory*, left a powerful legacy. It is the belief, endemic now, that all
political and military leaders are likely to have feet of clay. Haig's
personality and interests, or lack of them, Fussell says, are part of that.
"His want of imagination and innocence of artistic culture have
seemed to provide a model for Great Men."

Lord Haig certainly left no military legacy. Few officers of any army in the world after 1918 ever dreamed of following his bloody frontal-attack tactics. Yet he is not completely discredited in the eyes of history. Every now and then books or articles praising him appear. Their unanswerable question is, What policy *should* he have followed? Their premise is that his detractors freely damn his every act but never suggest possible alternatives.

Some historians uneasily go up and down on Haig. He remains a figure about whom it is difficult to make a definite judgment. After all these years it is unlikely that one will ever be made. He is largely forgotten in England. The man in the street never heard of him.

Walther Rathenau after his assassination remained very much present in the minds of Germans and those who studied Germany. There was always something sinister, dangerous, tragic, about the Weimar Republic; visitors sensed a profound illness, and many did not fail to connect it to the frame of mind which permitted much of the populace to applaud the shots and grenade which killed Rathenau. Ten years after his death, Weimar also died, the cause being partly murder, partly suicide, partly sickness, and Germany was seized by a man the illusions of whose followers almost perfectly paralleled those of the slain prophet. He became, of course, a slain devil in the lexicon of Hitler's Reich. A large tree which stood near where his car came to a halt as he suffered his death wound, known to Berliners as the Rathenau Oak and decorated with flowers on anniversaries, was cut down. The Second War came. When it was over, Rathenau was seen in the light of a man whose Policy of Fulfillment toward the First War Allies might if followed have prevented the second conflict. A plaque was put up in a little park near the scene of the assassination, and today there is no German town or city lacking its Rathenauplatz or Rathenaustrasse. No one reads his books. Too much has happened since they were written. His Berlin house, which he left for his last trip, survived the Allied bombings and has been subdivided for offices.

*   *   *

Marshal Pétain remains a figure of the greatest controversy in France. There is a committee to defend and extol his memory and upon occasion hold ceremonies honoring him. Former Resistance fighters, or people saying they are such, assault those who attend. The police intervene. France is uneasy with Pétain's ghost, for there are few who do not sometimes at least fleetingly wonder if he was entirely wrong in his acceptance of defeat in 1940 and of a post in which he tried to spare the French what he could. It is not forgotten that de Gaulle's early adherents in the immediate aftermath of the military catastrophe constituted a tiny handful, nor that many who today claim Resistance status flocked to him only when his American- and British-supplied tanks were practically within the suburbs of Paris.

Pétain died in 1951, within weeks of his Verdun opponent, the German Crown Prince. He was buried on the little island of Yeu in the Bay of Biscay which had been his home for six years of imprisonment. In 1966, President de Gaulle, back in power after twelve years of retirement, went to Verdun for ceremonies commemorating the beginning of the battle half a century earlier. There was widespread speculation that he would take the occasion to suggest that the Marshal at last be brought back to lie with his soldiers. Had he done so he would have made easier the minds of those French, not few in number, who have always wondered if it was completely correct to attempt to wipe out the memory of national shame and humiliation by denouncements of the man under whose wing they sheltered during times more difficult for France than any other. During the ceremonies de Gaulle did not mention Pétain's name.

On a cold and foggy January day two months after resigning as Prime Minister, Anthony Eden, broken and ill, sailed for New Zealand and its sunny skies. His ship had to go via the Panama Canal, for Suez was still closed. When he returned, he gave up the seat in Parliament he had held for more than thirty years. By then it was realized that what happened at Suez caused a complete change in the outlook and social structure of what is called the Third World, and made Europe and America look with different eyes at that entity.

England had its own special view. "In one week of senseless folly," wrote the British author Paul Johnson, "priceless assets, which it had taken scores of years—indeed, centuries—to accumulate, were reck-lessly cast away."

In 1961 Eden accepted the earldom routinely offered former Prime Ministers, and became Lord Avon. He raised prize cows, worked in his garden, wrote his memoirs. Privately he said that he wondered if the tone of British life was such as to indicate that the country missed too much the dead of the two world wars. In early 1977, visiting the Florida estate of W. Averell Harriman, he fell ill. He realized he was dying and said that he wished to do so in England. Prime Minister James Callahan arranged for a Royal Air Force plane to bring him home. He was gone on January 14, aged seventy-nine. The obituaries were tinged with sadness.

BIBLIOGRAPHY

Adams, Michael. *Suez and After*. Boston: Beacon Press, 1958.

Aron, Robert. *The Vichy Regime*. London: Putnam, 1958.

Aster, Sidney. *Anthony Eden*. New York: St. Martin's Press, 1976.

Barber, Noel. *The Week France Fell*. New York: Stein & Day, 1976.

Barnett, Correlli. *The Swordbearers*. London: Eyre & Spottiswoode, 1963.

Baudouin, Paul. *The Private Diaries*. London: Eyre & Spottiswoode, 1948.

Blond, Georges. *Verdun*. New York: Macmillan, 1964.

Bois, Elie. *Truth on the Tragedy of France*. London: Hodder & Stoughton, 1941.

Bolton, Glorney. *Pétain*. London: Allen & Unwin, 1957.

Bonham-Carter, Victor. *The Strategy of Victory 1914–1918*. New York: Holt, Rinehart and Winston, 1963.

Borden, Mary. *Journey Down a Blind Alley*. New York: Harper, 1946.

Brittain, Vera. *Testament of Youth*. London: Victor Gollancz, 1933.

Broad, Lewis. *Sir Anthony Eden*. London: Hutchinson, 1955.

Brooks, Howard. *Prisoners of Hope*. New York: Fischer, 1942.

Byford-Jones, W. *Oil on Troubled Waters*. London: Robert Hale, 1957.

Calvocoressi, Peter, and Moncrieff, Anthony. *Suez Ten Years After*. London: British Broadcasting Corporation, 1967.

Carlton, David. *Anthony Eden*. London: Allen Lane, 1981.

Cavenagh, Sandy. *Airborne to Suez*. London: William Kimber, 1965.

Chambrun, René de. *I Saw France Fall*. New York: Morrow, 1940.

———. *Pierre Laval*. New York: Scribner's, 1984.

Charteris, John. *Field-Marshal Earl Haig*. London: Cassell, 1929.

———. *At G.H.Q.* London: Cassell, 1931.

Churchill, Randolph S. *The Rise and Fall of Sir Anthony Eden.* London: Macgibbon & Kee, 1959.

Churchill, Winston. *Great Contemporaries.* New York: Putnam, 1937.

Cole, Hubert. *Laval.* London: Heinemann, 1963.

Cooper, Chester L. *The Lion's Last Roar.* New York: Harper & Row, 1978.

d'Abernon, Viscount. *The Diary of an Ambassador.* Garden City, N.Y.: Doubleday, Doran, 1930.

————. *Portraits and Appreciations.* London: Hodder & Stoughton, 1931.

d'Abernon, Viscountess. *Red Cross and Berlin Embassy.* London: John Murray, 1946.

Davidson, Sir John. *Haig, Master of the Field.* London: Peter Nevill, 1953.

Delmer, Sefton. *Weimar Germany.* New York: American Heritage, 1972.

Duff Cooper, Alfred. *Haig.* London: Faber & Faber, 1935.

Duncan, George S. *Douglas Haig as I Knew Him.* London: Allen & Unwin, 1966.

Eden, Anthony, Earl of Avon. *Another World.* Garden City, N.Y.: Doubleday, 1977.

Éditions Lorraines. *Verdun.* Verdun, n.d.

Everett, Susanne. *Lost Berlin.* Chicago: Contemporary Books, 1979.

Falls, Cyril. *The Great War.* New York: Capricorn, 1961.

Farwell, Byron. *Mr. Kipling's Army.* New York: Norton, 1981.

Federn-Kohlhaas, Etta. *Walther Rathenau Sein Leben und Wirken.* Dresden: Carl Reissner, 1927.

Felix, David. *Walther Rathenau and the Weimar Republic.* Baltimore: The Johns Hopkins, 1971.

Flanner, Janet. *Pétain, the Old Man of France.* New York: Simon & Schuster, 1944.

Friedrich, Otto. *Before the Deluge.* New York: Harper & Row, 1972.

Fussell, Paul. *The Great War and Modern Memory.* New York and London: Oxford, 1975.

Gardner, Brian. *The Big Push.* New York: Morrow, 1963.

Gordon, Bertram. *Collaborationism in France During the Second World War.* Ithaca, N.Y.: Cornell University Press, 1980.

Graves, Robert. *Good-bye to All That.* Garden City, N.Y.: Doubleday/Anchor Books, 1957.

Groot, Gerard De. *Douglas Haig*. London: Unwin Hyman, 1988.

Guedalla, Philip. *The Two Marshals*. London: Hodder & Stoughton, 1943.

Haig, Countess. *The Man I Knew*. Edinburgh and London: Moray, 1936.

Haig, Douglas. *Private Papers*. London: Eyre & Spottiswoode, 1952.

Hoover Institution on War, Revolution and Peace. *France During the German Occupation*. Stanford, 1957.

Horne, Alistair. *The Price of Glory*. New York: St. Martin's, 1963.

————. *To Lose a Battle*. New York: Little, Brown, 1969.

James, Robert Rhodes. *Anthony Eden*. New York: McGraw-Hill, 1987.

Johnson, Paul. *The Suez War*. London: Macgibbon & Kee, 1957.

Joll, James. *Intellectuals in Politics*. London: Weidenfeld & Nicolson, 1960.

Keegan, John. *The Face of Battle*. London: Jonathan Cape, 1976.

Kessler, Harry. *Walther Rathenau*. New York: Harcourt Brace, 1930.

————. *In the Twenties*. New York: Holt, Rinehart and Winston, 1971.

Liddell Hart, B. H. *Reputations Ten Years After*. Boston: Little, Brown, 1928.

Lottman, Herbert. *Pétain: Hero or Traitor*. New York: Morrow, 1985.

Ludwig, Emil. *Nine Etched From Life*. New York: Robert McBride, 1934.

Macdonald, Lyn. *They Called It Passchendaele*. London: Michael Joseph, 1978.

————. *Somme*. London: Michael Joseph, 1983.

Macmillan, Harold. *Riding the Storm*. New York: Harper & Row, 1971.

Marshall-Cornwall, Sir James. *Haig As Military Commander*. New York: Crane, Russak, 1973.

Martel, Francis. *Pétain: Verdun to Vichy*. New York: Dutton, 1943.

Maurois, André. *Tragedy in France*. New York: Harper, 1940.

Middlebrook, Martin. *The First Day on the Somme*. New York: Norton, 1972.

Morris, James. *Farewell the Trumpets*. New York and London: Harvest-HBJ, 1978.

Nutting, Anthony. *No End of a Lesson*. London: Constable, 1967.

Pachter, Harry. *Weimar Etudes*. New York: Columbia University Press, 1982.

Paxton, Robert. *Parades and Politics at Vichy.* Princeton, N.J.: Princeton University Press, 1966.

————. *Vichy France.* New York: Knopf, 1972.

Pertinax [André Geraud]. *The Gravediggers of France.* Garden City, N.Y.: Doubleday, Doran, 1944.

Pitt, Barry. *1918: The Last Act.* New York: Norton, 1962.

Porter, Roy. *Uncensored France.* New York: Dial, 1942.

Rathenau, Walther. *Notes and Diaries 1907–1922.* Oxford: Clarendon, 1985.

Robertson, Sir William. *From Private to Field-Marshal.* Boston: Houghton Mifflin, 1921.

Roy, Jules. *The Trial of Marshal Pétain.* New York: Harper & Row, 1968.

Ryan, Stephen. *Pétain the Soldier.* South Brunswick and New York: A. S. Barnes, 1969.

Salomon, Ernst von. *The Outlaws.* London: Jonathan Cape, 1931.

————. *The Answers.* London: Putnam, 1954.

Secrett, T. *Twenty-Five Years with Earl Haig.* London: Jarrolds, n.d.

Shirer, William L. *The Collapse of the Third Republic.* New York: Simon & Schuster, 1969.

Simonds, Frank. *They Won the War.* New York: Harper, 1931.

Sixsmith, E. K. G. *Douglas Haig.* London: Weidenfeld & Nicolson, 1976.

Spears, Edward. *Liaison, 1914.* London: Heinemann, 1930.

————. *Assignment to Catastrophe.* 2 vols. New York: A. A. Wyn, 1954, 1955.

————. *Two Men Who Saved France.* New York: Stein & Day, 1966.

Sweets, John. *Choices in Vichy France.* New York and Oxford: Oxford, 1986.

Sylvester, A. J. *Life with Lloyd George.* New York: Harper & Row, 1975.

Szaluta, Jacques. *Pétain: For and Against.* New York: Vantage, 1973.

Terraine, John. *Mons.* New York: Macmillan, 1960.

————. *Ordeal of Victory.* Philadelphia and New York: Lippincott, 1963.

————. *The Western Front.* London: Hutchinson, 1964.

Tournoux, Jean-Raymond. *Sons of France.* New York: Viking, 1964.

Watt, Richard M. *Dare Call It Treason.* London: Chatto & Windus, 1964.

Werth, Alexander. *The Last Days of Paris.* London: Hamish Hamil-
    ton, 1940.
Wolff, Leon. *In Flanders Fields.* New York: Ballantine, 1958.
Zuckmayer, Carl. *A Part of Myself.* New York: Harcourt Brace Jova-
    novich, 1970.

INDEX

The following abbreviations are used in this index: AE (Robert Anthony Eden); DH (Douglas Haig); HP (Henri Pétain); WR (Walther Rathenau).